IT COULDN'T HAPPEN TO A NICER TOWN

This is the place usually reserved for praise of the author.
Only, **PITTSBURGH: The Story of the City of Champions** isn't that kind of book.

It wasn't written. The plot, the characters, the crisis points, the happy landings and happy endings—everything—just happened. They happened in one glorious decade in one American city, **ours,** and the world wondered at the sight and sound of it.

How could one city, relatively small in total area as far as major cities go, manage to bring together the kind of owners, administrators, coaches and players it takes to win two World Series Championships, four Super Bowls, an NCAA National Football Championship, a host of MVPs, All Pros, All Stars, All League, All **Everything** performers.

As a member of one of those great Pittsburgh teams of the 70's, I say none of it would have happened without the staunch support of loyal fans. People who know and love their sports, and who cheer their teams on with an enthusiasm that is truly infectious. The kind of fans only **Pittsburgh** has!

I am proud to be one of them, a sports-loving, banner-waving, Pittsburgh-boosting resident of "The City of Champions." And I'm proud to be the spokesman for First Federal Savings of Pittsburgh, the people whose sponsorship helps bring you this exciting book of sports history.

The 10 incredible years of Pittsburgh's pre-eminence in athletics, recounted here, are unmatched in the annals of sports. It may never happen anytime, anywhere again. But here's one of Pittsburgh's adopted sons who says, it couldn't happen to a nicer town.

—Rocky Bleier

Photo by Harry Coughanour

PITTSBURGH:
The Story of the City of Champions

THE '70s—A DECADE UNMATCHED IN THE ANNALS OF SPORTS

Edited By JIM O'BRIEN and MARTY WOLFSON • Illustrated By MARTY WOLFSON

WOLFSON PUBLISHING CO., INC.
Pittsburgh, PA

DEDICATED

To my dear wife Irene, Paula, Marla, Todd, Karen and little Graham for their love, understanding and inspiration.

—Marty Wolfson

To my wife, Kathleen Churchman, our children, Sarah and Rebecca, and our families for their love, strength, inspiration, support and understanding.

—Jim O'Brien

A special dedication to all the wonderful fans in the City of Champions.

ACKNOWLEDGEMENTS

We are grateful to the following for their help and cooperation, unselfish service, hard-to-get photos and material, confidence and the best of luck: Ernie Buckman, Sam Nover, Dave Welty, Mayor Caliguiri, Justin Horan, Jim McKinnon, Neal Cohen, Nellie King, Bill Rush, Bill Smith, Bill Cox, Dan McCann, Ron Cichowicz, Kathleen Churchman, Dean Billick, Vince DiNardo, Sally O'Leary, Tom Bird, Jack Schrom, Joe Gordon, Cindy Himes, Charlie Strong, John Robison, Andy Russell, Dick Macino, The Golden Panthers, Walter T. Lease, Jr., Frank B. Fuhrer, Gary Murphy, Bob Heddleston, Paul Martha, Beverly Maroney, Charles Puskar, Ray Mansfield, A. J. Luppino, Harry Leach, Robert R. Toothman, Donald Bebenek, Pittsburgh Athletic Assn., Carol King, Don Clay, John Troan, Leo Koeberlein, Robert C. Todd, Jr., Larry F. Adams, Bill Connelly, John Paulus, William Fitz, Blair Gettig, Harold O. Drosethes, Steve Hansen, Dave Green, Rege McKenzie, Beth Adams, Pat Walters, Ross C. Feltz, Harry M. Carroll, Bob Yockel and Modern Reproductions.

Our special thanks and grateful appreciation to Art Gratz, Carl Cummings, Andy Komer and the entire staff at Herbick and Held and to all the people at First Federal Savings of Pittsburgh.

—Marty Wolfson and Jim O'Brien

Cover Photos by:
George Gojkovich (Pirates, Steelers, Pitt)
Paul Salva (Penguins)

Copyright© 1980 by Wolfson Publishing Co., Inc.

All rights reserved

Published by Wolfson Publishing Co., Inc.
Pittsburgh, PA

First Printing

Designed by Marty Wolfson

Manufactured in the United States of America

Printed by Herbick and Held
Pittsburgh, PA
Typography by Herbick and Held

Photo Reproductions by Modern Reproductions, Inc.

Library of Congress Catalog Card Number #80-52074

ISBN Number #0-916114-07-4

Photo by Al Church

TRIBUTE TO A CITY

"Pittsburgh: The Story of the City of Champions" is a prideful portrayal of the successful efforts and determination of our teams, players, coaches, managers, individuals and fans. It is a story that had to be told because it was a decade unmatched in the annals of sports. Nowhere in history has one city been so dominant in sports in one decade. During the decade of the '70s, Pittsburgh produced more champions and championships than any other city in America and throughout the free world.

A positive attitude more than any other single factor determined the championship status we achieved and maintained throughout the decade.

This then, is the story of a special city, its unique people, and its triumphant teams who showed absolute determination and dedication. They had a sincere belief in themselves that they could accomplish the impossible. They formulated the strong desire ... to WIN! We have endeavored to tell the story in human terms rather than in dry statistics alone.

We say it with pride, heartfelt thanks and love that Pittsburgh is truly a City of Champions ... in all ways.

Marty Wolfson

Marty Wolfson
Publisher

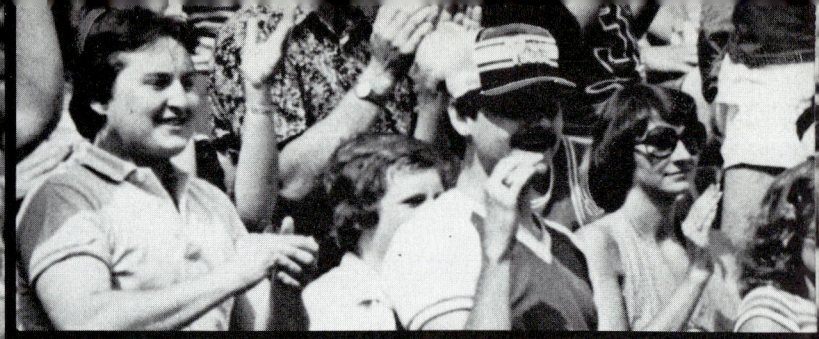

CONTENTS

Dedication and Acknowledgments	2
Tribute to a City by Marty Wolfson	3
Tribute to the Sports Fans in the City of Champions	5
Introduction	6
Mayor's Message by Richard S. Caliguiri	7
Championship Staff	8
Highlights of the City of Champions (1970-80)	10
Stadiums and Arenas	12

BASEBALL 16
The Pirates, A Dominant Force in the '70s
 by Bob Smizik 17
Pirate Profiles 37

BASKETBALL 54
Duquesne . . . Big Days During the Decade
 by Bob Smizik 55
Pitt . . . Had Its Good Knights 60
Carnegie-Mellon . . . Makes Its Mark 66
Robert Morris . . . Cream of Krop Rose to Top 67
Point Park . . . Conboy Puts It On National Map 68
Allegheny Community College . . . Becomes
 a Big Success 69
City High Schools . . . Winners of Four State Titles .. 70
Pro Basketball . . . Pittsburgh's Role by Jim O'Brien .. 73

FOOTBALL 82
Pittsburgh Steelers . . . Set Tone for '70s
 by Phil Musick 83
Steeler Sketches 95
Pitt . . . Comeback Story of the '70s by Jim O'Brien .. 134
Carnegie-Mellon . . . Turns Out Champs 152
Duquesne . . . Steps Up in Class 156

GOLF . . . In the '70s by Pat Livingston 158

HOCKEY . . . Penguins Push Toward '80s
 by Norm Vargo 162

TENNIS . . . Triangles Won World Team Tennis Title . 176

TRACK . . . ACC Outdistanced Everybody 182

OTHER HEROES . . . More Sources of Pride to
 Pittsburgh 184
 What Better Decade . . . Reflections by Sam Nover
A Tribute to Chet Smith 192

"I've been to some Steeler games, and I've been to some Pirate games, and I can't get over these people. Their enthusiasm is unreal. They belong in the movies."

—A movie producer while filming "Fighting Back," the Rocky Bleier story.

TRIBUTE TO THE SPORTS FANS IN THE CITY OF CHAMPIONS

The City of Champions Salutes its Steelers

City of Pittsburgh

The Chamber

INTRODUCTION

The Steelers were storming toward another touchdown. Rocky Bleier was running the ball and catching the ball and coming up with one big play after another. The Steelers were advancing toward the endzone where I was standing, along with several reporters. We had left the press box early in order to get to the dressing rooms right after the game was completed, as is our custom, to conduct interviews.

It was January 6, 1980, and this was the American Football Conference championship contest between the Steelers and the Houston Oilers. The crowd of 50,475 at Three Rivers Stadium was going crazy as the Steelers steadily marched toward one more touchdown. They were waving their Terrible Towels, which brought a beam to the face of an old friend, Myron Cope, who was standing nearby, and they were screaming and yelling. It was some scene. Then Bleier scored from four yards out, and Matt Bahr booted the extra point, and the final score was on the board. The Steelers had defeated the Oilers, 27-13. Only seconds remained on the scoreboard clock.

There were tears in my eyes, I must admit. The Steelers were going to the Super Bowl again. I could not believe how well things were working out.

Strictly from a selfish standpoint, I was overwhelmed by what was happening. The Steelers were going to the Super Bowl again, and I was going with them. It was unreal.

Less than nine months earlier, I had come home again to Pittsburgh after plying my trade elsewhere for ten years, first in Miami for a year, and then for nine years in New York. I was born in Pittsburgh and lived here most of my first 27 years, except for two years in the military service. I left in 1969 to seek my fame and fortune elsewhere. I returned a decade later—I thought the timing was right—and was able to enjoy, from firsthand experience, a continuing series of sports triumphs in what had become known in the interim as the City of Champions.

For starters, the Pirates beat the Baltimore Orioles to win the 1979 World Series in seven games, then the Pitt football team posted an 11-1 record and defeated Arizona to win the Fiesta Bowl and finish sixth and seventh in the wire service polls. Now the Steelers had won the AFC title, and they would go on to Pasadena and defeat the Los Angeles Rams, 31-19, to win the Super Bowl.

It was their fourth Super Bowl triumph in six seasons. For the Pirates, it was their second World Series victory during the decade. For Pitt, it was their sixth bowl appearance in the past seven seasons. In that glorious season of 1976, the Panthers won the national championship and their star performer, running back Tony Dorsett, won the Heisman Trophy.

No other city in the U.S.A. could say the same of its sporting teams. New York, in 1969, was the only other city in history to have its teams win the World Series and Super Bowl in the same year. But it couldn't claim a college team playing on a big-time basis, let alone a national championship team. Once-mighty Fordham had a good club football team, but Duquesne defeated Fordham during that decade, and also claimed the national club football championship in a game at Three Rivers Stadium in the winter of '73.

Then, too, there were the Triangles winning a World Team Tennis title during that marvelous span of ten years, and Frank Fuhrer coming back as the financier of another novel indoor game with the Spirit in the Major Indoor Soccer League before the decade came to a close.

Carnegie-Mellon and Point Park also produced championship teams, as did Allegheny Community College and Robert Morris, and so many local high schools won state scholastic titles in that time period.

The '70s were something else for the City of Champions. For the most part, I was a fan from a distance. I watched every time the Steelers and Pirates and Penguins and Pitt teams were on television. When they were in Miami and New York, I went to see them in action. At times, I traveled back home and had a chance to see them play.

I was in the stands, for instance, when Dorsett had two of his very best running days at Pitt—at Army in his junior season, and against Penn State at Three Rivers Stadium in his final game in Pittsburgh. I reported on several Steelers and Pirates and Penguins games. I was visiting Pittsburgh and able to attend the Eastern Eight basketball championship playoffs in 1979 when over 16,000 saw Rutgers beat Pitt for the title. That helped convince me to come back to Pittsburgh. Something special was going on here.

"When you went away," said Art Rooney, "we were fighting to see who'd get the first pick in the draft. We weren't very good when you were here. I hope you ain't the black cat."

So, there was personal pressure from the start, to prove that I "ain't the black cat."

For the most part, though, I had missed out on what happened on the Pittsburgh sports scene in the '70s.

Then Marty Wolfson called and said he wanted to talk to me about a book project he had in mind. Marty Wolfson was a name out of my past. An artist I had once worked with years ago. As a third grader at St. Stephen's Grade School in Hazelwood, I was invited to appear on Marty's TV Sketchpad show, to draw with him, to follow his lead at the easel. I've never forgotten that the nuns had scolded me afterward for saying "yeah" instead of "yes" when Wolfson said something to me.

I had learned my lesson.

Marty Wolfson wanted me to help him produce a book on Pittsburgh—The City of Champions—during the '70s. It would be a chance for me to recapture the period, to do research and relive this incomparable period in the city's history. I'd like the nuns to know that when Wolfson asked me if I'd do it, I said, "Yes." Ten times, I said, "Yes."

Jim O'Brien

MESSAGE FROM THE MAYOR

"We have another winner here..."

For nearly four decades, Pittsburgh has been striving to change its image as a blighted, smoke-polluted industrial town.

It has not been easy to communicate to the rest of the nation and the world the dramatic changes that have been made here since the mid '40s—the cleansing of our sky of its infamous smoke, the harnessing of our flood waters, the reshaping of our skyline and destiny. From an aesthetic and cultural standpoint, Pittsburgh has been one of the nation's best kept secrets.

But in the past decade, Pittsburgh found a powerful and unexpected ally in promoting its new image—a galaxy of sports champions. The phenomena focused the spotlight of national and international media attention on our City—giving us the opportunity to show off the new Pittsburgh to its best advantage. This was a most productive spin-off of the victories and trophies acquired by the Steelers, Pirates, Pitt Panthers and others performing under the Pittsburgh banner.

The story of the City of Champions decade—with all of its excitement, human drama, color, pride and courage—is chronicled within these pages by two men who share my abounding affection for our City of Champions, its loyal fans and its great teams—Jim O'Brien and Marty Wolfson.

Their combined talents have produced *another winner*—a very human, very factual and most entertaining account of the memorable happenings of a unique sports era.

In a very special way, they too are contributing to our continuing campaign to promote the real Pittsburgh. Hopefully, they will be able to produce an equally exciting sequel at the end of the decade of the '80s.

City of Pittsburgh
Richard S. Caliguiri, Mayor

CHAMPIONSHIP STAFF

MARTY WOLFSON AND FRANCO HARRIS

JIM O'BRIEN AND ART ROONEY

Born in Pittsburgh in 1924, **Marty Wolfson** is a man of many talents. A graduate of Fifth Avenue High School, Marty studied at the Royal Academy of Art in London, The Beaux Arts in Paris and at Carnegie Tech. He is president of Wolfson Publishing Co., Inc. and has published, co-authored, edited and illustrated over 20 books. He is a graphic designer, art director, illustrator and cartoonist; he is an advertising and public relations counselor. In 1970, he collaborated with Chet Smith on a book, "Greater Pittsburgh History of Sports," which received a Golden Quill Award for journalistic excellence in the field of sports, and this was the genesis for his installing the Three Rivers Sports Hall of Fame Museum and Theater in Three Rivers Stadium. He has been a TV producer and entertainer, having frequently appeared on WDTV, KDKA-TV, WIIC-TV, WTAE-TV and WQED during the past 20 years. Marty was the first to teach blind children to draw through the medium of television. He resides in Mount Lebanon with his wife, Irene, and daughter, Marla, and is the father of Paula and Todd, who live elsewhere.

Born in Pittsburgh in 1942, **Jim O'Brien** is a sportswriter-columnist for The Pittsburgh Press, and covered the Steelers in their Super Bowl XIV championship season. Joined the Press in April, 1979 after nine years at the New York Post, preceded by one year at The Miami News. Editor since 1969 of Street & Smith's Basketball Yearbook, and was contributing pro basketball columnist for eight years to The Sporting News. Regular contributor to Basketball Digest and Football Digest, as well as Goal and Hoop. Got start as sports editor at age 14 with Hazelwood Envoy. Graduate of Taylor Allderdice High and the University of Pittsburgh, where he obtained degree in English Writing and was sports editor for two years. Was co-publisher and editor of Pittsburgh Weekly Sports for 4½ years. Served in U.S. Army for two years as an editor of news services in Kansas City and Fort Greeley, Alaska. Resides in Upper St. Clair with wife, Kathleen Churchman, and daughters, Sarah, 7, and Rebecca, 3.

Born in Pittsburgh in 1920, **Pat Livingston** has been a sportswriter at The Pittsburgh Press since 1949 and sports editor since 1972. In 1979 he received the Dick McCann Award from the Professional Football Writers Assn. of America for long and distinguished coverage of pro football. In 1980, he authored "The Pittsburgh Steelers, An Illustrated History." He is the Pittsburgh correspondent for Sports Illustrated. Pat is a 1941 graduate of St. Francis College of Loretto, and has a law degree from Duquesne University, 1955. He served in the U.S. Navy from 1942 to 1946, and was discharged as a lieutenant (s.g.), 1946. He received the Hervey Award from Ohio State University in 1964 and the Keystone Award from the Pennsylvania Newspapers Publishers Assn. in 1977. He resides in Bethel Park with his daughters, Patty and Linda.

TONY DORSETT AND PAT LIVINGSTON

PHIL MUSICK

Born in Pittsburgh in 1937, **Phil Musick** is a graduate of Peabody High School and Duquesne University. He was a sportswriter-columnist at The Pittsburgh Press for four years and with the Pittsburgh Post-Gazette for five years as the sports editor-columnist. He has been named the Pennsylvania sportswriter of the year, and was the outstanding journalism graduate of Duquesne in 1969. He's authored three books and has been a contributor to SPORT, PRO! and countless other national magazines, all of which pay minimum wage, according to Phil. He served four years in the U.S. Air Force which, he says, "is slightly more liberal than the New York Times editorial page." He is married and the father of two and the stepfather of six. He and wife, Betty, and children are at home in Penn Hills.

BOB SMIZIK

Born in Pittsburgh in 1941, **Bob Smizik** graduated from Peabody High where he couldn't make the school newspaper so he played football. Graduated from University of Pittsburgh, where he was sports editor and associate editor of The Pitt News and obtained a degree in education. Taught in Pittsburgh public schools for four years. Joined The Pittsburgh Press in 1969. Covered high schools for two years, Penguins for one year, Pirates for six years, Pitt sports for two years. Won Golden Quill for best Pittsburgh sports story in 1972 for Roberto Clemente's 3,000th hit. Resides in Mount Lebanon with wife, former Nancy Homer of Baldwin Township, and son, Scott, 2.

NORM VARGO

Born in Munhall in 1934, **Norm Vargo** joined The Daily News in McKeesport in 1969, first as a general news and political writer, and moved to the sports staff in 1973. He was named sports editor in 1976 following the death of Luke Quay. He was the beat writer for the Penguins from 1973 through 1977, and the Steelers from 1976 to the present. During that span, he also covered World Team Tennis, the Spirit and the Pirates. He was chairman of the Pittsburgh Chapter of the U.S. Baseball Writers Assn. in 1978 and held office in the BBWAA for five years. He resides in North Huntingdon with his wife, Audrey, and their four children, Mike, Mark, Sandi and Gary.

CONTRIBUTING PHOTOGRAPHERS

George Gojkovich, Harry Homa, Bill Amatucci, Al Church, Rich Wilson, and Paul Salva.

●

Special thanks to The Pittsburgh Press for permission to reprint photos by: Albert J. Herrmann, Jr., Robert Pavuchak, Anthony Kaminski, Michael Chikiris

. . . and to the Post-Gazette for photo by Harry Coughanour.

●

HIGHLIGHTS OF THE CITY OF CHAMPIONS

1970
- Pirates' Dock Ellis pitches no-hitter in 2-0 victory June 12 at San Diego.
- Three Rivers Stadium opens with Pirates playing Cincinnati Reds, July 16.
- Pirates win Eastern Division championship. Danny Murtaugh makes successful return, winning Manager of the Year a third time (also 1958, 1960), and Dapper Dan Sports Award.
- Duquesne University basketball team in NIT.

1971
- Pirates' Willie Stargell wins National League's home run title with 48.
- Pirates' pitcher Dave Giusti wins Fireman of the Year award.
- Pirates win Eastern Division and National League pennants, and defeat Baltimore Orioles in World Series, taking final game of seven-game Series, 4-3. Roberto Clemente is named MVP of Series. First night game in World Series history is played at Three Rivers Stadium, Oct. 13.
- Duquesne's basketball team in NCAA tourney.

1972
- Pirates win Eastern Division title.
- Steelers qualify for playoffs the first time, winning American Football Conference's Central Division title. The "Immaculate Reception" by Franco Harris enables them to defeat Oakland Raiders, 13-7, in playoff, but they lose, 21-17, to Miami Dolphins in AFC Championship Game.

1973
- Former Pitt and Detroit Lion football star Joe Schmidt is named to Pro Football Hall of Fame.
- Sewickley's Carol Semple wins U. S. Amateur Golf Championship.
- Latrobe's Arnold Palmer wins Bob Hope Desert Classic in Palm Springs.
- Stargell sets National League record of 90 extra-base hits.
- Duquesne wins national club football championship, posting 10-0 record.
- Johnny Majors is named Coach of Year in first season at Pitt after Panthers improve record from 1-10 to 6-4-1. They go to Fiesta Bowl, where they lose, 28-7, to Arizona State.
- Bruno Sammartino regains World-Wide Wrestling Federation title by defeating Stan Stasiak at Madison Square Garden, Dec. 9.

1974
- Pitt's basketball team reaches NCAA Eastern Regional Finals, bowing to eventual champion N.C. State, 100-72.
- All-Star Baseball Game is played at Three Rivers Stadium, July 23.
- Carol Semple wins British Amateur Golf title.
- Pirates win Eastern Division title.
- Carrick's Danny Seemiller is rated No. 1 table tennis player in U.S.
- Pitt's football team wins Sun Bowl, beating Kansas, 38-19.
- Steelers win AFC's Central Division, and defeat Buffalo and Oakland in playoffs to win AFC title.

1975
- Steelers win first National Football League championship, Jan. 12, defeating Minnesota Vikings, 16-6, in Super Bowl IX. Franco Harris is MVP.
- Pitt's basketball team reaches second round of NIT at Madison Square Garden.
- Pittsburgh Triangles win World Team Tennis title; Vitas Gerulaitis is named MVP.
- Allegheny Community College wins first of three straight Junior College Team Marathon titles.
- Former Pirate Ralph Kiner is inducted into Baseball Hall of Fame in Cooperstown, N.Y.
- Pirates win Eastern Division title.
- Steelers win AFC Central Division title, and defeat Baltimore and Oakland in playoffs to win AFC Championship.

1976
- Steelers win second straight NFL Championship, defeating Dallas Cowboys, 21-17, in Super Bowl X, on Jan. 18; Lynn Swann is named MVP.
- Carol Semple wins U.S. Amateur and British Amateur championships, and her family is named U.S. Golfing Family of Year.
- Nancy Rubin wins 1st PGA National Jr. Girls' title.
- Carnegie-Mellon wins basketball and football championships in Presidents Athletic Conference.
- Pirates' John Candelaria pitches no-hitter in 2-0 victory Aug. 9 over Dodgers in Pittsburgh.

- Pitt wins national championship in college football, as Panthers are rated No. 1 in every poll. Also win Lambert Trophy as No. 1 team in East. Johnny Majors is named Coach of Year. Tony Dorsett wins Heisman Trophy, and is first amateur athlete to win Dapper Dan Award.
- Steelers win AFC Central Division title, and first playoff game at Baltimore, but lose to Oakland for AFC title.

1977
- Pitt defeats Georgia, 27-3, to win Sugar Bowl in New Orleans, Jan. 1.
- Pirates' Dave Parker wins National League batting championship with .338 average.
- Duquesne wins first basketball championship of Eastern 8 and advances to NCAA tournament; Norm Nixon is named tournament MVP.
- Carnegie-Mellon repeats as football champion of Presidents Athletic Conference.
- Steelers win AFC Central Division title.
- Pitt football team wins Gator Bowl, defeating Clemson, 30-17.

1978
- Pirates' Dave Parker named NL's MVP as he wins second consecutive batting championship with .334 average. He wins Man of the Year awards from Dapper Dan and Pittsburgh Jaycees.
- Carnegie-Mellon wins Presidents Athletic Conference championships in cross-country, basketball and football, gaining berth in Div. III grid playoffs.
- Pitt's football team invited to Tangerine Bowl, but loses, 30-17, to N.C. State.
- Steelers win AFC Central Division title, and AFC championship.

1979
- Steelers win third NFL Championship, Jan. 21, in Super Bowl XIII, defeating Dallas Cowboys, 35-31. Terry Bradshaw is named MVP.
- Johnny Unitas is named to Pro Football Hall of Fame.
- Pitt basketball team reaches finals of Eastern 8 tournament, before bowing to Rutgers.
- Point Park basketball team wins District 18 title and qualifies for NAIA tournament in Kansas City.
- Pitt's Sam Clancy is member of gold medal-winning U.S. basketball team at Pan American Games in Puerto Rico.
- Pirates win Eastern Division and National League pennants.
- Pirates beat Baltimore Orioles in seven games, winning final, 4-1, to win World Series.
- Willie Stargell shares NL's MVP award with Keith Hernandez of Cardinals, and Sports Illustrated's Sportsman of the Year award with Steelers' Terry Bradshaw. Stargell is named Man of the Year by Dapper Dan and Pittsburgh Jaycees, and The Sporting News. He is MVP of playoffs and World Series.
- Carnegie-Mellon wins PAC championship, and Lambert Bowl as best small college team in East, but loses out in Div. III national playoff semifinals.
- Pitt wins Fiesta Bowl, defeating Arizona, 16-10.
- Steelers win AFC Central Division title, and beat Miami and Houston in playoffs for AFC title.

1980
- Penguins defeat Montreal Canadiens and New York Islanders on consecutive nights to move into first place on Jan. 3 for first time in team's history.
- Steelers win fourth NFL Championship, defeating Los Angeles, 31-19, on Jan. 20 at Rose Bowl in Pasadena in Super Bowl XIV; Bradshaw is MVP.
- Spirit set MISL record with 13 straight victories.
- 10th Anniversary of Three Rivers Stadium, July 16.

Photos by Al Church

THREE RIVERS STADIUM SETS PACE FOR CITY'S BALLPLAYING SITES

"Without the new stadium, we'd never have been winners."

—Art Rooney

A new sports era in Pittsburgh began in the summer of 1970 with the opening of Three Rivers Stadium. The Pirates and the Steelers were the prime tenants from the start and Three Rivers became the center of sports excitement for metropolitan Pittsburgh and the Tri-State area.

With the success of the Pirates and Steelers in the '70s, unmatched by any other sports teams in a single city in America, it became a national sports showcase as well. TV viewers everywhere were treated to overhead views of the Stadium and the surrounding area—the Golden Triangle, the inclines of Mt. Washington, the steel mills and, of course, the three rivers, the Allegheny and Monongahela which meet to form the Ohio. Those spectacular aerial views were a great source of pride to Pittsburghers and, in particular, to Mayor Richard Caliguiri who complimented the TV networks for showing off the city at its best.

Three Rivers Stadium was officially opened July 16, 1970, and there were 48,846 fans in attendance. Tony Perez hit the first home run there to help the Cincinnati Reds beat the Bucs in the opener, 3-2. Willie Stargell hit the first Pirate homer and it earned him $1,000—a gift from a local lumber company.

Mike Bache, a 78-year-old gentleman from Braddock, was present for the Pirates' opener at Three Rivers Stadium. Four generations of his family were there for the event. "Being at a new park for an opening is something special," he said. "I remember going to the Forbes Field opener. I paid 50 cents and there were no seats left. I stood behind a rope in the outfield. I could have touched Fred Clarke."

Of course, the opening of Three Rivers Stadium meant a farewell to Forbes Field. That ballyard, with its ivy-covered brick wall in the outfield, stood alongside Schenley Park and was the scene of many thrills for sports fans in Pittsburgh for 61 years.

The Pirates closed down that wonderful baseball park on June 28, 1970 with a doubleheader sweep of the Chicago Cubs. The occasion was both significant and appropriate historically for it was with the same Cubs that Forbes Field was opened on June 30, 1909.

Part of the outfield wall, about 150-feet of the centerfield section, still remains intact, as a monument to Forbes Field, and can be found behind the new University of Pittsburgh Law School and Forbes Quadrangle which replaced the ballpark. Mazeroski Field, a Little League diamond, is also there. Many mementos from Forbes Field, and pictures of the famous players who performed there, can be found nearby in Frankie Gustine's Restaurant on Forbes Avenue.

Three Rivers proved a lucky charm for the Pirates and the Steelers in the '70s. In their second season in the new stadium, the Pirates won it all—beating the Baltimore Orioles in the World Series in '71, something they would do again in 1979.

The first night game in World Series history was played there on October 13, 1971.

Nobody enjoyed watching baseball and football games at Forbes Field any more than Art Rooney, the owner of the Steelers and one of the Pirates' most fervent fans. But the Steelers, or football for that matter, didn't really fit into Forbes Field. It was a pure baseball facility. And the Steelers were outsiders when they played at Pitt Stadium.

So Three Rivers Stadium—right in Rooney's neighborhood in Old Allegheny—was a significant development in the history of the Steelers. "Without the new stadium, we'd never have been winners," said Rooney at the outset of 1980, soon after the Steelers had won their fourth Super Bowl in six years. "We were a second-class club before we moved into the new stadium. That made us a first-rate club."

That's why Rooney wanted to make sure the Stadium was properly maintained and preserved for future generations of ballteams and their fans. Coach Chuck Noll shared his thoughts on the subject, believing that the Stadium was a key factor in the success of the football franchise.

Starting there in 1972, the Steelers began a string of qualifying for the playoffs eight straight seasons to tie a National Football League record established by the Dallas Cowboys. It was in 1972 that Franco Harris made his "Immaculate Reception" in the first NFL Playoff game ever played at Three Rivers as the Steelers surprised the Oakland Raiders, 13-7. It was there the following week, in the American Football Conference championship game that the Steelers were defeated, 21-17, by the Miami Dolphins.

That was to be the only playoff defeat to be suffered by the Steelers at Three Rivers in the '70s. Their post-season record on their home turf at the end of the decade was a dandy 8-1.

The Steelers' home record at Three Rivers during that span was 69-13—an .841 winning percentage—and they closed the decade by winning 16 straight home games, ten of those, including two playoff contests, in 1979.

During the same period, University of Pittsburgh officials considerably improved Pitt Stadium, to the point where today it's one of the finest college football facilities in the land.

It began with a modest refurbishing of the Stadium in 1969, Carl DePasqua's first year as head coach, when the original AstroTurf playing surface was installed. A 440-yard oval tartan track was installed around the football field.

Pitt Stadium was spruced up even more, inside and outside, after the arrival of Coach Johnny Majors for the 1973 season. Wooden benches gave way to aluminum seating in the latter years of the '70s, and the seats were widened—reducing capacity by 1,500 to 56,500. The concrete bowl built in 1925 was brightened by blue and gold paint. A new AstroTurf field was installed in 1978.

Beginning with the national championship season of 1976, the Panthers went unbeaten at home in three of their final four seasons in the '70s. They were 6-0 there during that sensational senior season of Heisman Trophy winner Tony Dorsett, and finished the regular schedule by beating Penn State for the first time in ten years in a nationally-televised night game at Three Rivers Stadium.

Pitt put together back-to-back 5-0 home records in 1978 and 1979 under Coach Jackie Sherrill. Altogether, they were 20-2 over the final four years of the '70s at Pitt Stadium.

During the same decade, Pitt refurbished Fitzgerald Field House, and increased its capacity to 5,308. At times, though, for big games with Duke and Duquesne, for example, there were closer to 7,000 jammed into the campus gym. With the hiring of a new basketball coach, Roy Chipman, at the start of the '80s, Pitt officials reaffirmed their desire to improve the basketball facility, and increase seating capacity to 7,500 in the not-too-distant future.

New physical education facilities and gyms were built during the decade at Robert Morris College and the Allegheny Campus of the Allegheny County Community College. Point Park College became a tenant of the ACC gym.

The Civic Arena underwent several face-liftings during the '70s to improve it and increase its capacity. The Arena opened its doors on Sept. 21, 1961 in the Lower Hill District.

Its seating capacity was increased from 10,700 to 12,500 in 1966 when the National Hockey League replaced the American Hockey League as the prime tenant in the building for the start of the 1967-68 season.

More seating additions were made in 1972 and 1973, and in that 1973 season 20 "super" boxes were installed in the rafters. Balconies were added for 1975 which increased capacity to 16,033, and the Penguins played to several sellout crowds of that number in the late '70s.

In addition to the Penguins, the Civic Arena was home to the Duquesne Dukes' basketball team during the '70s, and served as the home court for two seasons at the start of the decade for the Pittsburgh Pipers and Condors of the American Basketball Association, and for two seasons at the end of the decade for the Spirit of the Major Indoor Soccer League.

The Pipers had won the first title in the ABA while playing at the Civic Arena during the 1967-68 season. The Hornets had won the AHL's Calder Cup in the playoffs there the year before.

The Civic Arena was the scene for the city's most exciting college basketball events.

The Dapper Dan Roundball Classic, sponsored and promoted by the Pittsburgh Post-Gazette, annually draws sell-out crowds, and set a record with 16,649 on April 1, 1977.

The Eastern Eight playoff tournament found a home at the Arena late in the '70s, and drew several sellout crowds, topped by 16,172 for its semi-final card of Pitt vs. Villanova and West Virginia vs. Rutgers on Feb. 29, 1980.

Two weeks earlier, on Feb. 10, Duquesne defeated Pitt in a thriller before 14,416, the largest crowd ever to witness a regular season college basketball contest in the city.

On March 14, 1980, a record 16,661 turned out to see a wrestling show there which was topped by Pittsburgh's own Bruno Sammartino and Larry Zybisco.

Penguins' owner Edward J. DeBartolo expressed a desire to take control of the Civic Arena and make further improvements, while developing the surrounding area. There was also talk, as the '70s ended, that a National Basketball Association franchise was a future possibility for the Arena.

Boasting of fine sports facilities, the City of Champions looked to the '80s with more conquests in mind, and a desire to add to its stable of winners.

BASEBALL

THE PIRATES, A DOMINANT FORCE IN BASEBALL IN THE '70s

By Bob Smizik

"I wish I could explain to everybody what a real close family all of us on this ball club are."
—Willie Stargell

What they had done, not many people expected could be done. They had opened the baseball season as a distinct underdog, a team whose time was of an earlier era. By mid-season this belief was being confirmed. They were in fourth place, 7½ games away from the lead. This, everyone thought, was a baseball team in decline.

But here it was only three months later—Oct. 19, 1979 to be exact—and there were an estimated 25,000 people jammed into Market Square in downtown Pittsburgh to pay homage to them. They were not there to pay tribute to a fourth-place team. They were there to honor the World Champions.

The team of which so little had been expected had done so much. The Pirates were back in Pittsburgh after having defeated the Baltimore Orioles in the World Series.

They were World Champs and they were home in the City of Champions.

It is the story of many men and many years of hard work. But there was one Pirate who stood out. His name was Willie Stargell, or Pops, or Captain Willie. He answered to them all, and his efforts during the 1979 baseball season had earned him the respect of a nation and the love of a city and a team.

This was the baseball team that was a family. They adopted the Sister Sledge hit record of **"We Are Family"** as their theme song and, at first, it blared only in their clubhouse. Then in their stadium and then throughout the city. And as the Pirates progressed to a National League East championship and then a National League pennant and finally a World Series win, the rest of the country found out that this was truly a fam-a-lee.

And Captain Willie was the head of it. At the plate he was a batsman feared across the league. Off the field, he was the most respected player in the game. He came into the league almost two decades earlier. But his love of the game never diminished; his joy at being a Pirate only increased.

It was a spirit that proved contagious. His teammates followed his example. He was a man who led by word and deed.

And here he was on this nippy October day telling the assembled crowd, "You people are just as responsible for us winning as we are."

The crowd loved it as much as they loved Willie Stargell. But there had to be many among them who never felt they would be there in Market Square celebrating a World Series championship.

Less than a week earlier there wasn't any celebrating in the streets of Pittsburgh. The fam-a-lee was in a bad way. The team that had fought so courageously through the regular season, the team that had been so outstanding in dispatching Cincinnati in the National League playoffs, was upon hard times in the World Series.

Oh, those same powerful Pirate bats were around, delivering an abundance of base hits against the pitching of American League champion Baltimore. But in the field the Pirates were slightly short of pathetic, and their pitching, well, the pitching wasn't holding up as well as a lot of people thought it would.

And so it was on a cool Sunday afternoon that was October, 15, 1979 the Pirates faced the end of the season. They were down three games to one and needed to win three straight, a virtually impossible job considering the last two games of the Series—if they were necessary—would be played in Baltimore.

To make matters all the more disheartening for the Pirate fans, the matchup for that fifth game seemed to so heavily favor Baltimore that there was an excellent chance the Pirates' dream would end that afternoon on the turf of Three Rivers.

Pitching for the Pirates was Jim Rooker, once a man who thrived on such games, but who, at age 37, was in the twilight of a career. Twice during the regular season he had been on the disabled list. His 1979 record on a first-place team had been 4-7. His earned run average of 4.59 was no more encouraging. He had not even been used in the sweep of the Reds. There were, however, two reasons for optimism concerning Jim Rooker. For one, he had pitched 3⅔ innings of scoreless relief in the first game of the Series. And for another, there was his history of rising to the occasion. This was a man who wanted the ball in the big games.

"This is the kind of challenge I like," said Rooker characteristically.

Negating those reasons for optimism was Jim Flanagan, the Baltimore pitcher who not only had been the Orioles top winner during the regular season but who had beaten the Pirates in Game One.

The decision of Baltimore Manager Earl Weaver to pitch Flanagan surprised at least one Pirate. "I thought with a 3-1 lead they would give Flanagan an extra day off," said Rooker.

Weaver's strategy looked good in the early going. So did Chuck Tanner's as a crowd of 50,920 came out to Three Rivers to see if the Pirates could stay alive. Flanagan and Rooker were locked in a scoreless game through four innings. In the fifth, Baltimore pushed across a run on a double, a single and an infield double play. All of a sudden, the Pirates were five at-bats away from extinction.

As the National League had learned all season, however, this was not a team to die easily. Falling behind seemed to arouse the Pirates. In their half of the sixth, Tim Foli walked on a 3-2 pitch and moved to second on Dave Parker's single. Few managers would do what Tanner did next. He had his cleanup hitter, Bill Robinson, bunt. The sacrifice was successful and both Foli and Parker were in scoring position. Stargell did his job by scoring Foli with a sacrifice fly. Bill Madlock did his, too. He scored Parker with a single.

The Pirates were ahead and the World Series was headed in a dramatically different direction. No one dreamt it at the time—not even the staunchest Pirate fan—but Baltimore was on its way to defeat.

The two-run sixth not only put the Pirates ahead, but it forced Weaver to use a pinch-hitter for Flanagan, and once into their bullpen, the Orioles were in trouble.

The Pirates had no such problem with their bullpen. Rooker was lifted in the fifth for a pinch-hitter and Bert Blyleven came on to pitch with equal effectiveness. Tim Stoddard, Tippy Martinez and Dan Stanhouse could not do the same for Baltimore. The Pirates went on to a 7-1 win.

They were alive, well and looking forward to the challenge of playing two more in Baltimore.

"Before the game I said if we could beat Flanagan we just might win this," crowed Rooker.

Foli looked at the situation somewhat more objectively. "We've dug our own hole and we have to get out of it ourselves," he said. "This is the first game we've played completely. You have to hit and pitch and play well to win. We're not trying to kid anyone. It doesn't look good. But if we can go at them right from the get-go, we'll be all right."

The Orioles were hardly lacking in confidence as they returned home, needing only one win in two games. "We wanted to win the fifth game and get it over with," said Weaver. "But if somebody had told me we'd be leading three to two and going home with Palmer and Scott McGregor pitching, I would have said that would be nice."

The sixth game loomed as a classic. Jim Palmer, one of the premier pitchers of the '70s was coming off an injury-filled season, but was still regarded as Baltimore's money pitcher. Facing him was John Candelaria, unquestionably the man the Pirates wanted on the mound in a big game. "Candy is a money player," said Dave Parker. "He's the type who says, 'When there's a crucial game, give me the ball.' "

Candelaria, however, was far from healthy. An intense

JOHN CANDELARIA

pain in his side had been his constant companion for some time, and so unsure were the Pirates of whether he'd be able to pitch that Tanner had Bruce Kison warming up in the first inning.

The game was what people expected from Candelaria and Palmer. It was scoreless through six.

The Pirates struck in the seventh. Omar Moreno singled with one out and was running when Foli hit a bouncer up the middle. The ball ticked Palmer's glove and caromed towards Kiko Garcia, the Baltimore shortstop. It looked like a possible double play or at least a sure out at first on Foli, whose speed is average at best. But Garcia couldn't come up with the ball and the Pirates had two on.

Parker followed with a wicked bouncer at second baseman Rich Dauer. Again, a double play loomed. "My first thought was beat the double play," said Parker. But the ball got past Dauer as Moreno scored and Foli took third.

"It was a routine play. I should have had it," said Dauer, who was probably being too harsh with himself.

Stargell followed with a sacrifice fly and the Pirates led 2-0.

Candelaria had done his job. "He had the needle in his side again," said catcher Ed Ott. "He went out there on pure guts and won the game."

Tekulve relieved and shut out the Orioles the rest of the way as the Pirates made things even easier by scoring twice more in the eighth. "Candy pitched the toughest part of the game," said Tekulve. "There wasn't any score and a mistake becomes a run. I could afford to make some mistakes."

Neither team could afford a mistake the next day. Tanner sent Jim Bibby to the mound, Weaver came back with McGregor.

Baltimore jumped ahead in the third on Dauer's home run and the score remained 1-0 until the sixth.

It started quietly with a single by Robinson. And that brought up Stargell. Frank Merriwell couldn't have done it better. Once more Pops was to be the hero.

"He (McGregor) threw me a breaking ball," said Stargell. "I didn't want to commit myself on the pitch too soon. I was out in front of it, but I got the bat speed I wanted. At first I didn't think it would travel that far. When it did, I was thrilled."

No less so than an entire city and his teammates. Sitting in the bullpen, Ott, who gave way to Steve Nicosia when a lefthander was pitching, watched the flight of the ball.

KENT TEKULVE

"Rooker and I were talking about Willie hitting a home run into the bullpen," he said. "Then he hit it. It was high. It just hung up there so long. Rooker and I were pulling it, pulling it."

The Pirates had a lead and Tanner was confident. "I thought we had it then because we had enough pitching to hold them."

And he did. Just barely. Grant Jackson, who came on in the fifth and held the Orioles hitless for 2⅔ innings, walked two batters with one out in the eighth, and on came Tekulve. And up came left-handed pinch-hitter Terry Crowley, who had doubled with the bases loaded off Tekulve in the fourth game.

Stargell walked to the mound to talk to Tekulve. "I told him," said Stargell, " 'Teke, show the people why you're the best in the National League. And if you don't think you can do that, then you play first base and I'll pitch.' "

Tekulve thought he could do it. Crowley bounced out. Ken Singleton was intentionally walked to get to Eddie Murray, a big Baltimore hitter who had been a major disappointment in the Series. Murray cracked a drive to right that looked like trouble. It looked like even more trouble when Parker had difficulty with his footing.

"I slipped three times," said Parker. But he came up with the ball and the Orioles threat was over.

The Pirates scored twice more in the ninth and Tekulve had all the cushion he needed. There were two out in the ninth when Pat Kelly lofted a fly ball to Moreno. All eyes were riveted on center field except two. "I threw the ball and did not see the catch," said Tekulve. "I was so wrapped up in the game that it didn't hit me until the ball was in the air and Omar caught it. I then thought, 'World Championship. It's ours and nobody can take it away.' "

And so it was that the decade of the '70s ended on as upbeat a note as possible. The Pirates were World Champs, demonstrably the best team in baseball, and Pittsburgh was on its way to being known as the City of Champions.

Who'd have thought it would have ended that way. It most certainly didn't open up as a decade of promise. The '60s were turbulent times for the Pirates and left them staggering a bit as they came into the '70s. They won a World Series in 1960 and then mainly faltered through the remainder of the decade. The Pirates tumbled to sixth in 1961 and were eighth two years later. In despair, General Manager Joe L. Brown broke up his World Championship team by the mid '60s and later swung major deals for aging but not-yet-fading stars like Maury Wills and Jim Bunning. But nothing worked. The Pirates reached respectability by the end of the decade, but not much more.

When the '70s rolled around, the Pirates were a contender but lacking something. Brown thought he knew what it was. Larry Shepard was fired and in an astonishing move —one that shocked the entire baseball world—Brown re-hired Danny Murtaugh.

Brown made the most of his big surprise. Instead of having Murtaugh come directly to Pittsburgh for the announcement, he had him fly to Johnstown. "I knew darn well if his kisser appeared in the Pittsburgh airport everybody would pick it up," said Brown. Murtaugh came from Johnstown to Pittsburgh by car and spent the night at Brown's house in Mt. Lebanon. The next day, the Pirates ushered the media aboard the Gateway Party Liner to announce their new manager. No one suspected Murtaugh. As the boat headed toward the still unfinished Three Rivers Stadium, Brown took the microphone and said, "I

PITTSBURGH PIRATES 1979 WORLD CHAMPIONS

FRONT ROW, seated, left to right: Steve Nicosia, Batboy Steve Hallahan, Batboy Steve Graff, Phil Garner and Ed Ott.
SECOND ROW, seated, left to right: Ed Whitson, Trainer Tony Bartirome, Coach Al Monchak, Coach Harvey Haddix, Manager Chuck Tanner, Coach Bob Skinner, Coach Joe Lonnett, Jim Rooker and Enrique Romo.
THIRD ROW, standing, left to right: Grant Jackson, Rennie Stennett, Matt Alexander, Manny Sanguillen, Tim Foli, John Milner, Mike Easler, Dale Berra, Lee Lacy, Rick Rhoden and Traveling Secretary Charles Muse.
TOP ROW, standing, left to right: Bill Robinson, Bert Blyleven, Omar Moreno, Dave Parker, John Candelaria, Jim Bibby, Kent Tekulve, Willie Stargell, Bruce Kison, Don Robinson and Bill Madlock (inset).

PIRATES TURN IN A DANDY DECADE

When the calendar turned up the year 1980, it became fashionable to consider various happenings during the decade just passed—the '70s. Baseball is chock full of stats for the '70s, including those which indicate relative success by individual teams during those years. A look at that solidifies the Pirates' claim to being one of Major League Baseball's most competitive teams of the decade.

The Pirates amassed a 916-695 won-lost record from 1970-1979, for a .569 percentage. Only two big league teams topped that: Cincinnati (.592) and Baltimore (.590).

The Bucs and the Reds were the only teams in baseball to win six Divisional Titles, and each team won two World Championships, as did the New York Yankees. The only team to win more than two World Series? The Oakland A's.

The Pirates are the only National League team to have finished no lower than third in a season during the '70s, and they fell that low just one time—in 1973. The Boston Red Sox also have accomplished this feat, but they finished third five times.

By analyzing the final standings in both the National League and the American League over the past decade, a comparison of each team's cumulative "Games Behind" figure at the close of each season proves quite revealing.

The Pirates figure of 18 games back tops their closest rival, the Cincinnati Reds, who finished a total of 27½ games behind over the same period. The Baltimore Orioles are also in the top five, with a cumulative "Games Behind" figure of 31½, followed by Los Angeles (82½) and Boston (96).

All in all, for the Pirates . . . not a bad decade's work.

Last Game at Forbes Field, Pirates vs. Cubs, June 28, 1970.   Photos by Al Church

think most of you might know this man." With that, Murtaugh walked up a flight of steps and into everyone's view. The media were dumbfounded. Brown had his man.

The smiling Irishman, who was tough as steel on the inside, had managed the Pirates to a World Series win in 1960, but stepped down in 1964 because of ill health. He returned briefly to finish out the 1967 season when Brown fired Harry Walker. He had stayed close to the scene as a scout, troubleshooter and advisor to Brown. But no one ever dreamt he would return as a full-time manager. There was, however, no man in baseball Joe Brown respected more than Danny Murtaugh. He thought he had assembled a team that could win a pennant. Now he needed the manager to guide it, and, thought Brown, Murtaugh was his man.

Brown was right.

The '70s brought unparalleled success to the Pirates and Brown and Murtaugh were in the middle of most of it. The '70s also brought Pittsburgh a new stadium. Long talked about, and long being built, the stadium opened July 16, 1970. It sat over 50,000 people, some 17,000 more than Forbes Field held. It was located on the North Side where the Allegheny flows to join the Monongahela and form the Ohio. It was therefore called Three Rivers Stadium. Pirate Hall of Famer Pie Traynor had the honor of throwing out the first ball, and Dock Ellis delivered the first pitch that counted in the new stadium.

The fans flocked to the new stadium. Though they played only half the season at Three Rivers, Pirate attendance rose to 1,341,947, a significant improvement over the 769,369 that showed up at Forbes Field the previous year.

The Pirates didn't play all that much better baseball under Murtaugh than they did the year before under Shepard. They won 89 games in 1970 compared to 88 the year before. But 1969 was the miracle of the Mets. There were no Mets in 1970, the Pirates finished in first, five games ahead of the Cubs.

This was a team—as all the Pirate teams of the late '60s and early '70s were—of great hitters. The magnificent Roberto Clemente, of course, stood out. Though 36, Clemente hit .352, but played in only 108 games because of injuries.

There was much more than Clemente. Behind the plate there was the young Panamanian with the singing bat and the dazzling arm. His name was Manny Sanguillen and he hit .325. The great Bill Mazeroski, two years away from the end of his career, still was regarded as one of baseball's best fielding second basemen. Beside him was Gene Alley, three years earlier the premier shortstop in baseball but already fading because of injuries. The centerfielder was the once-magnificent batsman Matty Alou. But this was an off-year for Alou, who hit .297, and as Brown was soon to show, a player with the defensive deficiencies of Matty Alou would have to hit better than .297 to pull his weight in the lineup.

First Game at Three Rivers Stadium, Pirates vs. Reds, July 16, 1970.

LOG OF FIRSTS AT THREE RIVERS STADIUM

First Game—Pirates vs. Cincinnati Reds, July 16, 1970, before 48,846 fans. Pie Traynor, Pirate Hall of Famer, threw out the first ball.
First Pitch—Dock Ellis threw first pitch, a strike, to lead off batter Ty Cline of Cincinnati.
First Hit—Pirates' Richie Hebner, hit a one-out single in first inning.
First Extra Base Hit—Pirates' Al Oliver hit a two-out double in first inning, scoring Richie Hebner.
First Run—Scored by Pirates' Richie Hebner.
First RBI—Pirates' Al Oliver, doubling to score Richie Hebner.
First Pirate Home Run—Willie Stargell, none on, two out, sixth inning, into the second deck, right field stands, his 17th of the season.

Bill Mazeroski, Pie and Eve Traynor and Roberto Clemente.

AL OLIVER

There were three relative newcomers. At first base a big redhead from Maryland—billed as the next Ralph Kiner—had a mighty first season as a regular hitting 27 home runs and driving in 82 runs, though starting less than 100 games. His name was Bob Robertson. At third base was a left-handed power hitter who was to carry on a love-hate relationship with the fans throughout his Pittsburgh career. They loved his hitting, they hated his fielding. His name was Richie Hebner. The third was a young man who, at this point in time, was willing to play anywhere so long as he played. Shuffling between first base and the outfield, Al Oliver hit .270 and drove in 83 runs. Line drives leaped off his bat.

Oh, yes, in left field there was this 29-year-old power hitter who was already finishing up his eighth major league season. His name was Stargell and though he hit 44 home runs and drove in 119 runs there were much better days ahead.

On the bench, ready to play major roles in the years ahead were Dave Cash, who would succeed Mazeroski, Gene Clines and the popular veteran Jose Pagan.

The pitching was spotty. Luke Walker, before and after 1970 an erratic lefthander, led the team with a 15-6 record. Dock Ellis won 13, Bob Moose 11 and Steve Blass 10. A broad-backed righthander named Dave Giusti had come over from St. Louis as a starter but somehow wound up in the bullpen. It was a move of brilliance, a move that was to mean great success to the Pirates. Through the first six years of the decade, six years that brought five division titles, no Pirate save Stargell and possibly Oliver was to mean more to the team than David John Giusti.

This was the Pirate team that Brown assembled in 1970 and these were the men who were to play the major roles as the Pirates became a dominant team in baseball.

They were not, however, ready in 1970. The Eastern Division was one thing. The Cincinnati Reds, champions of the Western Division, were another.

DOCK ELLIS

The playoffs were like another season for the Pirates. Their mighty hitters were silenced. Only Stargell, 6-12, and Hebner, 4-6, hit over .300 among the regulars. But their questionable pitching was superb. The playoffs opened in Pittsburgh on Oct. 3. Ellis was magnificent. So was Gary Nolan of the Reds. The game was scoreless through nine. But the Reds broke through for three in the 10th and that's the way it ended with Cincinnati winning, 3-0.

The Pirates made another battle of it the next day. Walker and Giusti combined to hold the Reds to three runs, but Jim Merritt and fireballing 19-year-old Don Gullett held the Pirates to one run on five hits.

The series moved to Cincinnati, the outcome a foregone conclusion. The Pirates managed 10 hits but could get only two runs as Moose lost to reliever Milt Wilcox, 3-2.

Murtaugh was philosophical about the defeat. "We didn't lose this playoff," he said. "The Reds just went out there and beat us. The Cincinnati pitching was great and ours was outstanding. If someone had told me before this thing started that we'd hold the Reds to three runs a game and lose, I wouldn't have believed it."

The off-season was highlighted by two events. Murtaugh's announcement—amid speculation that he would once more retire—that he would return and Brown's trading of Matty Alou.

Murtaugh loudly pronounced himself fit and eager to go. Brown quietly pronounced Alou unfit and was eager to see him go.

Sensing he was close to another world championship, when the right deal came along, Brown pounced on it. He sent Alou and pitcher George Brunet to the Cardinals for Nelson Briles and Vic Davalillo. The Pirates got another starting pitcher in Briles and a dangerous pinch-hitter and dandy utility man in Davalillo, who despite advancing age was extraordinarily swift.

What about center field? Murtaugh had an answer for that. Oliver, the man without a position, would make the change. The man who had primarily been a first baseman was being asked to take over the most demanding position in the outfield. He relished the challenge. What he did not relish was the fact that Murtaugh would often platoon him with Clines.

The cast was set. The Pirates were ready to roll. And Stargell was out in front. He hit 11 home runs in April, a major league record. Twice in that month he hit three home runs in one game. It was an awesome performance, but an accurate indication of what was to come. Stargell would finish the year with 48 home runs and 125 runs batted in. On May 30, he became the first man to hit a ball into the top deck at Three Rivers.

But June 11 was the big day. Ellis defeated the Cardinals, 11-4, as the Pirates moved into first place and stayed there the rest of the season.

There were signs of the time along the way. Murtaugh was hospitalized after a May 20 game in Cincinnati. Mazeroski made his debut at third base on June 25. Clemente picked up his 2,800th career hit on July 6.

Two days later a skinny kid who had been burning up the International League beat the Reds, 7-1, for his first major league win. His name was Bruce Kison and he was to play a large role in the events that followed.

Nothing was stopping the team now. After Aug. 23, their lead was never less than five games and on Sept. 18, Blass shut out the Mets, 4-0, to clinch the National League East title. A young man up from the minors for a taste of big league life, hit his first major league home run. His name? Richie Zisk.

Three saves by Dave Giusti helped beat Giants in playoffs. Giusti, an Upper St. Clair resident, won the Fireman of the Year Award.

Stargell won the home run title, Giusti, with 30 saves, the Fireman of the Year award and for the first time since 1903 the Pirates led the league in homers.

Ellis carried the pitching staff early, coming up 14-3 at the All-Star Game and earning the start for the National League. When he faltered in the second half and finished with 19 wins, others picked up for him, Blass won 15, Moose 11 and Walker 10. And there was always Giusti.

The hitting remained superb. Stargell was no one-man show. Clemente, showing no sign of aging, hit .341 and drove in 86 while missing 30 games. Sanguillen hit .319 and drove in 81. Robertson hit .271 and drove in 72. Hebner and Oliver both hit over .270 and drove in more than 60 runs. Cash had taken the second base job away from Mazeroski and proved he deserved it with a .289 average. Clines came in at .308 and a pheenom up from the minors named Rennie Stennett hit .353 in 50 games. So deep were the Pirates in talented hitters that when the time came to return Pagan, who had broken his arm on Aug. 5, to the active list for the playoffs, Stennett had to be removed.

That was the team that went off to the playoffs to meet the San Francisco Giants. Compared to the Pirates of 1970, they had more poise, more confidence and—most importantly—more talent.

They had one other thing going for them as they entered the playoffs—rest. The Giants had battled furiously with Los Angeles to the last day of the season and their pitching staff was not ready for the playoffs. San Francisco Manager Charlie Fox could not use ace Juan Marichal until the third game. Murtaugh, with the luxury of an early clinching, had his staff ready to go.

There was, however, one series of facts that heavily favored the Giants. The Pirates had extreme difficulty beating them during the regular season. They could win only two of six at home and one of six in Candlestick Park, traditionally a nightmarish place for the Pirates. The playoffs, of course, opened at Candlestick.

And true to form, the Pirates lost. Blass had struck out nine and had a 2-1 lead going into the fifth. Home runs by Tito Fuentes and Willie McCovey produced four runs and the Giants went on to a 5-4 win.

The Pirates knew they needed a win in Game Two and they got a lift from a most unexpected source. Robertson went into a horrible slump at the end of the season and hadn't hit a home run since Aug. 25. He made up for all of that in one afternoon. He hit three home runs—still a playoff record—scored four times and drove in five. He was all the Pirates needed in a 9-4 win. Ellis, with relief help from Bob Miller, an Aug. 10 "pennant insurance" acquisition from San Diego, and Giusti.

The Giants were hardly dismayed. They were even at 1-1 in the playoffs and their best pitcher was set to go. Briles was Murtaugh's choice to face Marichal, but had to back off when a leg injury became too bothersome during warmups. Seven minutes before the scheduled start of the game, Murtaugh turned to Bob Johnson, a much-heralded off-season acquisition from Kansas City who finished a disappointing 9-10. The great Marichal against Johnson did not seem like much of a matchup.

Marichal was excellent. Johnson was more than excellent. Marichal allowed only four hits, but two of them were homers. Robertson hit his third straight in the second inning to give the Pirates a 1-0 lead. An error by Hebner allowed the Giants to tie it in the fifth. However, Hebner atoned for that error by homering in the eighth to put the Pirates ahead, 2-1. Giusti finished off the Giants in the ninth and the Pirates had the game 2-1 and led in the series by the same numbers.

It was Perry and Blass in the decisive game before 35,487 at Three Rivers on Oct. 6. Neither was on. The game

Bob Robertson missed the bunt sign and hit a 3-run homer giving Pirates a 5-1 win in Game Three of the World Series.

Bruce Kison allowed just one hit in 6⅓ innings, giving Pirates a 4-3 victory in Game Four of the World Series.

RECORD LOCAL CROWD OF 51,378 SAW BUCS BEAT ORIOLES, 4-3, IN THE FIRST NIGHT GAME IN WORLD SERIES HISTORY. GAME WAS PLAYED OCT. 13, 1971, AT THREE RIVERS STADIUM.

was tied, 5-5, after two. Blass was gone after the second inning, having allowed five runs and eight hits, Perry departed in the sixth. The difference was in the bullpen. Kison worked 4⅔ scoreless innings and Giusti added three more to that. Clemente singled home the go-ahead run in the sixth and Oliver followed with a three-run homer later in the inning. The Pirates had a 9-5 win and were off to the World Series.

They proceeded to be mightily embarrassed in the first two games. They were, in fact, something of a laughing stock by dropping the first two games to Baltimore, a team that came in with four 20-game winners, a magnificent defense anchored by Brooks Robinson and an offense led by Frank Robinson. When the Series moved back to Pittsburgh for the middle three games, the nation's sports writers were making jokes about the Pirates who lost 5-3 and 11-3 in the first two games.

A frustrated Clemente, who was four for nine in the first two games, had this to say: "It's like going against a fighter. You hit him and then he hits you. But then he hits you twice as hard and you get scared. You think he's going to kill you."

It was up to Blass to remove any fright. He righted the Pirates in Game Three, pitching a three-hitter, as Robertson, missing a bunt sign, hit a three-run homer in the seventh to break up a 2-1 game and take the Pirates to a 5-1 win.

Looking back on that game, Murtaugh said, "The most pressure-packed game was the third. Steve Blass won the third game, and if we'd lost, after losing the first two, it would have been the crusher."

Game Four looked like a repeat of the first two as Baltimore jumped on Walker for three runs in the first inning as a Pittsburgh crowd of 51,378 watched the first World Series night game in history. Enter Kison. The hero of the fourth playoff game became the hero of the fourth World Series game. Kison held the Orioles to one hit and no runs for 6⅓ innings. A pinch-hit single by rookie catcher Milt May in the seventh inning gave the Pirates a 4-3 win.

"If there was a turning point in the World Series it was the six innings Kison gave us," said Murtaugh. "He gave us a chance to go ahead in the game."

By now people had stopped laughing.

Murtaugh went to his fifth different starter in the fifth

game, giving Briles his first shot at post-season competition. The man who was too hurt to pitch in the playoffs was just fine for Baltimore. Too fine, in fact. Robertson led off the second with a homer and that was all Briles needed. He held the Orioles to two hits as the Pirates won, 4-0, to take the lead in the Series.

Figuring variety was the key to success, Murtaugh went to his sixth different starter in Game Six. Moose pitched a fine game, but Palmer was equally effective. The Pirates took a 2-0 lead on Robertson's single in the second and Clemente's homer in the third, but that was all they were to do against Palmer. Baltimore won it in the 10th when Frank Robinson walked, went to third on Merv Rettenmund's single and scored on Brooks Robinson's sacrifice fly. Weaver used three 20-game winners with Palmer pitching the first nine and Pat Dobson and Dave McNally relieving in the 10th.

He still had another 20-game winner available for Game Seven. Mike Cuellar, a tricky lefthander, faced Blass.

Clemente, capping one of the most marvelous Series in memory, homered in the fourth to give the Pirates a 1-0 lead. It was the 14th consecutive World Series game in which he had hit successfully. The score remained that way until the eighth when Stargell, running on aching legs

Nelson Briles shut out the Orioles, 4-0, on two hits.

Manny Sanguillen and Steve Blass celebrate team victory over the Orioles 2-1 in the final game of the World Series.

PITTSBURGH PIRATES 1971 WORLD CHAMPIONS

FRONT ROW, seated, left to right: Nelson Briles, Jose Pagan, Vic Davalillo, Ramon Hernandez, Coach Bill Virdon, Coach Don Osborn, Manager Danny Murtaugh, Coach Don Leppert, Coach Frank Oceak, Coach Dave Ricketts, Dock Ellis, Manny Sanguillen and Charlie Sands.

MIDDLE ROW, standing, left to right: Equipment Manager John Hallahan, Gene Alley, Bob Miller, Jack Hernandez, Dave Cash, Bill Mazeroski, Rennie Stennett, Roberto Clemente, Willie Stargell, Al Oliver, Milt May, Trainer Tony Bartirome, Team Physician Dr. Joseph Finegold, Traveling Secretary John Fitzpatrick.

TOP ROW, standing, left to right: Luke Walker, Carl Taylor, Dave Giusti, Bob Veale, Bob Moose, Bob Johnson, Bruce Kison, Steve Blass, Bob Robertson, Gene Clines and Rich Hebner.

---

that would soon require surgery, scored from first on Pagan's double. "I must of looked like a runaway beer truck going around those bases," said Stargell. His run proved to be the winner when Baltimore scored a run in its half of the eighth.

In the ninth, Blass retired the dangerous Boog Powell, Frank Robinson and finally Rettenmund on a bouncer to shortstop Jackie Hernandez.

Clemente's performance became a legend. He hit .414 with two home runs. But it was more than his hitting. And it wasn't only his marvelous throwing arm or his unexcelled skills in the field. It was his zest for the game. He took charge of the World Series and used it as a stage for his talents.

In the spotlight, Clemente had his say. "I want everybody in the world to know that this is the way I play all the time. All season, every season. I gave everything I had to this game."

In his book, "The Summer Game," Roger Angell wrote this of Clemente's 1971 World Series performance: "And then, too, there was the shared experience, already permanently fixed in memory, of Roberto Clemente playing a kind of baseball that none of us had ever seen before—throwing and running and hitting at something close to the level of absolute perfection, playing to win but also playing the game almost as if it were a form of punishment for everyone else on the field."

Pittsburgh went crazy—literally. The Pittsburgh Press quoted a motorcycle patrolman this way: "It was every man for himself. I never saw anything like it. It was terrible. The people ruined it for themselves. They jumped on the cars, blocked streets, grabbed at players. It was really frightening."

Four vehicles were overturned in downtown Pittsburgh and two were burned. Twenty to 25 display windows were smashed and two large fires were set. Nearly 100 persons were arrested.

Some six weeks after the World Series, the Pirates called a news conference. This time Murtaugh wasn't coming back. "Although the doctors have assured me my health is good, each succeeding season seems to take that much more out of me," he said.

To the surprise of no one, Bill Virdon, the Pirates' batting coach, was named to succeed Murtaugh. An outstanding centerfielder for the Pirates in the '60s, Virdon had served his apprenticeship. First as a minor league manager for the Mets and then as a coach for the Pirates. Joe Brown thought he had found a man to succeed Danny Murtaugh. Actually, as it was with all of his managers, he had found a man to preceed Murtaugh.

But on Nov. 23, 1971 no one could ever have believed that Danny Murtaugh would return again.

Virdon may have known something when he said, "We have the talent, it's a matter of going out and beating the other teams again."

Did they ever have the talent! There are people who insist the 1972 Pirates team was the best of the decade. Clemente was still going strong, Oliver was finding himself in center and Stargell was one of the game's premier sluggers. Hebner was established at third, Cash at second and Sanguillen behind the plate. Only at shortstop, where Alley and Hernandez shared the job, did there appear to be a weakness.

Soon enough another developed. Bob Robertson forgot how to hit. Virdon had the patience of Job with him, but nothing worked. By mid-season, Stargell was on first. It was said the move was a concession to his knees, but the mysterious failure of Robertson—who finished with a .193 average—to hit had to have something to do with it. Clines and Davalillo platooned in left field and both hit over .315 Even when a Achilles tendon injury sidelined Clemente for almost a month, the Pirates rolled.

After a slow start, they were in first place by June 15 and there to stay by June 19. The lineup was awesome and the bench almost as frightening. Murtaugh could call on the likes of Pagan, Mazeroski, May, Robertson, Stennett and Davalillo or Clines.

The pitching was the best it had been in many years. Blass won 19, Ellis 15, Briles 14, Moose 13 and Kison 9. The bullpen was the best in baseball. Giusti was 7-4 with 22 saves and a 1.92 earned run average. Ramon Hernandez, a Puerto Rican lefthander with previously unimpressive credentials for two other major league teams, was almost impossible to hit. He finished 5-0 with 14 saves and a 1.67 earned run average.

The Pirates led by 15 games in mid-September and the pennant race took a back seat to a far more dramatic event. Roberto Clemente was chasing his 3,000th hit. It was a feat achieved by only 10 other men in the history of baseball. He was, however, a reluctant chaser. "I don't worry if I get 3,000 hits this year," he said. "What I worry is for us to win. I'm not going to push myself for 3,000 hits. I'm not going to play doubleheaders for 3,000 hits. I'm not going to hurt myself for 3,000 hits. I would like to do it this year, but I'm not going to hurt myself for it."

Fortunately, Clemente made it to 3,000 in 1972. It was a cool September afternoon at Three Rivers. There was less than a week left in the season. The Pirates were priming themselves for the playoffs. Clemente, in with 2,999 hits, was playing only to get it over with and rest until the playoffs.

Only 13,117 came out to Three Rivers for what was to be a historic occasion. Roberto Clemente was about to join an exclusive club. At 3:07 p.m., he drove a Jon Matlack pitch into the left-center field gap. The crowd was on its feet. It was a patented Clemente liner to one of his favorite spots on the field. He had a double.

Characteristically, he first said, "I'm glad it's over. Now I can get some rest." Later, he said, "I dedicate this hit to the fans of Pittsburgh. They have been wonderful."

And with that bit of history out of the way, the world champs went into the playoffs to meet Cincinnati, rightfully bursting with confidence.

With Oliver driving in three runs and with Blass, for 8⅓, and Hernandez holding the Reds to one run, the Pirates took the opener at Three Rivers, 5-1. The second game was a nightmare for Moose. He never retired a batter. The Reds scored four in the first and that was enough as they went on to a 5-3 win. The series switched to Cincinnati for the final games. Briles, Kison and Giusti stopped the Reds in the third game, 3-2. The Pirates were one win away from another trip to the World Series. It was a win they'd never get. Ross Grimsley held them to two hits in the fourth game and the Reds won, 7-1.

It came down to Game Five. The Pirates had Blass, fast becoming the best money pitcher in baseball. The Reds countered with Gullett. Blass lived up to his reputation, taking a 3-2 lead into the eighth. With a runner on second and one out in the eighth, Virdon called for Hernandez to pitch. He did his job, retiring two lefthanders, Joe Morgan and Bobby Tolan.

With the score still 3-2, Virdon removed Hernandez and called for Giusti to start the ninth to face the righthanded power of the Cincinnati lineup. "I had a chance to win so I went with my best," said Virdon. It wasn't enough.

Johnny Bench led off the inning with a home run to tie the game. When Tony Perez and Denis Menke followed with singles it was clear that Virdon's decision to lift Hernandez had been a disaster. On came Bob Moose to face lefthanded hitting Cesar Geronimo. Geronimo flied to right, moving—most importantly—pinch-runner George Foster to

BILL VIRDON
Manager

third. The runners held as Darrel Chaney popped to short. The Pirates were one out away from going to extra innings.

Facing Hal McRae, Moose threw low and away. Too low. The ball bounced in front of Sanguillen and then skipped over his outstretched glove. Foster romped home with the run that sent the Reds to the World Series.

In the quiet of a crushed clubhouse, Blass told a group of writers, "Shed no tears for the Bucs, because we're not going to. We don't have to."

It was Clemente, though, who rallied the team. "Can you help it?" he roared to no one in particular. "Can you help it? Don't worry about it. What we need is a sense of humor. There's nothing you can do about it.

"Giusti! Damn you, Giusti. Look straight ahead. Pick up your head. We don't quit now. We go home and come back in February."

And they all did, except Roberto Clemente.

People coming home late on New Year's Eve heard it first. Others did not learn of the tragedy until the next morning. No one believed it. The radio said it and no one believed it.

Roberto Clemente was dead. On a mercy mission to aid earthquake victims in Nicaragua, Clemente and four other men were killed when their plane, badly overloaded with supplies, went down in the shark-infested waters off Puerto Rico.

A city mourned. It made the Steelers' loss to Miami in the AFC playoffs on Dec. 31 seem like a piddling thing. Losing a football game was one thing. Losing a great man was another.

"We lost not only a great ballplayer but a wonderful human being," said Joe L. Brown.

Clemente had shown little signs of slowing down though he was 38 when the season ended. He hit .312, and in August said he expected to play four or five more years. To those who watched him play, that did not seem out of the question.

The entire Pirate team went to Puerto Rico for a memorial service. Clemente's body has never been found. Who can forget the picture of a distraught Sanguillen standing in despair on the beach as the search for Clemente's body continued to be futile?

Clemente left behind a widow, Vera, and three sons.

He also left a team that missed him enormously.

It could be said that the Pirates were never the same. A leader through both word and action, Clemente could not be replaced. Virdon tried to make Sanguillen a right fielder and the experience flopped miserably. By June, Sanguillen, who more than any other Pirate missed Clemente, was behind the plate.

The Pirates lost another player that year. He didn't die, he wasn't even hurt, but nevertheless he was lost. On his way to becoming one of baseball's best pitchers, Blass mysteriously lost almost all semblance of control in 1973. The man who had won 34 games the previous two years, won only three in 1973. In 89 innings he walked 84 men. The previous year he had walked 84 in 250 innings. The Pirates tried everything. Nothing worked. Virdon stuck with him longer than most managers would have, but eventually he had to be taken out of the starting rotation.

Blass was symbolic of the team. They were 9½ back and tied for fourth on July 4. Slowly they rose in the Eastern Division race, more because no team took charge than on the strength of their own performance.

The team's ragged performance prompted Brown to look to the minors for help. On July 11 the call went out to Charleston. The Pirates were in San Diego when the help came. Dal Maxvill, a veteran shortstop who had joined the team only a few days earlier, took one look at the new man and said, "I don't even know who he is, but I'm glad he's on our side."

Dave Parker was in the major leagues. He hit .288 that year, but anyone who saw the 6-5 giant play knew that greatness was only a year or two away.

Parker helped some and the team continued to move up in the race. After losing to St. Louis on Sept. 5, the Pirates were in second place, three games off the lead.

And once again Joe Brown shocked the baseball world. Sept. 6 was an off day and Brown called a late afternoon news conference before the team left for Philadelphia. It was suspected by some that Brown was going to give Virdon a vote of confidence and extend his contract.

He did nothing of the kind. In what he called, "the most difficult decision of my baseball career," Joe Brown fired Bill Virdon.

He replaced him, of course, with Danny Murtaugh. "Joe put it to me in a way that I couldn't refuse him," said Murtaugh.

Once again Brown thought he had a chance to win a pennant and wanted who he thought was the best manager available.

Virdon, as expected, responded with class, "when you take this job you know some day you're going to get fired."

The players were stunned. "I can't believe it," said Oliver, who had been given a full-time job by Virdon.

The Pirates won seven of their first 11 under Murtaugh and even Blass started pitching more effectively. On Sept.

Rennie Stennett leaps for a high one.

17, Kison beat Tom Seaver and the Pirates were in first place by a game. But from that point, they lost 10 of their final 15 games and finished under .500. When what was supposed to be the final day of the regular season was over, the Pirates trailed the Mets by 1½ games. But because the Mets still had two games left with the Cubs and the Pirates one with San Diego, the season was extended an extra day.

The Mets went to Chicago and San Diego flew all the way to Pittsburgh, at the cost of $13,000, to play the Pirates. Only 2,572 showed up for that afternoon game at Three Rivers. It was all over by the fifth inning. The Mets had defeated the Cubs in the first game at Wrigley Field, clinching the title.

"Give the Mets credit," said Stargell, who had a heroic season, hitting 44 home runs and driving in 119 runs.

"We lost because we weren't good enough," said Murtaugh.

With that in mind, Brown, who had stood pat after the 1972 season, went looking for ballplayers. Cash went to the Phillies for left-handed pitcher Ken Brett. Milt May was traded to Houston for lefthanded pitcher Jerry Reuss. Briles went to Kansas City for utilitymen Ed Kirkpatrick and Kurt Bevacqua. Brown had strengthened the team considerably on the mound while not giving up all that much in the field. Cash was a valuable player, but Stennett was ready to be a regular. May had never progressed beyond being Sanguillen's backup.

Brown and Murtaugh liked what they had put together, but some questions remained. At shortstop, Maxvill, a light-hitting but previously dependable shortstop, was the incumbent. But Murtaugh saw signs of Maxvill's slowing. The season wasn't a month old when Maxvill was released. The shortstop job was given to two rookies, Frank Taveras and Mario Mendoza.

Also there was Blass. He had been sent to the Florida Instructional League after the '73 season and had, the Pirates said, been impressive. Steve Blass made one appearance for the Pirates that 1974 season. In five innings against the Cubs on April 17, he gave up five hits, seven walks and two home runs. He was sent to the minors and never pitched in another major league game.

The Pirates gave him a final shot the next spring. On March 24, pitching against the Chicago White Sox, Blass gave up two runs on four hits while walking three in his first three innings. In the fourth, he walked eight men. It was a tragic scene. After the eighth walk, Murtaugh came out to remove him. While on the field, he became so emotional that he got himself thrown out of the game for arguing with umpire John McSherry. McSherry, Murtaugh felt, should have been giving Blass more of the plate. Blass was fighting for his major league life and Murtaugh had wanted him to have every break.

The Pirates had no choice. A few days later Steve Blass was released. No one ever learned why his control so mysteriously deserted him. A resident of Upper St. Clair, he took a job selling school rings, and did occasional radio stints.

Back in 1974, the Pirates were off to yet another horrendous start. The city was down on the team. Attendance, which had climbed to 1,501,132 in 1971 was falling yearly. It was 1,427,460 in '72 and down to 1,319,913 the next year. With the team in last place on June 15, attendance continued to suffer. Even when the Pirates picked it up, as they surely did, the fans did not come back. By mid-July the team was in third place and on Aug. 25 it was in first.

Brett, though bothered by occasional shoulder problems, was a sensation. Not only did he make the All-Star team, he was the winning pitcher. And he hit almost as well as he pitched. Reuss, though less spectacular, became the team's most effective pitcher, winning 16. Rooker won 15 and Brett 13.

The Pirates and Cardinals were engaged in a furious pennant race. With three games left in the season, the teams were tied for first. Robertson's homer on the next-to-last game of the season put the Pirates in first by a game. The Cardinals were rained out on the final night and the Pirates needed a win to clinch the title. A loss and the Cardinals would play the next day to see if they could move back into a tie.

The Pirates trailed by two going into the ninth. Two outs later, they trailed by one and had a runner on third with Robertson at bat for Giusti. Robertson was no longer a regular but in this season he had proven himself a valuable reserve, time and again coming up with key hits. This time he came up with a key strikeout. When Robertson swung and missed for strike three, the ball got away from catcher Steve Swisher. Robertson, perhaps the slowest man in the National League, began lumbering to first. Swisher retrieved the ball and threw a perfect strike to first. It hit Robertson in the back. Sanguillen scored from third and the game was tied. The Pirates won in the 10th on Oliver's triple and Sanguillen's single.

The Pirates were back in the playoffs. But with the same success as in 1972. They were simply no match for the Dodgers and the pitching of Don Sutton and Andy Messersmith. Sutton beat Reuss in the opener, 3-0, Messersmith stopped Rooker in the second game, 5-2. Kison prolonged the agony by winning the third game at Dodger Stadium, 7-0. It ended painlessly the next afternoon. Sutton held the Pirates to three hits and the Dodgers won, 12-1.

"I guess the Dodgers proved they were the best in the National League," said Reuss. "They earned what they got. They beat a good club."

"They flat outplayed us," said the candid Oliver.

Believing he had the ingredients of another championship team, Brown did little off-season trading. There was, however, huge off-season news. Veteran announcer Bob Prince, a Pittsburgh legend, and his colleague Nellie King, a former Pirate pitcher, were fired. The dismissal brought a storm of protest from Prince's multitude of fans. But radio station KDKA held firm against the tide of complaints and later named Milo Hamilton and Lanny Frattare as replacements.

Well into spring training, Brown made a key move. He sent sore-armed pitcher Wayne Simpson to Philadelphia for outfielder Bill Robinson, a one-time schoolboy star at Elizabeth Forward. It was a trade that would still be reaping dividends five years later.

This was one year the Pirates did not mess around. They got out of the gate in a hurry, were in first place by late May and there to stay by June 6. They finished 6½ games in front of the Phillies. There were other good signs. The attendance, which had dropped to 1,110,552 the previous year, rose for the first time since 1971 to 1,270,023.

And there were some new faces on the scene. A big lefthander was called up from the minors in June and immediately impressed. John Candelaria won eight games that season and would soon be on to much better things. Zisk had established himself as an excellent hitter, though a bit of a liability in left field. And in the bullpen, a skinny righthander who had been floating around the minors for seven seasons was just beginning to be noticed. Kent Tekulve was 1-2 with a 2.25 earned run average that season.

Still, it was mainly the team the Pirates won a World Series with in 1971 that formed the nucleus of the club four years later. Stargell, Oliver, Hebner, Sanguillen, Robertson, Stennett, Ellis, Giusti, Kison and Moose were still around.

But it was not a team that could repeat that World Championship performance. They were no match for the Cincinnati Reds in the playoffs. The Reds swept the Pirates in three games. Cincinnati won the opener, 8-3, as Gullett topped Reuss; the second game, 6-1, as Fred Norman beat Rooker and the third game, 5-3, with reliever Rollie Eastwick getting the decision over Hernandez. The high point of the series was Candelaria's pitching in the final game. He set a playoff record by striking out 14 in 7⅔ innings. But that was about the only high point.

"We knew about their hitting and their speed and their defense," said Murtaugh, "but we didn't think their pitching would be strong enough to hold us. They just stopped our bats."

Brown went out looking for pitching and a gate attraction. He thought he had just the man, though he paid a dear price. Brett, Ellis and highly promising minor league second baseman Willie Randolph were traded to the Yankees for George "Doc" Medich, an Aliquippa native who had been a football star at Pitt and the winner of 35 games in the two previous seasons.

Ellis, who had refused to work in the bullpen and was suspended for almost a month late in the '75 season, had to go, but it was with reluctance that Brown parted with Randolph and Brett.

The trade boomeranged. Randolph became an All-Star and Ellis a big winner as the Yankees made it to the World Series. Medich never lived up to expectations, finishing 8-11, and the Pirates finished second to the Phillies. The Pirates charged from 15½ games back on Aug. 24 to move within three of the Phillies on Sept. 17 before faltering and finishing nine games back.

When the Pirates called a news conference on Sept. 29, it was widely expected that Murtaugh would announce his final retirement. Instead Brown shocked the city by resigning. "This is a joyous and sad occasion," he said. "I've had two great loves in my life, baseball and the little blonde girl I married. After 38 years I decided to devote most of my time to my wife, Din."

The man who had managed to show a cold posture to the public, but who was a warm human being, walked away from a job he had held since Nov. of 1955 when he succeeded the late Branch Rickey. "I've had enough challenges," said Brown. "I've come to a point in life where there was something I wanted to do and I did it."

Brown moved to California where he became a special assignment scout for the Pirates. Harding "Pete" Peterson was named vice president of player personnel and Joe O'Toole vice president of business administration. Joe Brown had simply been general manager, but it took two men to replace him.

The expected came three days later. For the fourth time, Danny Murtaugh retired. "My health was a factor," said Murtaugh. "This was one of my worst years of the last three. I was ill a few more times than people realized."

There were other reasons. "It's time for a younger man. And I want to spend more time with my grandchildren."

There would be no recommendation from Murtaugh concerning his successor. "The last time I stepped down everyone was in agreement it would be Virdon. But he didn't stay here too long, so since then I said I wouldn't do any recommending."

Less than three months later, Murtaugh was dead at age 59. He suffered a stroke at his Woodlyn, Pa. home and died two days later.

Back in Pittsburgh a new man was already on the job. He had, however, been hard to come by. He was Peterson's man right from the start but there were problems, to say the least. His man was Chuck Tanner, the New Castle native who already had a job managing Charley Finley's Oakland A's.

Finley, as Peterson was to find out, was a man you could deal with. But not at a small cost. When all the details were ironed out, Tanner came to the Pirates for Sanguillen and a reported $100,000.

"It's great to be managing the Pirates," said Tanner, all smiles. And a new era was upon the City of Pittsburgh.

It was run, run, run. Tanner and Peterson went away from the traditional Pirate formula for winning. They gave up hitting to get pitching, speed and defense.

At the winter meetings, Zisk was sent to the White Sox for Rich Gossage and Terry Forster, two relievers who stayed only a year. Another reliever, one who would stay around longer, Grant Jackson, was acquired from Seattle. The team was starting to change shape. The change became more dramatic in spring training. With Hebner having played out his option and signed with Philadelphia, the Pirates needed a third baseman. On the final day of inter-league trading the Pirates got their man. They dealt with Finley once again, and once again the price was high. Phil Garner came to the Pirates for Medich,

CHUCK TANNER
Return of the New Castle native

Giusti and minor leaguers Tony Armas, Rick Langford, Doug Bair and Mitchell Page. The last three have gone on to fine major league careers, but Peterson is having no regrets.

The Pirates fought the good fight in '77. Gossage was magnificent but was soon to go to the Yankees and big money. Candelaria became the first Pirate pitcher since 1960 to win 20 games and also led the league in earned run average and percentage. Parker came in to his own, winning the batting title. Stargell missed much of the season and there were whispers that he was through. The

DAVE PARKER

PHIL GARNER

Photos by George Gojkovich

BILL MADLOCK

BERT BLYLEVEN

OMAR MORENO

ED OTT

JIM ROOKER

TIM FOLI

Pirates led the league for a brief time in May, and finished second to the Phillies, five games back.

More changes were in order. In the winter meetings of '77, more hitting went for more pitching. Oliver, approaching his 10th season with the Pirates, was traded to Texas for Bert Blyleven and outfielder-first baseman John Milner. The fleet and defensively gifted Moreno was installed in center field. A championship team was being forged.

But there was still a way to go. They made another grand charge at the Phillies, coming from 11½ back on Aug. 12 to finish 1½ behind. Parker won another batting title and added the Most Valuable Player award. Stargell quieted the whispers by hitting 28 homers and driving in 97. But the best was yet to come.

When the Pirates started slowly in 1979, Peterson was quick to make changes. The moody Taveras was traded to the Mets in April for Foli, who had none of the physical talents of Taveras but all of the intangibles a championship team needs. The next big move came on June 28, with the Pirates in second place, 6½ games out of first. Three pitchers, none of whom figured big in the Pirates' plans, were sent to San Francisco for Bill Madlock, a two-time National League batting champ. The arrival of Madlock enabled Garner to move to second base, his best position, and where Stennett, never fully-recovered from a serious ankle break in 1977, was having problems.

The team was set. The Pirates hit first place on Aug. 5. And then it was a dogfight with Montreal. The Pirates were a half game behind the Expos when the teams opened a crucial four-game series at Three Rivers on Sept. 24. The Pirates took three out of four, with Blyleven, Rooker and Kison getting the wins. Kison clinched it on the final day by defeating the Cubs, 5-3.

The rest of the country was starting to recognize the fam-a-lee. "I wish I could explain to everybody what a real close family all of us on this ballclub are," said Stargell to a group of reporters after the Pirates clinched. "We love each other. I'm just so happy, not only for myself but for all of the guys." Personally, Stargell had much to be happy about. He hit 32 homers, drove in 82 runs and was fast becoming an American hero. His performance earned him co-MVP in the National League with the St. Louis Cardinals' Keith Hernandez.

And then for the playoffs. This was one October that the Reds were no match for the Pirates. Getting some revenge for the three defeats they had suffered to the Reds in past playoffs, the Pirates won in three straight. They won the opener, 5-2, in 11 innings, the second game 3-2, in 10 and the third, at Three Rivers, 7-1.

Stargell hit a two-run homer in the third inning of the final game and was called from the dugout by the crowd to take a bow. "If they took a picture of my body it would show goose bumps everywhere," said Captain Willie. "The good Lord let's us shed tears at touching moments and that's what transpired with me. I wish there was a way to thank every fan individually."

That, in effect, is what Willie Stargell and his teammates did in the weeks to come. They did it by winning a World Series and making Pittsburgh the City of Champions.

"WE ARE FAM-A-LEE"

PIRATE PROFILES
Text By Jim O'Brien
Illustrated By Marty Wolfson

JOHN GALBREATH

THE GALBREATHS & "FAM-A-LEE"

"Our owners are willing to do whatever it takes to bring a championship to Pittsburgh."
—Harding Peterson

John W. Galbreath gazed longingly at Roberto Clemente's last uniform, which is showcased in the trophy room at his huge country estate, Darby Dan Farm, just outside Columbus, Ohio, and offered, "Black and gold are great colors. Powerful. Frightening almost. That's important in sports."

If there's an edge, Galbreath wants it, whether it's in the baseball business, where he is principal owner and chairman of the board of the Pirates, or in the real estate business, where he made his fortune.

Galbreath, 82 at the start of the 1980 season in which his team would attempt to defend its World Series championship, is a man of great vision, a builder, a winner. He bought the ballclub in 1946 for $2,500,000. His partners were Pittsburgh attorney Tom Johnson, singer Bing Crosby, and Frank McKinney. In 1950, Galbreath bought out McKinney. Crosby's death left Galbreath and Johnson as sole owners, with Galbreath holding about 70 percent.

Their team has won three World Series titles.

Unlike Art Rooney, who resides in Pittsburgh, and is always present at Three Rivers Stadium or somewhere on the local sports scene, Galbreath has wider-ranging interests and commutes here only on occasion. He's not as well known to Pittsburgh sports fans. But the head of the Pirates' "Fam-a-lee" was profiled in the *Pittsburgher* magazine in a revealing manner by Jeffrey Zaslow.

A multimillionaire, Galbreath owns the Pirates, and a racing stable that has produced winners in some of the world's biggest thoroughbred races, including the Kentucky Derby twice. His real estate company has helped shape the skyline of many cities, and certainly he's left his mark in Pittsburgh in more ways than his team's World Series triumphs. In addition to the U.S. Steel Building, the tallest in town at 64 stories, Galbreath's company manages the William Penn Building, the Oliver Building, the Porter Building, the Blue Cross Building and 301 Fifth Avenue.

Galbreath's son-in-law, James Phillips, a vice-president in the real estate company, told Zaslow, "He can get tough when he has to, but I think he'd rather lay down the rules by his principles. And he'll go the extra mile to give a person an additional chance."

Sports Illustrated once carried an article in which it was stated, "If Galbreath has any detractors in sport or business, they are as hard to find as atheists in the Vatican."

One of the reasons Galbreath isn't a very visible ball-

DAN GALBREATH

TOM JOHNSON

VICE PRESIDENTS

HARDING PETERSON

JOE O'TOOLE

JACK SCHROM

club owner is because of his belief that "the owner hires the manager and the manager runs the team his own way. We (the owners) have the final say on all deals and trades, but decisions made in the dugout are not my business."

His son, Danny, a charming and affable gentleman, serves as president of the Pirates and is more responsible for the club's overall operation. "Danny could run the business if I never showed up another day," the father says of his sports-real estate empire. "He's got a fine mind. And he's honest, too."

Thomas P. Johnson serves as the club's vice-president and secretary, and he's been with the ballclub since it was purchased from the Benswanger family on Aug. 8, 1946. His two sons, Thomas and James, are also directors of the club.

The front-office brass includes three vice-presidents, all familiar to the fans these days. They are Harding Peterson, who runs the shop and is responsible for player personnel, Joe O'Toole, who's responsible for administration, and Jack Schrom, a more recent addition to the staff, who's in public relations and marketing. In the early '70's, of course, GM Joe Brown was the front-office boss of the Pirates and the architect of a championship franchise.

Peterson has been with the Pirates' organization as a player, manager, farm director and scouting director and you name it for over 25 years. O'Toole, once an Oakland kid and Schenley High grad, came out of the military service and joined the club in 1946. Schrom, a terrific golfer out of Ohio State—but not quite in a league with Jack Nicklaus—has had much to do with the Pirates' improved public image, and increased attendance.

"We do have a family here," said Peterson. "And our owners are willing to do whatever it takes to bring a championship to Pittsburgh."

ADMIRATION SOCIETY
Bucs' skipper Danny Murtaugh, Commissioner Bowie Kuhn and Orioles' Earl Weaver at '71 World Series Awards ceremony.

1979 WORLD CHAMPIONSHIP TROPHY

Joe Brown was GM of the Pirates in the early '70s, and the architect of a championship franchise. Here he displays the 1971 World Championship Trophy.

DANNY MURTAUGH

"He's been able to keep a fairly happy ship."
—Joe Brown

The image persists. Going to interview Danny Murtaugh, the manager of the Pirates, was like going to visit your grandfather. There he'd be, after a ballgame, sitting in a rocking chair in his office at Three Rivers Stadium, sipping on a glass of milk. Or spitting chew tobacco. Or both.

Murtaugh had a marvelous sense of humor, a twinkle in his Irish eyes, and he enjoyed jousting with sportswriters. Most of the time, anyhow. During the summer of '76, quite often he just looked pale and tired when you came upon him in his rocking chair.

He wasn't well, not really. We knew that. But none of us realized that his days were numbered. He had been ill before, on several occasions, but he had always bounced back, usually to manage his beloved Bucs once again.

He retired after that 1976 season. He suffered a stroke and died on Dec. 2, 1976, at age 59.

Murtaugh managed the Pirates on four different occasions—something no one ever did anywhere else in baseball—and led the team to four Eastern Division titles and two World Series triumphs—in 1960 and again in 1971.

His boss, general manager Joe Brown, once said of the dark-jowled Murtaugh: "He's not a flashy manager, but he always has a reason—a sound reason—for everything he does. And I think he's been able to keep a fairly happy ship."

In the third year of his first tour of duty, Murtaugh managed the Pirates to an unbelievable 1960 World Series victory over the New York Yankees. The team slipped to sixth place the next season, though, and then finished fourth, eighth and sixth again before Murtaugh was removed.

His successor, Harry Walker, was into his third season when Murtaugh was brought back to the bench. Murtaugh managed at a .500 pace in the Pirates' final 78 games, but they still finished sixth. He had been managing on an interim basis, and he gave way to Larry Shepard who had a two-year stint before Murtaugh came back a third time.

He came back in grand style. He directed the Bucs to an Eastern Division title in 1970, and was named major league manager of the year. He had been manager of the year twice before, in 1958 and 1959.

Murtaugh was named the Man of the Year for 1970 by the Pittsburgh Jaycees and won the Dapper Dan Award as the sports figure who did the most to promote Pittsburgh that year.

He wasn't in good health, though, and he stepped down in favor of his right-hand man, Bill Virdon, who led the team to another Eastern Division title in 1972. Virdon's team was struggling the next season, and Murtaugh was brought back for the final 26 games.

Murtaugh's finest managing job may have come in the 1974 season. The Pirates lost 10 of their first 12 games, and were 18-32 at one point. They put on an incredible drive and won 51 of their last 76 games and won the pennant on the final day of the season. It was their fourth division championship in five years.

Murtaugh made it five for six the next summer as the Pirates won another pennant. His team finished second in his final season of 1976. Altogether, his teams won 1,115 games and his .540 winning percentage ranks him among the game's greatest managers.

He's dearly missed on the Pittsburgh sports scene.

**DANNY MURTAUGH'S LAST GAME
OCTOBER 3, 1976**

Made from actual body measurements, this statue of Roberto Clemente is the work of Pittsburgh artist Ivo Zini. The original was presented to Clemente on "Clemente Night" (July 24, 1970) and is now on exhibit in the Sports Hall of Fame at Three Rivers Stadium. After Clemente's death, Pittsburgh Jaycees commissioned the above duplicate which was presented to the Baseball Hall of Fame.

ROBERTO CLEMENTE

"I was born in 1934, and again in 1955, when I came to Pittsburgh."
—Roberto Clemente

He was always a heroic figure, a sleek, compact-muscled man who could do it all on a baseball field, whether it was Forbes Field, Three Rivers Stadium or some distant outpost in this country or his native Puerto Rico. It took awhile for Pirate fans to truly appreciate him, and it took his untimely death in an air tragedy in 1972 to properly focus attention on his marvelous feats, both on and off the playing field. Real fame came to Clemente late in life, and more so when he was gone.

Roberto Walker Clemente came to the Pirates in 1955, brought here by Branch Rickey, and he played 18 summers—sometimes spectacular summers which stretched into falls, and found the Pirates winning the World Series—and he set the standards for the Willie Stargells and Dave Parkers to push toward these days.

He was something else, something special, an athletic marvel. Sometimes he was hard to understand, and to fathom, but this may have added to his mystique more than anything else. Clemente cried out to be loved, to be lauded, to be cheered, to be crowned as one of the game's greatest players.

He came from Puerto Rico, but Clemente became a big part of Pittsburgh. "In a way, I was born twice," Clemente said when he was honored in special ceremonies on July 25, 1970 at Three Rivers Stadium, his night at the ballpark. "I was born in 1934 and again in 1955, when I came to Pittsburgh. I am thankful I can say that I live two lives."

He didn't live either of them long enough, however.

Clemente was killed in an airplane crash on Dec. 31, 1972, one mile off the shores off San Juan, Puerto Rico, attempting to fly relief supplies to earthquake victims in Managua, Nicaragua.

His image was such among his good friends and teammates that one of them, Manny Sanguillen, fully expected Clemente to come walking out of the water, and return to play for the Pirates. It's no wonder that Clemente's life is scheduled to be made into a TV movie.

He was with the Pirates so long, yet he was gone too soon, leaving his wife, Vera, and their three children, as well as his many admirers, behind him. He left us with many cherished memories.

The rule requiring a ballplayer to be retired five years before becoming eligible for Baseball's Hall of Fame was waived, and Clemente was enshrined during ceremonies in the summer of '73 at Cooperstown, the sleepy and picturesque little community in upstate New York where Abner Doubleday was believed to have invented the game of baseball.

A life-like wax figure of Clemente was presented to Baseball's Hall of Fame on September 8, 1973, by the Pittsburgh Jaycees and the people of Pittsburgh expressing their love and admiration for a great athlete.

Those who can't make it to Cooperstown, or can and want to see more memorabilia heralding Clemente's many achievements with the Pirates, ought to check out the Three Rivers Sports Hall of Fame Museum and Theatre. A life-size wax figure of Clemente, as well as Honus Wagner and Pie Traynor, are on exhibit there in a shrine of tri-state area sports figures and lore that was created and co-ordinated by Pittsburgh artist and publisher Marty Wolfson.

Clemente became an "overnight sensation" with his sterling performance in the 1971 World Series. He led the Pirates to a comeback championship series victory over the favored Baltimore Orioles as only he could. He hit .341 for the season and .414 for the World Series.

The Pirates dropped the first two games of that Series in Baltimore, but bounced back to win the next three, then dropped the sixth game, so the Series was squared at three games apiece. Clemente had hit a home run in that sixth game, but it wasn't enough as the Orioles prevailed, 3-2.

In the deciding seventh game, Clemente gave the Bucs a 1-0 lead with his second home run of the Series. It was also the 14th consecutive World Series game in which Clemente had hit safely. He'd done the same thing when the Pirates won the World Series in 1960. He was only the second player ever to pull off that feat.

The Pirates won that seventh game, 2-1, and Clemente became a national sports hero. He was 37 years old at the time, and felt that such recognition had been long overdue. He felt neglected. "How come they call Pete Rose in Cincinnati Charlie Hustle?" asked Clemente. "I hustle just like Pete Rose and they don't call me nothing."

One thing they did call him was a hypochondriac, but again he felt it was undeserving. He was a thoroughbred. People generally conceded that he was a hitter of great consistency, a runner of consummate speed and that he had an arm of pure gold.

He joined baseball's elite on September 30, 1972—during his last season with the Pirates—when he doubled against New York's Jon Matlack to become only the 11th player in baseball history to get 3,000 hits. He hit .312 that year.

At the close of the '70s, Clemente remained the Pirates' all-time leader in games played, at-bats, hits, singles, total bases and runs batted in.

He won 12 Gold Glove awards, batted over .300 in 13 different seasons, and was selected for 12 All-Star games. He led the league's outfielders in assists five times, tying a major league record.

He had back-to-back 5-hit games against the Los Angeles Dodgers on August 22-23, 1970.

He was the National League's MVP and Player of the Year in 1966 when he batted .317 and had 119 RBIs.

He is still an inspiration to the Pirates. Willie Stargell speaks of him often, and is among those who most dearly miss the man. When Sanguillen came through with a game-winning performance in the 1979 World Series triumph, he said he did it in memory of Roberto Clemente.

Even in death, Roberto Clemente aids the Pirates' cause, and contributes to winning the World Series, and enhancing Pittsburgh's reputation as the City of Champions.

"You know all about him," said Baltimore's Brooks Robinson during that 1971 World Series. "But in real life he's even better."

Roberto Clemente's youngest son, Enrique, says goodbye.

ROBERTO CLEMENTE was enshrined in Baseball's Hall of Fame in the summer of '73 at Cooperstown.

CHUCK TANNER

"Happiness is what it's all about."
—Chuck Tanner

Chuck Tanner had an eventful year in 1979. He experienced the greatest highs and lows of a lifetime, all in one October week. While he was piloting the Pirates to a World Series triumph over the Baltimore Orioles, his 70-year-old mother Anna died.

Imagine that, and what a man might go through under those circumstances. It required a man like Tanner, who is always so enthusiastic and optimistic about things, no matter how dejected or pessimistic others might get around him, to survive such an emotional roller coaster ride.

His mother and dad, Charles Tanner, instilled and helped nurture the dream of this exceptional young man from New Castle to become a big league baseball player and, eventually, a big league manager.

It was his dream to come back home and manage the Pirates, which he did in 1977, and then, at age 50 in 1979, he guided them to a World Series victory that turned the City of Champions upside down. The Pirates' victory, coupled with the Steelers' earlier Super Bowl decision over the Dallas Cowboys, meant that Pittsburgh was the first city since New York in 1969 to claim champions in pro football and baseball in the same year.

"I'd love nothing better than to go back to Pittsburgh," Tanner once said when he was managing the Chicago White Sox. So you can imagine what it must have meant for him to accomplish the ultimate in his sport in his native diggings. During his days as an all-around athlete at Shenango High School, he used to run home from school to listen to the radio broadcasts of the Pirates' games, when Rosey Rowswell and Bob Prince were at the mike.

He was a Pirates' booster, from the beginning.

In 1979, Chuck led the Bucs to their most wins since 1909 by winning 98 games. Tanner had finally made it to the top. Twice before his Pirate teams had finished runner-up in the Eastern Division of the National League, and he had teams at Chicago and Oakland which finished runner-up in the Western Division of the American League. He had always been a successful manager in the major leagues, after joining the White Sox in that capacity at the tail end of 1970.

The '70s were quite a decade for the Pirates' popular skipper, and he was well-liked wherever he worked. "I've been fortunate that all of my life I've been involved in baseball," he says to explain his eternal smile. "Not only has it been good to me, but the friendships I've made are something else. I know doctors and lawyers who'd trade positions tomorrow to be in sports."

His 1978 Pirates mounted an unforgettable surge on the division-leading Philadelphia Phillies, coming back from an 11½ game, fourth-place deficit on August 12, and getting as close as one game out on September 19, before the Phils finally clinched it in the season's next-to-the-last game in head-to-head competition with the Pirates. The Baseball Bulletin named him 1978 Manager of the Year.

He led the 1977 Pirate club to its most wins (96) since the World Championship 1971 season. So he's done quite a job here.

"You can have money piled to the ceiling," Tanner tells you, "but the size of your funeral is going to depend on the weather. So happiness is what it's all about."

WILLIE STARGELL

"This is a city of nothing but champions."
—Willie Stargell

Willie Stargell could do no wrong in 1979. At times, it seemed like he could do it all. Everyone knows he led the Pirates to a National League pennant and a World Series triumph, but there were times when he also seemed to be inspiring the Steelers toward another Super Bowl.

There were times when Stargell was pushing and prodding, and back-patting his friends on the Steelers to another successful season. He was captain of all the sports teams in Pittsburgh. This is a unique, heart-warming man who is a cheerleader for the Pirates, the Steelers, Pitt and Pittsburgh at large.

Wherever he went in the winter of '79, and he went everywhere, he was an ambassador for the City of Champions. "This is a city of nothing but champions!" he told a Market Square gathering at a World Series celebration.

He was named the Man of the Year—not just in sports, but overall—by the Pittsburgh Jaycees, and he won the Dapper Dan Sports Award. He praised Pittsburgh and its people to the hilt—"there's a nice feel about Pittsburgh; it's my home now," he told everyone—and he urged them all to spread the good word.

He passed out stars to everyone.

"I think it's great to be working in a city with such a winning atmosphere," said Stargell. "It's good for everybody. We kinda spoil the people, but I'm hoping we can spoil them as long as we can."

Stargell spoiled the faithful fans in 1979, that's for sure. At age 38, he came through in Hall of Fame fashion in the Pirates' pennant push and ultimate triumph in the World Series.

He won three prestigious Most Valuable Player Awards. He shared the regular season award with Keith Hernandez of the St. Louis Cardinals and was the unanimous choice in both the National League playoffs and World Series. He drove in the Series winning run in the sixth inning of Game 7 with a two-run homer. He led in so many categories, including most extra-base hits (with 7) in a Series.

For the season, he led the Bucs in home runs (32) and was second in RBIs (82). He also led the NL in fielding percentage (.997) for first basemen and pinch-hitting (.467 average).

The year before, in '78, Willie was named NL Comeback Player of the Year by The Sporting News and UPI, batting .295 with 28 home runs and 97 RBI.

His best seasons, statistically, were in 1971, when he led the league with 48 homers, drove in 125 runs and hit .295, and 1973, when he led the league in homers (44) and RBI (119), hit .299 and set a NL record of 90 extra-base hits in one season.

As he entered the '80 season, Stargell said he was far from finished, and planned to pad all his Pirate totals. With Willie, nothing seemed out of reach.

Gold Glove Award Winner

"I hustle and play hard all the time. I give the fans 110 percent all the time."
—Dave Parker

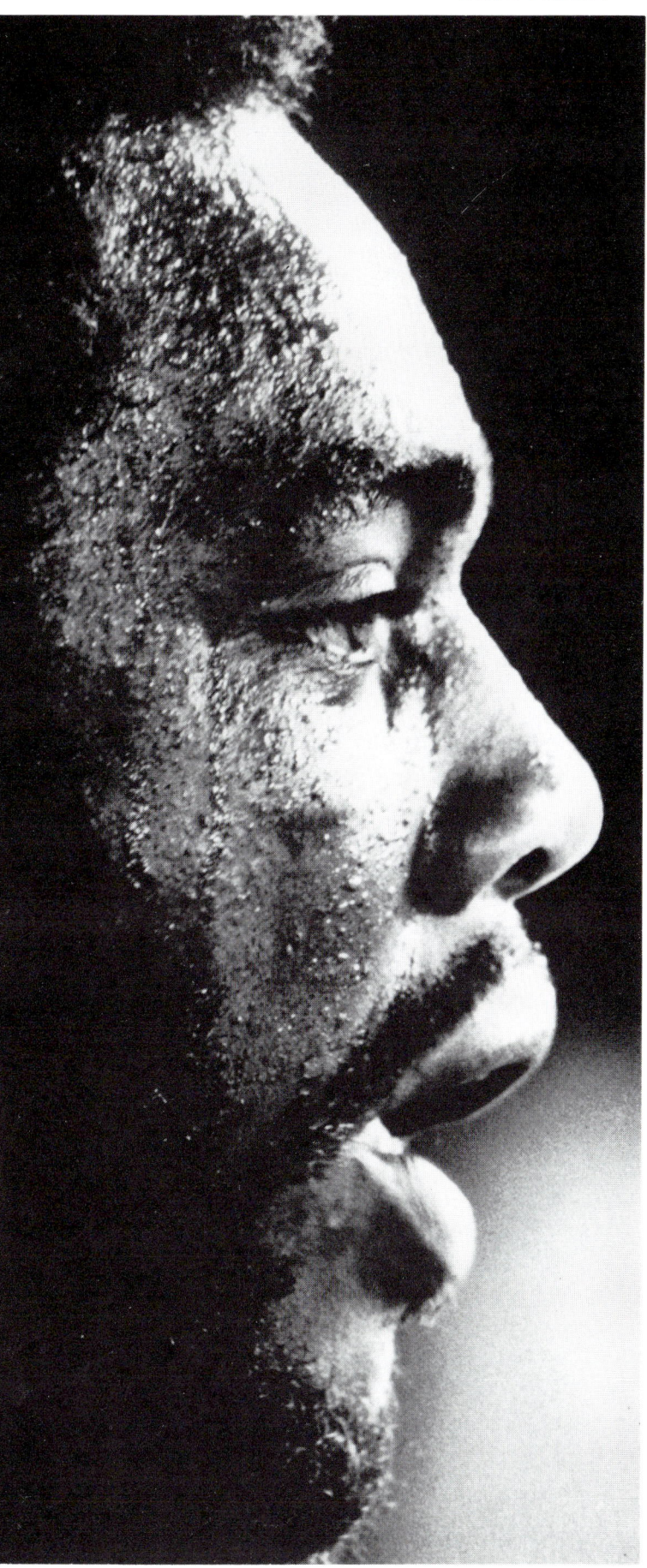

DAVE PARKER

The scene was at Al Lang Field in St. Petersburg, Fla., and the Pirates were in to play the Mets in an exhibition game during spring training in 1972. This big guy was coming to bat for the Pirates, and Charlie Feeney, the baseball writer for the Pittsburgh Post-Gazette, came scrambling through the press box to inform his friends from New York: "Watch this guy!" offered Feeney. "He's going to be something else! Look how big he is! Wait'll you see him hit the ball! Wait'll you see the speed this big guy's got!"

Just then, the big guy, Dave Parker by name, got his bat on a pitch and drilled the ball to deepest center field. It cleared the head of Tommie Agee and rolled to the wall. Parker took off, and ran the bases with the speed one doesn't expect to find in a man his size—6-5, 230 pounds back then—and he pulled into third with a standup triple. Feeney beamed in the press box.

The Pirates were so deep in talent in 1972, and Parker so young (not yet 21) that he didn't make the parent team. Instead, the Mississippi-born, Cincinnati-bred outfielder was sent to Salem in the Carolina League.

All he did there was lead the league in hitting (.310), at-bats (523), runs (91), hits (162), doubles (30), runs batted in (101) and stolen bases (38). He was, easily enough, voted Player of the Year in the Carolina League.

He divided the next season between Charleston in Triple A ball, where he batted .317, and Pittsburgh, where he hit .288 in 139 at bats. After that, he was a full-time Pirate.

By 1977, he led the National League in hitting with a .338 average, in hits with 215 and in doubles with 44. He also hit 21 home runs. He led outfielders in assists, with 26, to win his first Gold Glove Award. He followed that with his finest season, leading the league once again in hitting with a .334 average, and had 30 home runs and 20 stolen bases.

Following that fantastic 1978 season, he was named the NL Player of the Year by The Sporting News and Baseball Bulletin. The Pittsburgh Jaycees named him 1978 Man of the Year in Sports, and he was the 1978 recipient of the Dapper Dan Man of the Year Award.

He also signed a six-year contract with the Pirates that made him one of the best paid players in the game. It was a reported $6 million contract. It also put a lot of pressure on him to prove he was worthy of it.

He struggled for awhile during the 1979 season, but batted .310, and led the league in extra-base hits (77) and sacrifice flies (9), and was second in total bases (327), tied for second in runs scored (109), third in doubles (45), fourth in assists for an outfielder (15) and in the top ten in most other offensive categories. He contributed in post-season play to winning the World Series.

"I hustle and play hard all the time," points out Parker. "The fans haven't been cheated. I give them 110 per cent all the time. Everyone should know that I'm always trying to do my best.

"Our ballclub reflects the city. It's tough, hard-working and we're expected to produce on schedule. I stayed in Pittsburgh because it's my kind of town. I want to end my career with the Pirates."

BASKETBALL

DUQUESNE HAD ITS BIG DAYS IN BASKETBALL DURING THE DECADE

By Bob Smizik

"That 1972 was really something. It was a very satisfying year."
—Red Manning

Few universities in the country have a more grand basketball tradition than does Duquesne, and as the decade of the '70s opened it seemed certain that the Dukes would carry on as a national power.

Red Manning was the coach in those days, and following a school-record 15-loss season in 1967, the Dukes were immediately righted and went cruising into the '70s with 18 and 21-win seasons. The first four years of the new decade were equally outstanding. The Dukes won 17, 21, 20 and 16 games. Counting the last two years of the '60s, over a six-year period Duquesne won a truly outstanding 76 percent of its games.

Something happened as the decade moved towards its middle. Turmoil replaced calm. The school that had only three coaches in 50 years all of a sudden had three in five years. It was a difficult period. The once-proud program suffered through four straight non-winning seasons. But as the '70s ended, Duquesne seemed once more headed in the right direction. Mike Rice, a former outstanding player for the Dukes, an enthusiastic, charming guy who looks much younger than his 41 years, was the coach, and his recruiting successes the first two years on the job were an indication of much better days ahead.

That's exactly how it looked when the '70s opened. Manning, on the job since 1958, and himself a former Duquesne player, had weathered a few off-seasons, but mainly the Dukes were highly successful.

Billy Zopf, a superb guard from Monaca, was finishing up an excellent career. The Nelson twins, Barry and Garry, two 6-10 giants from Blawnox, were juniors who provided the strength, and on the wings there was sophomore Mickey Davis and junior Jarrett Durham. It was some team and they rolled to 16-7 season. It was good enough to earn an NIT invitation.

Despite the presence of the Nelsons and the 6-7 Davis, the Dukes couldn't handle Georgia Tech's big Rich Yunkus and lost, 78-68, in the first round of the tournament. Yunkus scored 28. Zopf's 18, 15 by Davis and 11 by Durham weren't enough.

Zopf was the only serious loss off that team and the Dukes were loaded in 1971. Both Nelsons were back along with Durham, Davis and Mike Barr. Up from the freshman team were Jack Wojdowski and Reuben Montanez. A transfer from Miami, Dave Rodi of McKeesport, also got some playing time.

The team rolled to a 21-3 record in the regular season and, of course, received a bid to the NCAA Tournament. This was a team, people felt, that had a chance to do something. But the luck of the draw matched Duquesne against Penn, the Ivy League champ, in an opening game at Morgantown. Penn came into the game undefeated. And it went out the same way.

When 6-7 Bob Morse went outside for long jumpers, the Dukes let him have them. "We didn't adjust quick enough," remembers Manning. At Penn, they called those long one-handers "Morse layups." They were enough to propel the Quakers to a 70-65 win and the season ended abruptly for Duquesne.

The Dukes were ravaged by graduation. The Nelsons, Durham and sixth-man Steve McHugh all left. The crushing blow, though, was Davis, who gave up his final year of eligibility to turn pro.

Manning was virtually stripped of players. There was talent returning, but in sheer numbers the Dukes were hurting. They had Barr, Wojdowski, Montanez, senior Darnell Roebuck, and up from the freshman team a true standout, 6-10 Lionel Billingy—the Big Train.

Beyond that, there was little. Rodi was sixth man and Dan Slater of Monaca, a seldom-used seventh man.

That was it, but that was enough. They started winning and winning. They moved up in the polls. They caught the fancy of the country. These were truly Iron Dukes. Manning seldom went beyond his sixth man. Billingy was excellent, on his way to averaging 21.6 points. It looked like clear sailing to another NCAA Tournament bid.

Late in the season, however, a newspaper story revealed that Rodi had played sparingly in his sophomore season at Miami. Duquesne claimed it was unaware of this. Rodi, it turned out, was in his fourth year of competition. The Dukes were afoul of the rules. They offered to forfeit no games; no one asked them to do so.

They got the message soon enough. They were a 20-5 team, but when bids went out they were bypassed first by the NCAA and then by the NIT. To this day, no one will

NORM NIXON takes shot during double overtime victory against Detroit. Flanking Norm are referee "Dutch" Shample and teammate Lonnie McClain.

say it was because of Rodi's ineligibility. But how else can a 20-5 team going uninvited be explained?

Despite the disappointment of not receiving an invitation, Manning looks back on that year as one of his most satisfying. "Those two years back-to-back were very exciting for me," he says. "We went from a wealth of talent to thin personnel. That 1972 team was really something. It was a very satisfying year for me."

The years were to become less satisfying after that. With Montanez averaging 17.8 points to lead the team, the Dukes were 16-12 the next season. When Billingy got hurt and missed seven games the next season, the Dukes slumped to 12-12.

Red Manning had enough. After four years as the assistant and 16 years as the boss, he announced his retirement from coaching. His record of 247-138 speaks for itself. He ranked as one of the best coaches in the country.

Duquesne was quick to promote Manning to athletic director, but it wasn't so quick to name his successor. Just as Manning had succeeded Dudey Moore, it was expected that John Cinicola, for 14 years the assistant coach, would succeed Manning.

Manning quit on Feb. 18, 1974. On March 13, Cinicola was given the job. "I waited 14 years, what's another month," he quipped.

Cinicola improved on Manning's 12-12 record by going 14-11 in 1975 as Kip McLane led the Dukes with a 14.7 average. It was, however, to be Cinicola's only winning season. It was hardly his only moment of glory.

JOHN "RED" MANNING
Head Coach 1958-74

Familiar quartet (l. to r.) Garry Nelson, Mickey Davis, Jarrett Durham and Barry Nelson helped take the Dukes to the NIT in the early '70s.

JOHN CINICOLA
Head Coach 1974-78

The Dukes staggered in at 12-13 the next season, but there was a distinct bright spot. A flashy guard from Georgia was coming into his own. Now a junior, Norman Nixon did not have a national reputation, but those who saw him play for Duquesne came away believing that this was a *player.* Nixon averaged 21 points as a junior.

He averaged 22 the following year, but the Dukes finished 12-14. They went off to the first Eastern Eight Tournament given almost no chance of winning.

They drew Penn State in their first game at Philadelphia's Spectrum. "I figure this thing is up for grabs," said Nixon. Nixon made good on those words by scoring 18 as the Dukes beat Penn State, 65-55. Don Maser, a 6-4 senior whose career had been pronounced "finished" two years earlier because of a kidney disorder, scored 15. For Maser, who hadn't started until February, it was the beginning of a memorable tournament.

The Dukes got a break when Massachusetts upset first-ranked Rutgers, 78-74. After losing by 13 to Massachusetts in January, Cinicola had said, "I'd like another chance to play them."

MIKE BARR (1970-72) takes it to the hoop. Mike went on to play in the ABA and NBA.

NORM NIXON

He got his chance in the semi-finals. UMass was sky-high after beating Rutgers. They were thinking title not Duquesne. "They had a look in their eyes that was looking right past us to the finals," said Maser. Nixon scored 20, Lonnie McClain 18 and Maser 14 as the Dukes moved to the finals with an 89-82 win.

It did not hurt Duquesne that their opponent in the finals, Villanova, was without its best player, Larry Herron, who suffered an ankle injury in the semi-finals.

Nixon was magnificent. He made 13 of 17 shots from the field and was credited with eight assists. The Dukes totally astounded just about everyone by taking the Eastern Eight championship with a 57-54 win. Nixon had 65 points and 18 assists for the tournament and was named MVP. Maser finished with 37 points, 24 rebounds and only five turnovers.

"We had good, tough defense and intensity in our all-around play," said Cinicola. "We also maintained our poise and were able to keep it under pressure."

It was on to the NCAA Tournament where the first-round opponent was VMI, which came in with a 25-3 record.

Nixon gave it his all, scoring 27 points and making 13 of 24 shots from the field. It wasn't quite enough. VMI won, 73-66. "Nixon couldn't do it all," said VMI Coach Charlie Schmaus, a Ford City native. "I guess he got tired."

The foul line may have had something to do with the outcome. The Dukes shot five free throws and made two. VMI was 15 for 20.

The Eastern Eight win had saved Cinicola's job, but when the Dukes came home 11-17 the next season, he

MOE BARR   RED MANNING   GARY MAJORS

DUQUESNE EASTERN EIGHT COLLEGIATE BASKETBALL CHAMPIONSHIP TEAM OF 1976-77

MIKE RICE
Head Coach

became an ex-coach. In a bitter battle, well documented in the newspapers, Manning overruled the school's athletic advisory committee and fired the popular, gentlemanly Cinicola.

It was a bit of a surprise when Rice, for two years Cinicola's assistant, was named the new coach. Rice went right to work and had an outstanding recruiting season, bringing in Doug Arnold and Bruce Atkins, the two most sought-after players in Western Pennsylvania.

Both moved into the starting lineup and the inexperience of the entire team showed. Though junior B. B. Flenory averaged 20.4 points and led the league in scoring, the Dukes finished 13-13 for the 1978-79 season. To make matters worse, they lost in the first round of the league tournament.

But the Dukes moved into the '80s with confidence.

BRUCE ATKINS
Big hope for the '80s

OFTEN A RIDL, PITT HAD ITS GOOD KNIGHTS

By Bob Smizik

BUZZ RIDL
Head Coach

"What we set as goals when we came here have been reached."

—Buzz Ridl

It was a decade of highs and lows for the Pitt basketball team. It was a decade that had a 25-win season and a decade that had a five-win season. It was a decade of two post-season tournament appearances and a decade of numbing losses to the mighty and the meek alike.

It was a decade of Buzz Ridl and Tim Grgurich, of Billy Knight and Mickey Martin, of Keith Starr and Tommy Richards, of Kent Scott and Kirk Bruce and of Sam Clancy and Sammie Ellis.

It was a decade that began with Pitt in, er, the pits. The school had long treated basketball as a bit of a lark, something to occupy the time between the end of the football season and the start of spring practice. But when Bob Timmons resigned after the 1968 season, Pitt hired Buzz Ridl from up the road at Westminster, a highly successful small college coach, and thoughts of putting a consistently good basketball team on the floor danced in the heads of some people.

The Pitt press guide came out for the 1969 season announcing the school's basketball stock "was on the rise." And Pitt responded with a 4-20 season. The man who had won 216 and lost 90 at Westminster was finding the major college level considerably more difficult.

But Buzz Ridl was not a man easily put off. He and his energetic assistant, Grgurich, hit the recruiting trails hard. The 1970 freshman class included Jim Bolla, a 6-8 center from Canevin, Mickey Martin, a 6-5 forward from Baldwin and a 6-6 smoothie from Braddock named Billy Knight.

The foundation was being laid. Buzz Ridl was going in the direction he wanted. "I always thought we could do big things with players from Western Pennsylvania," said Ridl.

Freshmen were not eligible at the time, so Ridl took a team that had largely been recruited by Timmons into the 1970-71 season. Timmons had left behind one gem in Kent Scott, a bone-skinny deadeye from Raytown, Missouri. Scott's average fell off three points from the year before to 13, but Pitt started to take off. With Paul O'Gorek, a center from Indiana, and Mike Paul, a forward from Baldwin, also making important contributions, Pitt, despite losing its last three games, finished 14-10.

"After that season I saw we could do it," said Ridl.

There was a backward step the next season. Knight was all that people thought he would be, averaging 21 points and pulling down double the rebounds of any teammate, and Scott came through with 17 points a game, but the Panthers fell to 12-12.

Martin and Bolla were not yet ready and they waited, along with Kirk Bruce, a freshman from South Hills, for their chances.

HOME OF THE PANTHERS: Fitzgerald Field House filled to capacity (5,308)

A look at Pitt's won-loss record in 1972-73 season would indicate another step backward, but Ridl didn't see it that way. The team finished 12-14, with Knight averaging 23.7 and Martin 12.5, but Ridl liked what he saw. "We were in so many games," he said. "We were much better than our record. I was confident we'd have a good season the next year."

With Knight and Martin as seniors, Bruce and the redshirted Bolla as juniors, and Tom Richards and Keith Starr as sophomores, Pitt was eager for the 1973 season. A junior college transfer from Virginia, Lew Hill, was added to the cast, and two virtual unknowns, Willie Kelly, a walk-on from Philadelphia, and Ken Wagoner, a defensive specialist from Beaver Falls, also were to play key roles.

The season opened with a loss to West Virginia and then came the deluge. Twenty-two straight wins. They won the Steel Bowl, they won the Razorback Classic and they won at Virginia.

"After we won those two tournaments and then beat Virginia," said Ridl, "the team really came on. It did wonders for our confidence."

The team moved to as high as seventh in the national rankings, unheard of for a Pitt team. The streak ended at Penn State, 66-64, on a controversial call, but with a 23-3 regular-season record, the Panthers were off to the NCAA tournament for the first time since 1963.

In first-round NCAA play, Pitt defeated St. Joseph's, 54-42. From there the Panthers moved on to the Eastern Regional where Furman was dispatched, 81-78. They were one step away from the final four, but it was a mighty step. Their next opponent was North Carolina State, the team of David Thompson, Tom Burleson and Monty Towe, the team that was to win the national championship.

The Panthers played the Wolfpack tough in the first half, trailing, 47-41. Thompson played only 10 minutes before injuring himself in a spectacular fall.

He wasn't missed a bit in the second half as the Wolfpack pulled away to a 100-72 win. Knight had 19, Martin 12 and Richards 10 for Pitt, but those totals were no match for Burleson's 26, Towe's 19 and the 17 scored by Mo Rivers.

"North Carolina State just played a great game," said Ridl. "They obviously had a very good basketball team."

It was the end of a career for Knight, perhaps the greatest career in Pitt basketball history. His 1,713 points are third on Pitt's all-time list, his 938 rebounds are second.

"Bill's points and rebounds were not all he gave us," said Ridl. "He gave our entire team tremendous confidence. Just his being there meant so much to our players. When we needed the big basket, he got it. When you have a super player who never rocks the boat, it means something to the team. He just had the complete respect of the other players."

An era had ended at Pitt. The team would never rise to such heights again in the decade.

Bruce, Starr, Richards, Hill, Bolla and Kelly were all

And that was it for Buzz Ridl. "I could have stayed as long as I wanted," said Ridl on his departure. "I was told that last year and again this year. But certain things tell me it's time to go. Coaching limits you, and there are some things my wife and I would like to do.

"I feel good about this. What we set as goals when we came here have been reached."

To no one's surprise, Grgurich, an assistant at Pitt since 1965, was named to succeed Ridl. Almost from the start, a black cat followed him around. No sooner had he been named coach than Bennett, a player who could have carried Pitt for three more seasons, signed a pro contract with the Virginia Squires of the American Basketball Assn.

But, Starr, Richards, Kelly and Harris, destined to become Pitt's all-time leading scorer, were coming back and this was a strong nucleus. But not for long. In an exhibition game with the Yugoslavian National team, Starr went down with a knee injury. He was lost for the season. Richards, an excellent outside shooter, played most of the season with a broken wrist. His scoring average fell from 11.4 to 8.0, his shooting percentage from 48 to 43.

But they scraped, my how they scraped. This was to become the trademark of Grgurich's team. While Ridl always had a player who could put the ball in the basket, Grgurich would always have a player who could dive for the ball.

They finished 12-15 and the list of teams they almost beat was impressive. They were a player away from winning 18-20 games and Starr or Bennett could have been that player.

More bad news the next season. Starr elected not to take his final year of eligibility and signed with the Chicago Bulls. Grgurich had a great recruiting year, but this team needed a senior, not a group of freshmen.

Harris averaged 22.9 points and freshmen Sonny Lewis and Michael Rice were also in double figures. But with the exception of a stunning one-point win over nationally ranked Cincinnati, the season was a disaster. Pitt finished 6-21.

The house that Buzz Ridl built was in disarray.

BILLY KNIGHT

back the next season along with two freshmen of unlimited potential—Melvin Bennett and Larry Harris. Bruce, Starr, Richards and Bennett all averaged in double figures and Bennett did the same thing in rebounding.

The team finished 17-10 in the regular season and was invited to the NIT. They beat Southern Illinois, but lost to Providence.

MELVIN BENNETT

KEITH STARR

More bad news the next season. Rice became academically ineligible and Lewis quit the team in mid-season. But the Panthers fought back. And they had a fighter leading them. Despite Harris' presence, freshman Sam Clancy became the leader of the team. Harris averaged 20.6 and Clancy 14.0. Clancy added 12.1 rebounds and was named Player of the Year in the city. Terry Knight, Billy's brother, was developing into a fine player in his own right and averaged 10.2 points.

LARRY HARRIS

TIM GRGURICH
Head Coach

The team finished 16-11, a record which included a win and a loss in the Eastern Eight Tournament. It was the second year for the league, but the first year the tournament was held in Pittsburgh. It was an immense success. Pitt beat George Washington in the first round before losing to eventual champion Villanova in the semi-finals. A crowd of 13,376 attended the semi-final doubleheader, a shock to some but an indication the league was a hot-item in Pittsburgh.

It was the end of Harris' career, and Grgurich had to find a way to replace 1,914 points.

It wasn't easy, but Pitt was a better team in 1978-79. Sammie Ellis, a j.c. recruit from Georgia, joined Clancy and Knight to give Pitt a super-quick front line, one that most teams could not match up with. There was a nine-game winning streak that included a two-point win at Duke and a more successful Eastern Eight Tournament.

The Eastern Eight Tournament really took off this year.

SAM CLANCY

The crowd for the semi-finals was 15,208. That was expected because of advance ticket sale. What wasn't expected was the crowd that came out for the finals, where only one game was played and where only one Pittsburgh team was represented. The figure was 16,009, a Pittsburgh college basketball record, for a Pitt-Rutgers final.

The Panthers finished the 1978-79 season at 18-11. During the summer a significant honor came along. Clancy was chosen as a member of the United States team in the Pan-American Games and came home with a Gold Medal.

But later that summer, he was struck down with a serious and mysterious illness that left him in intensive care for a brief time.

Clancy was not the same player the following season. His statistics dropped, but Ellis and Carlton Neverson picked up the scoring slack. The Panthers made it to the semi-finals of the Eastern Eight Tournament where they lost to Villanova, 72-59, as a record crowd of 16,172 watched.

Pitt was invited to the NIT, where it lost in the first round to Duquesne.

A day later, Grgurich, coming off a 17-12 season, shocked the city by resigning.

The Panthers marched off into the '80s with a new coach in Roy Chipman and an optimistic outlook, and with fond and somewhat mixed memories of the previous 10 years.

ROY CHIPMAN
Pitt's Coach for '80s

TERRY KNIGHT

HARVEY AND MALONEY MAKE THEIR MARK AT CARNEGIE-MELLON

"We've proven in all sports that we can have winning teams at Carnegie-Mellon."
—Dave Maloney

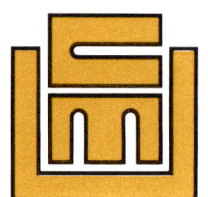

When Dave Maloney, an unknown high school coach, accepted the basketball coaching job at Carnegie-Mellon in 1975, a newspaper story called him a masochist. The job seemed hopeless. Maloney's immediate predecessor, Rudy Yaksich, compiled an 8-56 record in three seasons, including one year of 1-22. Before Yaksich, Jim Brown was 9-27 for two years.

Carnegie-Mellon had not had a winning season in nine years. This was a program as low as Panther Hollow.

It didn't get all that much better in Maloney's first year. The Tartans finished 6-14 and the future looked bleak.

After that difficult first year, Dave Maloney has been a bit of a miracle worker for the Tartans. CMU was 54-33 over the last four seasons of the '70s.

The highlights of the decade came in 1977 when a team led by George Harvey, the school's all-time leading scorer, finished with an 18-6 record and won the championship of the Presidents' Athletic Conference.

It was quite a season. CMU not only ended its 10-year losing streak, it won its first-ever title in the PAC. To top it all off, Harvey was named a Division III All-America by *The Basketball News*, the first Carnegie-Mellon basketball player ever to achieve that honor. The fact that the team lost in the first round of the NCAA Division III tournament did nothing to diminish its accomplishments.

Harvey was joined on that team by Lester Harper, Larry DiCicco, Greg Chambers and Marty Costa.

"Some people thought I was moving into an impossible situation," said Maloney. "But I think we've proven in all sports that we can have winning teams at Carnegie-Mellon."

With Harvey returning, the Tartans slipped to 14-7 the next season, but it was still good enough for second place in the PAC. They ended the decade with an 11-9 record in 1979, also good enough for second place in the league.

"We've had some fine players here," said Maloney. "Of course George Harvey was the best, our first All-America, but there have been others. Larry Hufnagel was an academic All-America and Marino DeFilippo was a three-year starter."

Hufnagel, a South Hills Catholic graduate, scored over 1,000 points in his career. DeFilippo led the PAC in assists in his senior year.

It was a decade that started on the lowest of possible notes and one that ended on a high note. Dave Maloney was no masochist. Just a good basketball coach.

DAVE MALONEY
CMU Coach

GEORGE HARVEY

LARRY HUFNAGEL

CREAM OF KROP ROSE TO TOP IN EARLY '70s AT ROBERT MORRIS

"We had so many good kids it's hard to pick out just one ... It was a great era."
—Gus Krop

The glory years of the '70s were the early years for Robert Morris. And, my, how they were glory years. With the volatile Gus Krop, a demon on the floor, a pussycat off it, doing the coaching, the Colonials began the decade as a national junior college power and never budged from that position.

For the first seven years of the decade, Robert Morris won 159 games, an average of 23 a season. Krop's team won the regional junior college tournament twice and lost in the finals four other times.

All that glory came to an end, however, in 1976 when the Moon Township college made the giant leap from junior college to Division I of the NCAA. It was too big of a step. Maybe that was so because it was made without Krop. The popular coach announced his retirement when RM moved up to major college status. The program hasn't been the same since. In four years as a Division I team, Robert Morris had a 31-71 record and had yet to have a winning season. The closest the Colonials came was 13-14 in 1978-79.

Krop, a cop all of his life, still heads the security force at Robert Morris. He looks back fondly on those excellent teams of the early '70's.

RM'S JONATHAN MARSHALL and RON HIGHTOWER

"Of course the best team we ever had was in 1968-69 when we lost in the national finals," says Krop. "But we had some terrific teams after that. People around here say the best team was in '73-'74. We beat Vincennes at Vincennes, we beat Mercer at Mercer. Those were two of the best teams in the country. Mercer went on to win the national championship. I guess that team lacked just one more player. We didn't have quite the depth we needed."

Two players who later went on to fine careers at Canisius, Tim Stokes of Ringgold and Craig Prosser of South Side Catholic, were the stars of that team which finished 23-5 and lost to Allegheny Community College in the regional finals, 80-79.

Another team that Krop remembers well is the 1970-71 club. And small wonder. It won 28 games and finished seventh in the national tournament. From that team, Jonathan Marshall of Clairton and Jim Dashield of Ellwood City went on to play at Penn State and Ron Hightower of Allegheny High at Cincinnati.

"We had so many good kids it's hard to pick out just one," says Krop, "but I guess the guy with the most talent was Hightower."

Hightower twice made All-America honorable mention. Other RM players to gain that status were Stokes (1974), Jeff Butler and Pat Hill (1975) and Jesse Hutson (1976).

RM closed out its junior college program in 1976 with a 22-6 record. From that team, Earl Cureton went on to an outstanding career at Detroit, Lovell Joiner to Eastern Kentucky and Hutson to West Virginia.

But after that, the glory was gone. With Matt Furjanic coaching, Robert Morris is hoping for more of those great days in the '80s, but a tough road lies ahead.

Behind, though, lies a memorable one. "It was a great era," says Krop.

GUS KROP
Colonials First Coach

CONBOY PUTS POINT PARK ON NATIONAL HOOP MAP

"We reached a lot of milestones. We did a lot of things people thought we couldn't do."
—Jerry Conboy

Jerry Conboy arrived on the scene at Point Park College in 1969, fresh out of a high-powered program at Davidson, where he was an assistant to Lefty Driesell, and full of ambition and grand plans.

He talked about making Point Park a national power. He talked about going to the NIT.

Then the basketball season began, and Jerry Conboy found out that this wasn't Davidson. The Pioneers were 11-14 that first year and 7-17 the next. But things were not to remain that way for long. Jerry Conboy was not a man used to losing.

"What happened," recalls Conboy, "is that as soon as I got here I upgraded the schedule but I couldn't get the talent in to meet the schedule. We didn't have much to sell at the time."

Conboy worked as hard as three men and soon the wins started to come. The Pioneers were 13-12 in 1972 and 15-9 the next year. It was that season the Pioneers began a streak of reaching the NAIA District 18 tournament that continued throughout the decade.

"We're very proud of the fact that we've gone to the tournament eight straight times," said Conboy. "We consider that a fine achievement."

But the finest achievement was made by the 1978-79 team. In the last year of the decade, the Pioneers had their finest hour.

With Terry Peavy, Sonny Lewis and Melvin Paul leading the way, the Pioneers roared to a 24-4 record in the regular season. They moved through the District 18 playoffs, defeating Clarion, 97-84, and Westminster, 78-69.

For the first time in Point Park's history, it was on to the NAIA tournament. And heartbreak. With Peavy, who was later to be selected in the NBA draft, scoring 34 points in a marvelous exhibition, Point Park lost in the first round to Henderson State, 70-69. Henderson went on to reach the finals.

Conboy looks over the decade with pride in his voice. "We reached a lot of milestones," he says. "We did a lot of things people thought we couldn't do."

Helping Point Park achieve those goals were some excellent players. Conboy remembered some of the best.

He cited Bob Rager, Larry Anderson, Jim Ney, Bobby Franklin, Peavy, Lewis and Paul.

Rager (1974), Ney (1975) and Peavy (1979) were honorable mention NAIA All-Americas. Franklin (1977) was second team All-America.

Conboy takes special pride in Franklin, a four-year regular who holds almost every Point Park record. "He's the greatest college scorer the city of Pittsburgh has ever had," says Conboy. "He's the only player in the city to ever score more than 2,000 points." Franklin scored 2,020 points, some 400 more than Paul, the school's No. 2 all-time leading scorer.

Maybe Point Park didn't reach the goals that Jerry Conboy set for himself at the start of the decade. But the school located in the middle of Pittsburgh's downtown area has made its mark on the college basketball scene.

"At the start of the decade no one knew who we were," says Conboy. "Now we get letters from kids in other states wanting to come to Point Park. We've come a long way."

Coach JERRY CONBOY watches intently along with his Assistant LARRY ANDERSON.

BOBBY FRANKLIN **SONNY LEWIS** **TERRY PEAVY**

LITTLE ALLEGHENY COMMUNITY COLLEGE BECOMES A LARGE SUCCESS STORY

"We're not only proud of the fine teams and players we've had, but of the fine people we've sent out into society."
—Bill Shay

BILL SHAY
ACC Coach

There could be little doubt that the most successful college basketball played in Pittsburgh in the '70s was played on the junior college level. And no team won more often than did the Allegheny Campus of the Community College of Allegheny County, known as ACC.

Bill Shay, a basketball player at Pitt in the '60s, came to ACC for the 1969-70 season and posted a 13-13 record. It was the last time ACC would have anything approaching a losing record.

For the next three years, ACC was 19-7, 20-7 and 24-3.

But it was the following year that ACC had its greatest success. Led by Harold Johnson, who later went on to a fine career at Oral Roberts, and Ralph McClelland, the Cougars finished 25-5. They advanced to the junior college region 20 finals where their opponent was cross-town rival Robert Morris. In an earlier game, Robert Morris won, 80-79. This time, ACC won, 80-79.

ACC needed one more win to advance to the national tournament. This time the opponent was Mercer of New Jersey. Bill Shay remembers it well. "We lost by two points," he said. "From there Mercer went on to win the national title. They won in a breeze. They won by 20, 25, 20 and seven points. I don't think I'd be wrong in saying we were the second best team in the country and didn't even make it to the national tournament."

ACC has not won the region since, but its success continued to be large. They were 20-4 the next season and finished off the decade with years of 21-5, 28-7, 17-8, 18-12 and 23-6 in 1979-80.

"It's been a very satisfying experience," said Shay. "We're not only proud of the fine teams and fine players we've had, but of the fine people we've sent out into society."

Pressed to name his top five players, Shay came up with this list: Harold Johnson, Ralph McClelland, who had a fine career at Pitt, Gene Turner, an all-time great at Carnegie-Mellon, Terry Peavy, one of Point Park's best players ever, and George Harvey, Carnegie-Mellon's all-time leading scorer and a Division III All-America.

It was a great 10 years for Shay and ACC and nothing figures to change in the '80s.

CITY HIGH SCHOOL BASKETBALL: WINNERS OF FOUR STATE TITLES

By Bob Smizik

Schenley High and the emergence of the City League is the basketball story of the '70s. This was the decade that made Schenley not just a team known throughout the city and throughout the state, but throughout the country.

Maurice Lucas at Schenley in '71.

There are almost 200 high schools in the state of Pennsylvania that play Class AAA basketball. Twelve of those schools are in the City of Pittsburgh. That comes out to something like six percent. With such a statistic, it would not figure that Pittsburgh would be making much of a noise when it came to winning state championships. In the decade of the '70s, however, with the odds considerably stacked against them, City of Pittsburgh teams won the state championship four times.

Once more, on the scholastic sports scene, Pittsburgh proves itself to be the City of Champions.

On the high school basketball level, at least, it owes much of that reputation to Schenley High. The powerful Spartans, starting with Maurice Lucas and Ricky Coleman and finishing with Larry Anderson and Dave Thornton, dominated the state in the '70s, winning titles in 1971, 1975 and 1978.

Schenley's one-time neighbor at the other end of The Hill District, Fifth Avenue High, won the state title in 1976. Fittingly, it was the last year of Fifth Avenue's existence.

To add to the city's luster on the high school basketball floor, two teams from the nearby suburbs also won state titles during the same decade. General Braddock was the champ in 1973 and Fox Chapel in 1977. Going a little farther away from the city, but certainly staying in the western end of the state, Beaver Falls won the state title in 1970, Farrell in '72 and Valley High of New Kensington in 1979.

Schenley High and the emergence of the City League is, however, the basketball story of the '70s. This was the decade that made Schenley not just a team known throughout the city and throughout the state, but throughout the country.

The marvelous team of 1971 had much to do with it. Three players from that team went on to play major college basketball. Lucas went to Marquette, Coleman to Jacksonville and Jeep Kelley to Nevada-Las Vegas. But this 1971 team, coached by Spencer Watkins, did more than produce great talent. It ended a myth. It was the team that won respect for the City League. For years there has been a theory across the state that city kids could not play the disciplined game that was necessary to win on the state level.

And, at first, Schenley didn't help erase that theory. In 1970, on a team that had Coleman and Lucas and Clarence Hopson, who went on to a fine career at St. Francis, Schenley held a large lead over Beaver Falls at halftime of the state semi-final. The Spartan players left the Johnstown War Memorial floor with arms raised and waving to their friends at the half.

Beaver Falls went off business-like and returned to win the game.

It was a lesson Schenley never forgot. It was a lesson the City League never forgot.

A year later Schenley, with Watkins a year wiser, was back in the same Johnstown War Memorial for the same state semi-final. Only this time the opponent was perennial champion Farrell coached by the legendary Eddie McCluskey. Farrell and McCluskey, the feeling went, would teach those Schenley kids another lesson.

Instead, it was Schenley doing the teaching. With Kelley, only a sophomore, scoring 19, Lucas 18 and Coleman 15, Schenley led Farrell by 16 points before settling for a 74-63 win.

"The best team won," said a crushed McCluskey. And a dynasty of City League greatness was born.

Norm Frey's Peabody High School team, led by Mel Bennett, reached the state finals two years later, only to lose to Abington.

WTAE's Bill Hillgrove hosts Schenley coach Fred Yee.

Schenley students signal 'We're No. 1' in 1978.

The next year, Schenley and Fifth Avenue battled in the state semi-final. It was a classic Pittsburgh confrontation. The two City League teams had beaten back all other competition from the western end of the state to reach this spot.

Fifth Avenue had won both regular season games, but the Spartans had come back through the state playoffs for another chance. This time they brought Sonny Lewis, Kelley's step-brother who had missed the two regular season games with a broken foot. Lewis scored 20, as did 6-11 Kelvin Smith, and Schenley advanced to the state final with a 78-63 win.

Once in the finals, it was revenge for the City League. The team that beat Peabody the year before, Abington, came oh, so close to making it two straight but Schenley prevailed, 65-64. The Spartans, with Wayne Williams joining Smith and Lewis to form a superb trio, had their second state title of the decade.

There was to be no stopping Fifth Avenue the next season. Not even a teacher's strike which had robbed the Archers of vital pre-season play. Sam Clancy, only a junior, and Bill Clarke gave Fifth Avenue a devastating inside game. On the outside there were juniors Warner Macklin and Puffy Kennedy. It was a team of all-staters. And it was a team, not surprisingly that would not be beaten.

The Archers finished 15-0, defeating Farrell, 58-46, in the semi-finals and Norristown, 53-42, in the finals. In the semi-finals Clarke scored 24 points, which prompted McCluskey to say, "Part of our game plan was to concentrate on Clancy and hope Clarke had a bad game. It looks like we concentrated on the wrong man."

Maybe Norristown was concentrating on Clarke the next night because Clancy scored 22.

It was the last game for Fifth Avenue. The students would be bussed to the new Brashear High the next season. With Clancy, Macklin and Kennedy coming back, another state title was in the offing.

Maybe Clancy had a feeling that night: "We could win it for Brashear next year, but it wouldn't be the same as winning for Fifth Avenue."

And it wasn't. Brashear was stopped by Beaver Falls, which, in turn, lost to Fox Chapel. With Rick Keebler coaching and Stu Lyons starring, Fox Chapel finished 29-1 and defeated Steelton-Highspire, 81-71, in the state finals.

The next year once again it was Schenley, this time with

Fifth Avenue's Sam Clancy shows his stuff in '75-'76 season.

Fred Yee coaching. By the narrowest of margins. With Thornton scoring 29 and James Smith 18, the Spartans slipped past Erie Prep in the semi-finals, 67-66, in overtime. Schenley trailed by six with 90 seconds left. Anderson hit a 20-foot jumper from the corner with four seconds remaining to send the game into overtime. Smith's three-point play in the closing seconds of overtime provided the margin of victory.

In the finals, the Spartans had to face the great Sam Bowie of Lebanon High. Though only a junior, the 6-11 Bowie was regarded as one of the best high school players in the country. Bowie got his 24 points, but Schenley got a 51-50 win.

Schenley was a favorite to repeat in 1979, but ran into an exceptional Valley team, led by Bill Varner, and was eliminated in the quarter finals. Valley went on to beat Allentown Allen in the state finals.

The City League does not field teams on the Class AA level, a classification that was dominated in the '70s by Midland High of Beaver County. Coached by Ed Olkowski, Midland, with a student body that often dipped below 200, won the state title in 1971, 1973, 1974 and 1976.

And when all the state titles are done with, the Roundball Classic holds forth in Pittsburgh. The brainchild of Trafford's Sonny Vaccaro and Jeannette's Pat DiCesare—started in 1966 by the Post Gazette Dapper Dan Club—the Roundball Classic has generally matched the best players in Pennsylvania against the best players from the rest of the United States. It was one of the original scholastic showcase contests and the most respected. It plays to a full house at the Civic Arena every year. And every year Pennsylvania gives the U.S. All-Stars all it can handle. And more often than not, it is players from Pittsburgh who are leading that Pennsylvania team.

Former Pitt and Braddock High basketball star Billy Knight fights off one-time idol Walt Frazier

PITTSBURGHERS PLAY CHAMPIONSHIP ROLE IN PRO BASKETBALL IN THE '70s

By Jim O'Brien

From Norm Van Lier to Norm Nixon, and Maurice Stokes to Maurice Lucas, Pittsburgh has always had a special place in pro basketball.

During his student days at the University of Pittsburgh, Braddock's Billy Knight papered the walls of his dormitory room with pictures of his favorite professional basketball players.

They included Julius Erving—"Dr. J" was Knight's No. 1 favorite—Rick Barry, Kareem Abdul-Jabbar, George McGinnis and Walt Frazier, among others.

"Those guys are my heroes," Knight once told a visitor to his room.

Several years later, on February 13, 1977, to be specific, at Milwaukee, Knight was playing in the 27th annual all-star game of the National Basketball Association with all of his heroes.

Erving, McGinnis and Monroe, as well as John Havlicek, Elvin Hayes, Pete Maravich, Bob McAdoo and George Gervin were playing for the East All-Stars.

The West All-Stars looked like the Western Pennsylvania All-Stars to a courtside observer who hailed from Pittsburgh. It was easy to feel proud, seeing Knight, an All-America at one's alma mater, out there with the best in the business.

His teammates on the West All-Stars included Norm Van Lier, who once teamed with Simmie Hill to lead Hank Kuzma's Midland High School Leopards to the Pennsylvania State Basketball Championship in 1965, and Maurice Lucas, who led Spencer Watkins' Schenley High Spartans to a state title, along with Ricky Coleman and Jeep Kelley, during the 1970-71 season.

Knight was now the No. 1 scorer for the Indiana Pacers, Lucas was the league's premier power forward with the Portland Trail Blazers, and Van Lier, who was a starting guard for the West All-Stars, was among the top playmakers in the pro ranks for the Chicago Bulls.

If you were a basketball fan from Pittsburgh, those three had to bring back memories, of exciting contests at the Pitt Field House, the Civic Arena and high school gyms scattered throughout Western Pennsylvania. If you knew Press Maravich, and remembered him from the days he was coaching at Ambridge High, rather than at Clemson University or Louisiana State University, then you could also take pride in "Pistol Pete" Maravich, his son, who was born in Aliquippa. Pete's dad was among the pioneers in professional basketball, playing for the Pittsburgh Ironmen back in the mid-1940s.

Yes, Pittsburgh has a professional basketball heritage, even if it has seldom had a solid pro franchise. There were the Ironmen of the 11-team Basketball Association of America, which was later absorbed into the National Basketball Association, there were the Rens (or Renaissance, to be more formal) of the American Basketball League, which began play in the 1961-62 season and collapsed midway through the following campaign, the Pipers of the American Basketball Association, who won the ABA's first championship at the end of the 1967-68 season, then moved to Minneapolis, and returned to Pittsburgh a year later, calling themselves the Condors.

The Condors called Pittsburgh home for two years, during the 1970-71 and 1971-72 seasons, before flying the coop, or folding the franchise.

For the most part then, pro basketball fans in this area have always had to follow the game on a long-distance basis, taking particular pride in the achievements of young stars such as Billy Knight, Maurice Lucas and Norm Van Lier, or those of two adopted sons, Connie Hawkins and, more recently, Norm Nixon.

Hawkins grew up in Brooklyn's Bedford-Stuyvesant section, but came to Pittsburgh at age 19 to play for the Rens, and won the scoring title that first season (1961-62) with a 27.5 scoring average.

NORM VAN LIER   "PISTOL PETE" MARAVICH
Pros from Midland and Aliquippa clash in NBA.

"THE HAWK"

Pittsburgh's adopted son, CONNIE HAWKINS, starred in three different pro leagues.

Later, The Hawk got his second shot at pro ball when the American Basketball Association came into being in 1967, and he led the Pipers to that league's first championship, and topped the ABA in scoring with 26.8 points a game.

In between the ABL and the ABA, Hawkins spent some time touring with Abe Saperstein's Globetrotters, and could even be seen—after a 50 cents donation at the door—playing for Porky Chedwick's All-Stars, along with former pros Ed Fleming, Jim McCoy and Walt Mangham, at the YMHA in Oakland.

He played his last season in the ABA, 1968-69, for the Minnesota Pipers. All the while he was prohibited from playing in the National Basketball Association, where he should have been displaying his tremendous talents all along.

It's a story that's been told many times, but Hawkins had been entangled in a college basketball "fixing" scandal and bounced out of the University of Iowa after his freshman season. He was barred from the NBA because of his alleged involvement with New York gamblers.

He came to Pittsburgh and played for the Rens and then their spiritual successors, the Pipers. Two Pittsburgh attorneys, David and Roslyn Litman, believing in his innocence, prepared a $6 million suit against the NBA. The Rens were owned by Dave's brother, Lennie Litman. In June of 1969, the Litmans brought the NBA to its knees. The Litmans made Hawkins a millionaire overnight.

Hawkins was absolved of taking part in the 1960-61 college betting scandals. He signed a five-year $400,000 contract with the Phoenix Suns and, as part of the settlement with the NBA, it was agreed that he would receive an additional $600,000 in annuities starting at the age of 45.

It was Friday the 13th of June, but it was hardly an unlucky day for Hawkins. He had been making $30,000 the previous year with the Minnesota Pipers. When the Litmans told Connie the good news, he broke into tears.

So pro basketball returned to Pittsburgh at the start of the '70s, but without The Hawk, the team had no chance of succeeding. It lasted only two years.

The lanky 6-8 Hawkins, however, was finally entering the big league of basketball. He couldn't have been happier; those were tears of joy.

In his first NBA season, at age 27, Hawkins led the Suns in scoring with a 24.6 average and was the starting forward for the West in the NBA All-Star Game and won first team honors on the league's year-end all-star five.

"If he hadn't got such a bad deal," Bill Russell once remarked about him, "you would mention Hawkins with Elgin Baylor and Bob Pettit."

"He has the biggest hands I've ever seen," said Dave DeBusschere of the New York Knickerbockers. "He handles a basketball as though it were a baseball. He doesn't run, he floats. Inside, he's one of the best scorers in the league."

To which Jerry Colangelo, the general manager of the Suns, added: "I've never seen anybody with so much ability, the hands, the tools, the size! How many guys 6-8 can bring the ball up the floor like he can?"

For four years, Hawkins represented Phoenix—as well as Pittsburgh—in the NBA All-Star Game. Early in his fifth season, Phoenix sent him to the Los Angeles Lakers. He stayed there two years, then moved on as a free agent for one final season with the Atlanta Hawks.

He attempted to join the Knicks, and go home again for one last fling, but the Knicks were not interested.

pittsburgh condors

SUITE 193 CARLTON HOUSE   PITTSBURGH, PENNSYLVANIA 15219   AC 412-566-1800

For Immediate Release

Stew Johnson scored a <u>record 62 points</u> as the Pittsburgh Condors whipped The Floridians last Saturday afternoon (March 6) and the 6-8 "local" boy from Clairton

 **The Pipers no longer play, and the Condors are extinct, but we won't soon forget them...**

JACK McMAHON	**JOHN BRISKER**	**STEW JOHNSON**	**GEORGE THOMPSON**	**MIKE LEWIS**

GEORGE CARTER	**CHARLIE WILLIAMS**	**CRAIG RAYMOND**	**ARVESTA KELLY**	**DAVE LATTIN**

During his absence, pro basketball floundered and failed in Pittsburgh. Gabe Rubin, an engaging Pittsburgh theatre entrepreneur, tried but didn't succeed in selling pro basketball at the Civic Arena. Gabe gave way to a New York conglomerate that owned Jack Frost sugar, among other things. The sweet-talking owners didn't fare any better than Rubin.

They brought in Marty Blake, who'd once been the front-office boss of the Hawks in St. Louis and Atlanta, and Mark Binstein, who'd been hustling for a buck every which way before coming to Pittsburgh, to run the show. Jack McMahon was the coach; Buddy Jeannette the business manager; Dick Groat, the executive vice-president; Fred Cranwell, the public relations director; Ray Melchiorre, the trainer.

The Condors' cast of thousands included John Brisker, a brilliant scorer from the University of Toledo, but a bust later on when he skipped out on the ABA for the NBA's Seattle SuperSonics; George Thompson, who also joined the Condors as a rookie, out of Marquette, and put in two solid, high-scoring seasons; and Simmie Hill, who came home for awhile, a reminder of that wonderful Midland High team, but too late to recapture the glory that once was.

There was another local high school hero, Stewart Johnson of Clairton, a 6-9 sharpshooter who got his pro start in the ABA and lasted its lifetime on the strength of uncanny long-distance shooting accuracy.

The lineup also included the likes of Mike Lewis, Charlie "Helicopter" Hentz, Charlie Williams, not to be confused with Chuck Williams, Charles "Chico" Vaughn, George Carter, Daddy Lattin, Arvesta Kelly and Mickey Davis.

There were other Pittsburgh and Western Pennsylvania connections elsewhere in pro basketball at the start of the '70s.

One of the best was Jack Marin, who grew up in Sharon and played for Eddie McCluskey at Farrell High School. He was not as highly-regarded as ex-Steelers Willie Somerset and Brian Generalovich when he graduated, but he turned out to be better. He was a first round draft pick by the Baltimore Bullets when he came out of Duke University in 1966.

He played 11 seasons in the NBA, was twice in the all-star game, and finished his career as one of the top 50 scorers in the history of the league. The only local player to do better was Jack Twyman, who came out of Central Catholic High School in Oakland and the University of Cincinnati, to play 11 pro seasons with the Royals, first in Rochester and then in Cincinnati, and, as the '70s ended, was one of only 30 players ever to score over 15,000 points in their NBA careers. Like Marin, Twyman played 11 pro seasons.

Marin's best season was 1971-72 when he averaged 22.3 points for the Bullets. During the off-season that followed, he was traded to the Houston Rockets in exchange for Elvin Hayes, and Jack averaged 18.5 points that year with the Rockets.

Stu Lantz, a 6-3 guard, graduated from Uniontown High School and the University of Nebraska, to become an NBA performer with five teams in eight seasons. In his heyday, he averaged 20.6 points a game with San Diego in 1970-71, and 18.5 points with Houston in 1971-72.

Freddie Lewis, a little guy at an even six feet, played for Neenie Campbell at McKeesport High School, went to Arizona State University when none of the local schools

FREDDIE LEWIS
Little Tiger From McKeesport

Photo by George Gojkovich

KENNY DURRETT
Former Schenley High standout moves on Nate "The Great" Thurmond

showed interest in him because of his size, and surprised a lot of people when he made the grade with the Cincinnati Royals for the 1966-67 season. A year later, Lewis jumped to the newly-formed ABA and played in all eight of that league's seasons, mostly with the Indiana Pacers, whom he directed to three ABA championships, with short stints at the end of his career with the Memphis Sounds and Spirits of St. Louis.

Stew Johnson, the hotshot from Clairton, also was an ABA pioneer and played throughout its lifetime, once averaging over 19 points per game with the New York Nets. His last season was 1975-76 with the Memphis Sounds, and then he went off to Europe to continue his jump shooting.

Two outstanding players, with local roots, whose pro careers spanned the '70s, were Maravich and Van Lier.

Maravich was the greatest scorer in the history of college basketball, breaking Oscar Robertson's records, while playing for his dad, Press, at LSU. He was a three-time collegiate scoring champion and All-America.

He was the first draft choice of the Atlanta Hawks in 1970. Later, while playing for the New Orleans Jazz, Maravich won the NBA scoring title, averaging 31.1 points during the 1976-77 season. This writer was at courtside one night in the Superdome in New Orleans that season when Pete popped in 68 points against Walt Frazier of the Knicks. Pitt's Billy Knight, then with the Indiana Pacers, finished second in scoring to Maravich with a 26.6 average, followed by Abdul-Jabbar, David Thompson and Bob McAdoo.

Van Lier was among the assists leaders in the NBA that season. Van Lier starred for Johnny Clark at St. Francis of Loretto, and was a third round draft choice of the Chicago Bulls in 1969. The Bulls traded him to the Cincinnati Royals right off the bat, and he played there 2½ seasons,

"STORMIN' NORMAN" VAN LIER
Challenges Kareem Abdul-Jabbar

MOE BARR
Ex-Dukes' star challenges Knicks' Dick Barnett at Madison Square Garden

Photo by Jim O'Brien

then went back to the Bulls for 6½ seasons, and completed his pro career with one season with the Milwaukee Bucks.

Out of his ten NBA seasons, Van Lier's best was his second season in Cincinnati, the 1970-71 season, when he averaged 16 points a game and led the league in assists with 10.1 a game.

Simmie Hill, whom Lewis told his teammates was the best high school player to ever come out of Western Pennsylvania, got his start in the ABA with Los Angeles and then Miami in 1969-70, and later saw service with the Dallas, San Diego, Pittsburgh and San Antonio teams.

With the start of the '70s, several Duquesne University players had brief trials in the NBA. Jarrett Durham, later an assistant coach at his alma mater, had the briefest fling, seeing action for less than a minute with the New York Nets in 1971. Moe Barr, from Penn Hills and Duquesne U., played 31 games with the Cincinnati Royals during the 1970-71 season.

Billy Zopf, a nice little brainy backcourtman from Monaca, also came out of Duquesne to play 53 games with the Milwaukee Bucks during the 1970-71 season, went into the military service and missed being with the Bucks when they won the NBA championship at season's end, with Kareem Abdul-Jabbar and Oscar Robertson showing the way.

Barry Nelson, who along with his 6-11 twin Garry had come from Fox Chapel to give the Dukes two pillars under the boards for three strong seasons, played 28 games during the 1971-72 season with the Bucks, as a backup to Abdul-Jabbar. Garry failed a tryout with ABA's Dallas entry.

That same season, Monaca's Mickey Davis departed Duquesne U. after his junior season to sign as a "hardship case" with the Condors. It was a move that left all parties unhappy. Davis moved on to Milwaukee the following year and played four seasons as a reserve forward-guard with the Bucks, averaging about five points per season.

During the 1971-72 season, Walt Szczerbiak, who had starred at St. Casimir's in Catholic Class B competition on the South Side, as well as George Washington University, played for the Pittsburgh Condors. He continued his pro career in the European League, and, as the '70s drew to a close, was the top star in Spain with the Real Madrid team.

In that same 1971-72 season, Kenny Durrett, a 6-7½ forward from LaSalle University, who had led Willard Fisher's Schenley High team to the state title in 1967, was the No. 1 draft choice of the Cincinnati Royals.

Bob Cousy, the coach of the Royals, felt he would be a great one. After all, Durrett had averaged 27 points his senior season at LaSalle. Jack McKinney, the coach at St. Joseph's, had called Durrett the most complete player LaSalle had since Tom Gola. Durrett signed a five-year, $1 million, no-cut contract with the Royals.

But Durrett was a big disappointment. He had injured his knee in his senior season and never played to his potential. The team moved to Kansas City in his second season. In four years, Durrett played in only 93 games.

"Durrett had the most ability of any city kid," claims Cleveland Edwards, a one-time rival from Fifth Avenue who became an assistant coach at Pitt. "He shouldn't have played that first year in the pros, not with his knee."

Three former local high school heroes and one Duquesne U. dandy broke into the pro ranks for the 1972-73 season. Two of them, Denny Wuycik and Steve Previs, came out of the University of North Carolina in 1972 and signed with the ABA's Carolina Cougars. George Karl came out of North Carolina that same season and signed with the San Antonio Spurs. Mike Barr went from the Dukes to the Virginia Squires.

Wuycik, who had teamed with Dickie DeVenzio to win a state title for Chuck DeVenzio's team at Ambridge High in 1968, played a couple of seasons with the Carolina Cougars, and one more with the Spirits of St. Louis in 1974-75. Previs, from Bethel Park, played just one year with the Cougars, but caught the eye of club owner Tedd Munchak, and became the president of a meat packing firm Munchak operates in Atlanta.

Karl, who starred for Dick Misenhelter's team at Penn Hills High, played five seasons with the San Antonio Spurs, three in the ABA and two in the NBA. The heady backcourtman then became an assistant coach and scout in the Spurs' organization.

Mike Barr, a 6-3 backcourtman from Canton, Ohio, left the Dukes for two years with the Virginia Squires, two more with the Spirits of St. Louis, and a final season (1976-77) with the Kansas City Kings.

Wilbert Robinson, who grew up on Pittsburgh's North Side and moved to Uniontown to play for "Horse" Taylor at Laurel Highlands High School, which he led to a state title, joined the Memphis team in the ABA for the 1973-74 season and had a short stint in the pros.

The 1974-75 season was the start of something big, as far as young basketball pros from Pittsburgh were concerned. A total of 16 pro players hailed from the Pittsburgh area that winter. Only ten years earlier, when there were nine pro teams rather than 25, Pittsburgh had only two representatives in the pro ranks, Duquesne grad Sihugo Green with the Baltimore Bullets and Jack Twyman, the pride of Pittsburgh's Central Catholic, with the Cincinnati Royals.

During the 1955-56 season, Green and Twyman were teammates on the Rochester Royals. Also on that team were Maurice Stokes, an all-NBA performer from Westinghouse High School and St. Francis of Loretto College; Dick Ricketts, an All-America at Duquesne University; Ed Fleming, from Westinghouse High and Niagara University, and Dave Piontek, another Western Pennsylvania product who played at Xavier University.

A young man in Pittsburgh could identify with that team, since Pittsburgh had no pro team of its own at the time. The same could be said about the ABA's Spirits of St. Louis during that 1974-75 season.

**MAURICE LUCAS—THE PRIDE OF SCHENLEY HIGH
In ABA Days...**

The Spirits' squad included McKeesport's Freddie Lewis, Ambridge's Denny Wuycik, Schenley's Maurice Lucas, Duquesne U.'s Mike Barr and Uniontown's Gus Gerard. Lucas and Gerard had both left college after their junior seasons to turn pro.

Gerard starred at Laurel Highlands and put in three years at the University of Virginia before signing a lucrative multi-year contract with St. Louis. The 6-8 forward averaged 15.7 points as a pro rookie, and was with five different teams in six years in the '70s, including Denver, Buffalo, Detroit and Kansas City.

Lucas may be the best pro basketball player to come out of Pittsburgh proper with the exception of Stokes.

Lucas started out as a six-foot guard as a sophomore at Schenley, played forward as a junior and was a 6-8 center as a senior when Schenley finished 26-2 and won the state championship. Lucas averaged 29 points and 24 rebounds. He grew 6½ inches in the summer after his sophomore year.

He went to Marquette University where he became the most dominant freshman in the school's history, playing for colorful Al McGuire. He averaged 28.6 points and 16.8 rebounds. Then he went on to two more varsity seasons, leading his team to a second-place NCAA finish to North Carolina State and David Thompson in 1974. He scored 21 points and had 13 rebounds in the championship game.

After his junior year, he decided to take the "hardship" route, and was drafted No. 1 by the Chicago Bulls. He couldn't come to a contract agreement and signed instead with the Spirits of St. Louis. In his second season, he was traded to the Kentucky Colonels in exchange for Caldwell Jones. He teamed up with Artis Gilmore in Kentucky, and

BILLY KNIGHT

finished runner-up to Gilmore in ABA rebounding.

The ABA's four best teams were absorbed into the NBA for the next season and Lucas, one of the leftovers, was picked up by the Portland Trail Blazers. Now, he was teamed with another great big man, 6-11 Bill Walton of UCLA. The 6-9 Lucas became a domineering frontliner in the NBA.

"He is the premier power forward in the game," said Paul Silas, no slouch himself under the boards.

Walton and Lucas led the Blazers to the NBA championship that first season together. Lucas led the Blazers in scoring during the regular season with a 20.2 average, and was even better in 19 playoff games with a 21.2 average and .519 shooting from the field. He finished ninth in the league in rebounding with an 11.4 average.

It was a rags-to-riches story for the 25-year-old athlete from Pittsburgh who once thought that swimming was going to be his best sport, and who fooled around with boxing at boys' clubs in his native Hill District neighborhood.

Portland pulled in nothing but sellout crowds while Walton and Lucas were there, but by the end of the '70s both had departed Portland and gone elsewhere to work.

Billy Knight came out of college the same season as Lucas, and met with more immediate success in the pros, playing for the Indiana Pacers. He teamed with George McGinnis to give them an all-star frontline.

Knight is as nice a guy as you are ever going to meet. He played ball for Moe Becker at Braddock High School, then Buzz Ridl and Tim Grgurich at Pitt. In 1974, he led Pitt to the Eastern regional finals of the NCAA playoffs, losing out to David Thompson and the eventual champion N.C. State squad.

Photos by George Gojkovich

...In NBA Days

Knight was the No. 1 draft pick of the Pacers in 1974, and he had some very nice numbers when he played for the Pacers. He averaged 17.1 points as a rookie, 28.1 in his second season to finish runner-up to his hero, "Dr. J," in the ABA scoring race, and 26.6 in his third season, second in the NBA only to Pete Maravich, and appeared, along with Lucas, in the 1977 NBA All-Star Game. He had contract difficulties after that, and ended up the following season with the Buffalo Braves, with whom he averaged 22.9 points. He divided the 1978-79 season between the Boston Celtics and the Pacers, returning to Indianapolis where he was happiest playing pro ball. McGinnis had made a similar return home since then. For some reason, Knight was not starting and scraping to score in double figures as the '70s came to a close.

At his best with the Pacers, the 6-6 Knight was called by Coach Bobby Leonard "one of the finest offensive forwards in pro basketball."

Lionel Billingy of Duquesne came into the ABA the same season as Knight and Lucas, but left after one season with the Virginia Squires.

Melvin Bennett, who played for Norm Frey at Peabody High School, was a prize recruit for Grgurich at Pitt and was the heir apparent to Knight's No. 1 starring role for the Panthers. But Bennett pulled out of Pitt after only one season to sign with the Squires. The beefy 6-7, 200-pound forward signed a multi-year contract. He played a year with the Squires, then two more seasons with the Indiana Pacers, and moved on to Hawaii of the Continental Basketball Association.

Another Western Pennsylvania product who left college early to turn pro, and ended up in the Continental Basketball Association, with the Anchorage, Alaska team, no less, was Monaca's Brad Davis, the kid brother of Mickey Davis.

The younger Davis was a delightful 6-3 guard at the University of Maryland, and was one of the best playmakers in the college game. Brad went "hardship" after his junior season and was a first round draft pick of the Los Angeles Lakers in 1977. He was with the Lakers only one season, and then went to the Indiana Pacers.

Duquesne's Norman Nixon succeeded where Brad Davis failed. The Lakers had two No. 1 draft choices in 1977, and used the second of those to name Nixon—the 22nd and last player taken on the first round.

A 6-2 guard, some thought Nixon was too small for the NBA when he came out of Duquesne. He set an all-time assist record at Duquesne, and was second in scoring for one season only to Sihugo Green (by one point), and was named the MVP in the Eastern Eight's first playoffs when he rallied a .500 Dukes team, coached by John Cinicola, to the league championship.

With the Lakers, Nixon averaged 13.7 points a game as a rookie, really developed under West, who was one of the game's great guards after an All-America career at West Virginia University, and averaged around 17 points his next two seasons. He was the Lakers' lead guard during that time, and was always among the league leaders in assists and steals.

He was teamed with Earvin "Magic" Johnson at the start of the 1979-80 season and it was one of the league's best backcourts. "I knew I could play in the NBA," Nixon tells people. "'I knew I was never a great player, but I knew I could play."

Asked what the big difference was between playing at Duquesne and in the NBA, Nixon smiled and said, "There's no homework in the NBA!"

Ron Carter, 6-5, from Perry High and Virginia Military Institute, was the No. 2 pick of the Lakers in 1978, but stayed only one uneventful season.

With Nixon, Knight and Lucas all going strong, the '70s ended on a positive note for NBA followers in Pittsburgh, but the decade started on a sad note for local fans.

Maurice Stokes, all-rookie in the NBA in 1955-56, second team all-NBA in 1956-57, died in 1970 at the age of 36

JACK MARIN
Farrell

DENNIS WUYCIK
Ambridge

BARRY NELSON
Fox Chapel

MICKEY DAVIS
Monaca

KENNY DURRETT
Schenley

BILLY ZOPF
Monaca

GEORGE KARL
Penn Hills

BRAD DAVIS
Monaca

RON CARTER
Perry

GUS GERARD
Laurel Highlands

following a heart attack. At the end of the 1957-58 season, he was struck with encephalitis, a crippling brain disease. It turned Stokes into an invalid.

He was in a coma for a long time. One of his teammates on the Royals, a fellow Pittsburgher, Jack Twyman, looked after him, became his legal guardian, and teamed up with Milt Kutsher of Kutsher's Country Club in the Catskills to raise money for "Mo" Stokes during a long and often frustrating rehabilitation program.

Theirs was a special relationship, and it's one that has been documented in a movie—"Maurie"—that sometimes shows up on the late night movies on TV.

A scholarship fund was set up at Stokes' alma mater at Pittsburgh's Westinghouse High, and a special Maurice Stokes Room was established at the Basketball Hall of Fame in Springfield, Mass.

So Pittsburgh has a special place in basketball's shrine. From Norm Van Lier to Norm Nixon, and Maurice Stokes to Maurice Lucas, Pittsburgh has always had a special place in pro basketball.

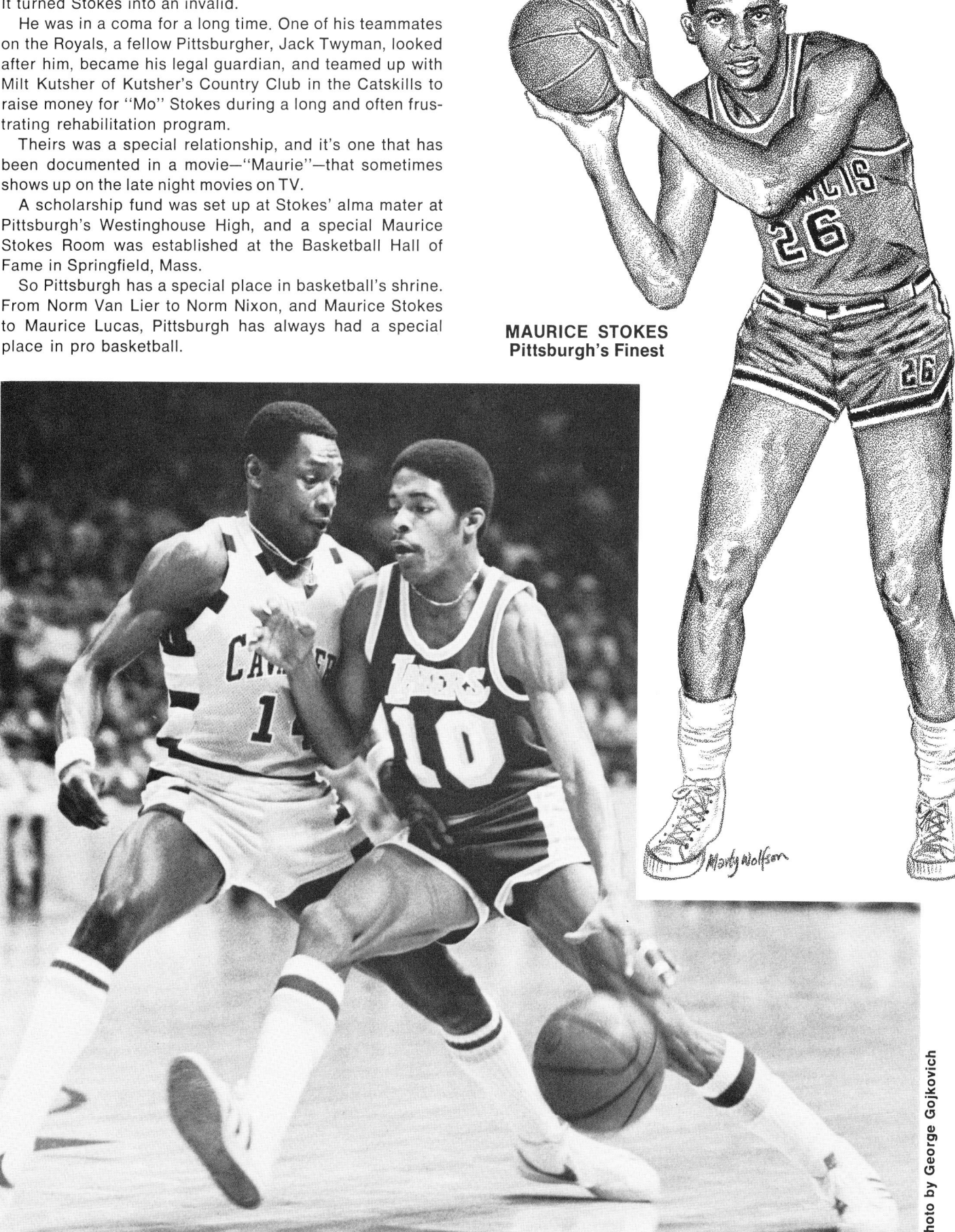

MAURICE STOKES
Pittsburgh's Finest

Former Duquesne MVP NORM NIXON, now with Lakers, drives on Cavaliers' "Foots" Walker

FOOTBALL

STEELERS SET THE TONE FOR CITY IN SENSATIONAL '70s

By Phil Musick

"Our football team won't be satisfied with just winning four Super Bowls."
—Chuck Noll

Success had finally turned his head.

On the occasion of his Steelers' unparalleled fourth Super Bowl triumph, Charles Henry Noll, the pre-eminent coach in all of football history by virtue of his accomplishments and the era in which they were recorded, danced and sipped champagne and smiled and did all the other frivolous things people do when they peer down upon the world from that marvelous vista of total success.

The year before, Noll had leaned close to assistant coach Woody Widenhofer and talked X's and O's as another such party swirled around him. After winning his first Super Bowl, it was widely reported Noll had formally shaken hands with his wife, Marianne. After the second, there was speculation Marianne had gotten a kiss and Noll rewarded himself with a few glasses of fine white wine. But, in the early hours of Jan. 20, 1980 in the shimmering expanse of the Newport Beach Marriott ballroom, Chuck Noll partied.

Escorting his wife from the celebration, Noll ran into a couple of newspaper types. He looked swozzled. Not drunk. To envision Noll drunk is to conjure Bo Derek in a reducing salon or the Pope in a house of ill repute. No, he was swozzled. Smile-button face flushed with ebbing excitement, spirits loosened a notch, thinning hair askew. In toto, a likeable man thoroughly pleased with life.

"Vince who?" asked a reporter and longtime Noll antagonist, who was also somewhat swozzled. "Congratulations. You had a hell of a year."

Make that decade. Charles Henry Noll had a hell of a decade. Because he did, the Steelers did. Few franchises in the history of games played for money equaled the Steelers of the 1970s. In Pittsburgh, the Sweet, Swinging, Sensational '70s. Sure, there were the Yankees of the 1920s and the Celtics of the 1960s and the Canadiens of several decades.

And there were the Pittsburgh Steelers of Chuck Noll. Four Super Bowl triumphs, fashioned in perhaps the most demanding crucible in professional sport. Four Super Bowl rings. Back there at the turn of the decade, who would've ever thunk it. Art Rooney's pointy-headed Steelers, those woeful children of scorn, four times the champions of the National Football League, so dominant that Commissioner Pete Rozelle would say one year "it would be better for the league if another team won" and to Rooney at the next presentation of the Lombardi Trophy, "Art, we have to stop meeting like this."

The snow would swirl around our ears and my old man would stare steadily out at them as they fumbled and stumbled their way to yet another pitiful loss, and he would take a long bite of bourbon from his flask, and he would say "Damn!" He was the gentlest of men, but when it was over, he would grab me by the jacket and hustle me out of Forbes Field toward the streetcar stop, and anyone who made eye contact with him, would move from our path.

Damn! The price of the tickets took a hunk from a 1940s' paycheck and a man had bills, and Rooney was foisting these stiffs on the public as professionals. "Why the hell doesn't he get some ballplayers." my old man would ask rhetorically. He knew the answer. "Too damn cheap."

Arthur J. Rooney must awaken some mornings wondering where it all went right. For almost four decades, he wore his football team around his neck like a millstone. Its nickname gradually lengthened, ironically but understandably, to the international symbol of distress . . . S.O.S. . . . Same Old Steelers. A civic embarrassment most noted for historical eccentricity. To wit:

• A coach named Johnny Blood, who once misread the schedule and went to Washington to scout the Redskins on the day the Steelers were playing Philadelphia.

• An inability to recognize mercurial quarterbacking talent which cost the Steelers the services of, among others, John Unitas, Sid Luckman, Len Dawson and Jack Kemp.

• Being originally financed by Rooney's racetrack, and some say poker, winnings.

• Having had five coaches in its first seven years, two of whom were later rehired.

• Being first nicknamed the Pirates, then due to World War II, the Phil-Pitt Steagles and the Card-Pitts, an amalgamation of the Steeler and Chicago Cardinal clubs quickly and rightfully labeled the Carpets.

• And Rooney's quirky decisions, motivated by either a shortage of cash or an abiding sense of honor, which saw him sell the league's best passer without telling his coach and thereby blowing the 1938 championship, transporting his team clear across the country by train because of a promise to an old friend and then returning it just in time for the most critical game of the year and the one which

83

THEIR FAVORITE TEAM ALL THE WAY TO CALIFORNIA!

Myron Cope's Magic Creation

85

cost it a second title, and his sale and repurchase of the team in 1940.

Ernie Holmes sat on a bed in a tiny room in the barred-door section of Western Psychiatric Hospital. A week before, after a bizarre incident in which he had shot at truck drivers on two state turnpikes, he had wounded a policeman. His life was a shamble, he was facing jail, his football career seemed over, he was badly confused. He held to one thought as a judge and a psychologist pondered his future: "Mr. Art Rooney's going to help me. He's like my father. I love him."

"We've been lucky," Arthur J. Rooney has said many times, usually in the presence of the Super Bowl trophy. True. There has been great good fortune, all of which dates back to the year preceding the Sensational '70s and the hiring of Noll.

To understand what Noll has meant, you have to understand something of Arthur J. Rooney. To The Chief, professional football was always fun. He is a personal man, which means he invariably shakes your hand and inquires after your wife and asks—and really wants to know—"how are ya?" His friends were his coaches and the sportswriters. He conducted a personal business. Which meant that if he still refers to Joe Bach as "that bullheaded Irishman," and if he found it necessary to knock Bach down following serious differences of opinion, he also twice hired Bach as his coach. As he did another pal, Walt Kiesling.

Rooney's coaches were friends, confidantes. Hamhanded, affable men who thought football was a game won by pounding the opposition flatter than a puddle; men who

ERNIE HOLMES

PITTSBURGH: A CITY OF BIG SHOULDERS

liked to sit around and drink beer and argue with their employer and tell stories and laugh a lot. Personal men. "We had more fun in the old days," Art Rooney has said many times, although rarely in the presence of the Lombardi Trophy.

The fun ended, or rather was drawn to the narrow perspective of victory, with the hiring in 1969 of Noll, a 36-year old assistant coach with the Baltimore Colts and reputed to be something of a defensive wizard.

Noll was not Art Rooney's type of coach. He was the new breed. Bright, dedicated only to winning, disciplined, fraught with innovative ideas, and not given to sitting around joking with the boss. "A nice boy," Art Rooney remembers. But, as many have said since, not a guy you'd go get a beer with.

Dan Rooney had picked up jocks and repaired equipment and handled tedious front-office chores through years of Steeler ineptitude. He wasn't interested in drinking beer with the coach who would replace the fired Bill Austin, a throwback to Bach and Kiesling who won only 11 of 42 games. Dan Rooney was interested in winning.

Having taken over the operation of the club short of determining matters of major policy—"the old man *still* does that," a club official would say 10 years later—Dan Rooney conducted the search. It ended at 7 a.m. on January 27, 1969. After a fretful night's sleep, Dan Rooney rolled out of bed and reached for the telephone. His mind was made up. He had talked to experienced National Football League coaches looking for work. They had all promised a winner immediately, if not sooner. Noll had come to Pittsburgh two days after Baltimore lost Super Bowl III, surveyed the situation, studied the roster, and told Dan Rooney the truth: The Steelers were a wreck, the rebuilding process would take at least three years and maybe five, only a few of the players were talented enough to play for a good NFL team, and the club was operated in a manner befitting a loser.

"The job's yours, if you want it," the sleepy Rooney mumbled into the telephone.

"I want it," Noll said.

He is the oldest of the five Rooney boys, who it is generally agreed will never be the man their father is. And he will forever be "Art's kid . . . whatshisname?" Both are harsh labels for a man to live with, but Dan Rooney has handled them well. There is about him, even at 47, in the year 1980, a boyishness unmarred by graying temples. It is at once his charm and his power. How could a man smile so winningly and be so unfailingly nice, and wield the power Dan—still Danny to those who've known him a decade or more and, revealingly, to many who work for him—does? It could be a hustle. Call it, rather, a soft con. Or Irish charm.

In the turbulent '70s, the players and owners renting the game over economic differences which at times seemed irresolvable, Dan Rooney became a bridge. Players' association officials had grown to personally loathe their NFL Management Council counterparts, ex-Baltimore Colt John Mackey and Dallas general manager Tex Schramm could literally not stand to be in the same room with the other. Dan Rooney was Commissioner Pete Rozelle's choice to negotiate a peace which would not strangle the golden goose. Quietly, skillfully, cajolingly, he did. He has been Art's boy, perhaps, but he is no one else's. An observation: In one 1979 game, the Steelers were being beaten. The Dan Rooney smile had long been lost to the obvious out-

DAN ROONEY

come. There was a minor error on the scoreboard. Dan Rooney seethed. "Val . . . Val!" he shouted at NFL director of television Val Pinchbeck, who sat a row in front in the press box watching a mini-TV set, earphones squeezed tightly over his ears. When Val Pinchbeck didn't respond, Dan Rooney threw a notebook at him. "Damn it, Val, the board's wrong." A better observation: Dan Rooney's name appears once in the Steelers' media guide. In 8-point type.

The sensational '70s began there, with the son ascending to the throne and a young assistant come to power to exercise all of the thousands of football theories which had been running pell-mell through his mind for years.

A messenger guard and linebacker for Paul Brown's Cleveland Browns and an assistant under Sid Gillman and Don Shula in the pros, Noll came to the job well-schooled and with certain foundational ideas which he has not yielded.

A team is built through the draft. "No one wants to trade you quality," he says, having not made a major trade in his 11 seasons. "You build with draft choices. You find people with talents adaptable to your plans and then you teach them to do things the way we do them."

Joe Greene was the first of them. A 6-5, 265-pound defensive tackle from North Texas State, he was called a Fort on Foot. An injury had kept him out of the two most prestigious college all-star games as a senior, but Noll had seen him dominate the line of scrimmage for the South in the Senior Bowl. Greene was as quick a defensive lineman as Chuck Noll had ever seen. It was being won on defense in the NFL at the end of the 1960s. This kid would be the foundation of that defense.

"We are going to build a championship team in Pittsburgh," Chuck Noll promised the day after the draft, when a Pittsburgh newspaper headline screamed in 48-point type, 'Joe Who?' "Joe Greene is going to be the cornerstone of that defense."

Greene started all 14 games in 1969 and was named the NFL Defensive Rookie of the Year. It was the lone Steeler boast entering the '70s. The Steelers won their first game under Noll, lost the next 13 and the only consolation was having the first pick in the college draft.

"The best way to describe the 1969 season is that we decided we had to do certain things to win a championship and we decided to do them, even though we knew some of the personnel couldn't handle it," Noll said.

But the personnel would shortly change . . . drastically.

TERRY HANRATTY

The needs were many. A quarterback. Even if Noll had drafted Terry Hanratty in the second round the year before, evidence insists he was pressured into it. He never had faith in Hanratty's ability to be a winning NFL quarterback. If Greene was to be a cornerstone, Terry Bradshaw, a kid from Louisiana Tech whose arm was best defined in calibre rather than inches, was the turning point.

Sure, he would need time, nurturing, the supporting cast. But when Bradshaw became the first player selected in the 1970 collegiate draft, the success which later became a torrent, started to trickle. In his debut, Bradshaw completed just four of 16 passes, was replaced by Hanratty, the Steelers were whipped and he sat in the parking lot after the game and wept. Noll didn't. He had a quarterback whose ability to run would torment defenses susceptible to a scrambler able to run over defensive backs. It was a matter of education. The talent was there. "Watching Terry play quarterback is like watching a rose bloom on slow-motion," thought tight end Bob Adams.

Under Bradshaw, the 1970 Steelers were young and unpredictable. Cold (they lost their first three), hot (won four of five), cold (lost five of six). Still, they were moving. Bradshaw was learning, and the draft had also brought gifted wide receiver Ron Shanklin and cornerback Mel Blount, whom his colleagues immediately dubbed "Supe" in recognition of obvious superior athletic skill.

The draft was working its magic. Art Jr., second oldest of the five sons of Art Rooney, ran the personnel department and served as a buffer between Noll and the scouts, between whom there was little affection. "Coaches always think they can scout better than we can," Artie Rooney would chuckle, "and we think we can coach better than they can."

Despite some differences—scouts like to drink beer and tell stories and none of them ever indicate a belief in Chuck Noll's infallibility—the Steelers got the talent. In perhaps the pivotal draft in the club's history, the real nucleus of the Super Bowl clubs was born in the spring of 1971: receiver Frank Lewis, linebacker Jack Ham, tight end-turned-tackle Larry Brown, guard Gerry Mullins, defensive linemen Dwight White, Ernie Holmes, and Craig Hanneman, and safeties Mike Wagner and Glen Edwards. In all, 11 rookies made the club.

GERRY MULLINS

For much of the 1971 season, the Steelers fought Cleveland for control of the AFC Central Division. The teams were tied with 5-5 records before inexperience and a lack of overall talent caught up with the Steelers, who lost three of their last four and their bid for the first championship of any kind in their history.

It happened in the third game. Everything that would follow was crystallized in that third game. They beat San Diego, 21-17, in a mean, gritty game. And they did it with two goal-line stands, the Chargers failing once after getting a first down at the one. They began to learn how not to lose that day. For the first time in anyone's memory, the Steelers, faced with imminent collapse, had held fast. When it was over, linebacker Andy Russell slowly unpeeled tape from his ankles and nodded his head with satisfaction. "We're coming of age, we're getting there," the thoughtful linebacker mused. "Two years ago, we would've lost this game."

"Just wait," promised Joe Greene.

The waiting ended the following season. Franco Harris arrived in the draft, along with tackle Gordie Gravelle, tight end John McMakin, linebacker Ed Bradley, defensive end Steve Furness, defensive back Denny Meyer and a slender quarterback from a black college whose arm would one day seduce even the disciplined Noll, Joe Gilliam. Harris was drafted in the first round over the objections of Noll, who wanted to opt for a fireplug back named Robert Newhouse, who would become a dependable runner but no Harris for the Cowboys.

In 1972, Bradshaw finally asserted himself in the huddle, Harris stuttered and slithered and danced for more than 1,000 yards rushing, and the front four harassed opposing quarterbacks unmercifully. In that unforgettable year, 1972, the millstone finally slipped from Arthur J. Rooney's aging neck.

They had to win this one. They had not beaten the Cleveland Browns for a decade and now, the first weekend in December, with a division championship hanging in the balance, they had to beat Cleveland.

Even a sportswriter was rooting . . . and sportswriters don't root. It's part of the job, like you being in Toledo and your suitcase being in Tampa. Rooting is for the fans. I rooted. For my town, Paris hard by the pollution, the Vienna of erector-set architecture. My town. I rooted for all the times I played hook to watch Pat Brady loft those incredible punts into the low-hanging clouds over Forbes Field, and for the times my old man and I had sat in the end zone sipping a little sour mash and watching them blow another one and learning something of that complicated business of father and son.

I rooted for justice, by God. Cleveland had 25 assorted championships; my stiffs were looking for their first one.

I rooted for a guy I knew, who worked with his hands, worked the split-shift so that he never knew whether it was time for breakfast or Archie Bunker, took his lunch in a tin pail and talked about the Steelers over chipped-on-rye and Tuesday's leftover cake.

Like the mortgage payment and the car that overheated and the kids with colds, they were his . . . and underneath my objective veneer they were mine, too. We rooted them past the hated Browns that Sunday, and a city where people say "watch it, Mac," instead of "excuse me" when they bump one another on the street; where the gut drink is PM-and-a-beer; where the game is football, took the first big step toward becoming a city of champions.

FRANCO HARRIS

The pointy-headed Steelers, who had never won anything, won the Central Division championship in San Diego on the last Sunday of the season and, a week later on the strength of the most bizarre, electrifying play in the NFL's history, immortality.

They had pounded Cincinnati (40-17) and Cleveland (30-0) at home enroute to an 11-3 record, best in their history, and Three Rivers held sway in the playoffs. "The great God, Tar-Tan, won't let us down," center Ray Mansfield predicted the day before the playoff game against Oakland, and if the Tartanturf didn't rise up in the Steelers' behalf, there were obviously *some* mysterious forces at work against the Raiders.

They led 7-6 with 22 seconds left in the game when Bradshaw rifled a desperate fourth-down pass at running back Frenchy Fuqua. He and Raider safetyman Jack Tatum went up for the ball as one and what occurred then was quickly dubbed **The Immaculate Reception.** The ball deflected from either Tatum (legal) or Fuqua (illegal) into the hands of Harris, who tightroped a foot inside the sideline

TERRY BRADSHAW   **CHUCK NOLL**

for a game-winning touchdown which triggered a debate that still ensues.

"That ball hit Frenchy . . . he *knows* it did!" Tatum still wails. The Frenchman, a free spirit who wore boots in which goldfish swam contentedly in plastic heels, remains silent. "I'm going to write about it and put it in a time capsule," Fuqua grins of the remarkable play.

Art Rooney was probably the only person in Pittsburgh who didn't see it. He was en route to the locker-room to, as he had so often before, console the troops. "You won, you won," a security guard screamed at Rooney as he departed an elevator near the dressing-room. "How do you like that?" Rooney replied calmly. After 39 years of owning the Steelers, he was impervious to surprise.

In the AFC title game, the bloom quickly left the rose and the Steelers lost to Miami, but only after Noll gambled on rushing only one outside man on a punt and Dolphin kicker Larry Seiple's run had set up the deciding points in a 21-17 victory. Still, could the Super Bowl be far away?

At least another winter, as it turned out. Injuries claimed Bradshaw, Harris, Hanratty and Fuqua for large parts of 1973 and the Steelers staggered to a 10-4 record and into the playoffs, where Oakland summarily dismissed them, 33-14.

Patient through five seasons, except for the odd occasions when he would grab Bradshaw and shake him along the sideline after a particularly onerous mistake, Noll lost his cool when the players struck just before the 1974 training camp opened. The previous season was a mistake he planned to rectify; the strike was interfering.

Neither Bradshaw nor Hanratty would cross the picket line and the gifted but troubled Gilliam inherited the regular quarterback job. If he was inconsistent, if he was using the drugs which would shortly wreck a promising career, Gilliam could throw the football and Noll, logic lost to his passion over the strike which badly disrupted camp, used him for six games. Jefferson Street Joe Gilliam, an 11th round draft pick, sat in the Three Rivers dugout after a mini-camp workout and all but seethed confidence.

"I can play, man . . . I can play," he said over and over, a compulsion to do so as a starting quarterback in the NFL born years before under the tutelage of his father, a college coach. "I can do it. I can beat out Bradshaw. Believe me."

A reporter lifted Gilliam's arm up to his eyes and asked a question: "What color do you see?"

"Yeah, I know," Joe Gilliam.

But the coach was color-blind. "I'm not prejudiced, at least I don't think I am," Chuck Noll said one afternoon, watching Gilliam fire streaks across the July sky. Two years later, for a couple of months during which his judgment was marred by emotion, Noll thought his young black quarterback's arm and a defense best-described as ominous would prove matchless.

Gilliam, who had presumptuously thrown 11 straight passes in his first Steeler scrimmage, was 4-1-1 early in 1974, but lost his job to Bradshaw after completing just five of 18 passes in a shaky win over Cleveland.

Returned to grace, Bradshaw shortly became the quarterback Noll had envisioned him becoming years before.

Through his apprenticeship, he was thought stupid. Local sportscaster Sam Nover—perhaps hoping controversial commentaries would lift WIIC from a very poor third in the TV news rankings locally—seriously questioned whether Bradshaw possessed the intellectual capacity to lead a winner in the NFL. But anyone familiar with the situation realized Bradshaw's I.Q. had nothing to do with his early problems. Simply put, he lacked poise. The pressure of being the first player chosen in the draft had been too much.

"I wanted so badly to win, to show them they hadn't made a mistake," he would say years later. "I'm not dumb, but I pushed too hard." So he did, at a team barbeque days after he was drafted, Bradshaw had stood around, drinking beer and telling dirty jokes. "He was trying to be the leader before he ever put on a uniform," one Steeler mused. "To us, he just seemed like a scared kid."

They were not sold on Terry Bradshaw until he had won them a Super Bowl, until he quit becoming rattled. Once, in his rookie year, Bradshaw had come unhinged to the point that receiver Ron Shanklin was forced to call plays in the huddle. Once, he was so nervous he vomited on tight end Bob Adams' hands. Once, in a third-and-17 situation, from the Steeler 17, in the final moments of a 1971 game they had to win to remain in contention for the division championship, he had called an off-tackle running play. A veteran Steeler lineman grabbed Bradshaw and roared, "God damn it, call something else." Bradshaw called for a pass, was too nervous to throw it and was sacked. "If we do ever get to a Super Bowl, Terry'll be so shook that we won't even get a first down," that veteran said in 1972.

There were moments of continuing struggle for Bradshaw during the 1974 season, but he sensed Noll's unwavering confidence in him. Their relationship, far more discordant than was ever publicly known, became more comfortable.

"He let me know I was his quarterback," Bradshaw says. "What I had lacked was confidence . . . I was pressing, trying to do too much. In 1974, Chuck took the heat off me."

And Bradshaw applied it to the Steeler opponents. An offense which had set a club record 343 points two years before, was equally powerful and the Steeler defense was simply perhaps the finest defensive unit in the game's history.

The Steelers buried Buffalo in the playoffs, then went to Oakland for what had become a holy war with the Raiders. The defense was so dominant that Oakland got just 29 yards rushing in 21 carries and it pushed the Steelers into their first Super Bowl.

LOREN TOEWS   **JOE GREENE**   **L. C. GREENWOOD**

As the teams in Super Bowl IX lined up in the tunnel prior to the pre-game introductions, Joe Greene winked at Viking defensive tackle Alan Page and said, "You guys are in for a long afternoon."

Greene was right. Minnesota never got an offense untracked. L. C. Greenwood, irritated at pre-game remarks by Ron Yary, made a revolving door of the all-pro tackle and spent the day with his hand seemingly growing from Viking quarterback Fran Tarkenton's face. Greene dominated the line of scrimmage to the extent that Noll, who treats adjectives with the respect most people reserve for large denomination bills, said afterwards, "I never saw a defensive lineman play as well as Joe has this year."

The Vikings, of course, were merely the beginning. A year later, the Steelers lost only two of 14 regular-season games, a 30-21 decision to Buffalo when O. J. Simpson ran wild for 227 yards and a meaningless finale in Los Angeles. The '74 draft had brought Lynn Swann and Jack Lambert and in their third seasons, they were possibly the dominant players at their positions. Jack Ham had blossomed into the finest outside linebacker in the game. The defense continued to shut down the run in every important game and Harris continued to get his 100-plus in every important game. A playoff tone had been established: Control the football, make them stop Harris. No one could and the Steelers rolled into Super Bowl X against Dallas. An

Ernie Holmes' hit put Baltimore quarterback Bert Jones out of action in the first playoff game and the Steelers dominated it; Lambert recovered three fumbles the following week against Oakland and the last one set up the deciding touchdown. In Super Bowl X, more of the Noll philosophy prevailed.

"Hang tough and wait for the good things to happen to you," he'd been telling them for years. Against the Cowboys, the Steelers did, Reggie Harrison sticking his upper lip in front of a Dallas punt with the Steelers trailing, 10-7, in the final quarter. Following two Roy Gerela field goals, Bradshaw stood up under a safety blitz and threw a 64-yard touchdown strike to Swann to decide the issue and give Noll his second Super Bowl win and credibility to his coachly philosophies.

The Noll method was now obviously successful. One Super Bowl could've been a product of sheer talent and luck; a second obviously indicated coaching genius. It existed in the form of adhering unblinkingly to certain basics. The draft. Unhesitating discipline which ruled out favoritism. Communication which demanded that *all* announcements affecting the team would first be made in team meetings. Noll's total control over football matters, to the degree that he chose hotels and menus on the road, selected even the smallest types of equipment, okayed the hiring of anyone who conceivably could affect his players, passed on the club's public statements, and exercised the sort of overall authority which brought the unerring response to all decisions of, "Let's see what Chuck thinks about it."

The draft produced 43 of the 47 players on the first Super Bowl roster. It was the obvious foundation and when the Steelers went on to win their fourth Super Bowl championship, it was with an entirely home-grown roster.

No single Steeler had ever received any sort of preferential treatment since Noll had fined Greene for walking into a training camp dormitory one minute past curfew. Eyeing a flat, white cardboard box in Greene's hands, Noll had smiled "I hope that pizza's good, Joe, it just cost you $25," and the message had never needed repeating.

Players who could not or would not conform to Noll's methods were dispatched when replacements became available. Cornerback John Rowser swore at defensive coordinator Bud Carson one afternoon and Carson said later, "believe me, he's gone. It may not be for a while, but he's gone." Rowser was traded several months later. Defensive back Jimmy Allen roiled the waters publicly in a contract dispute. He was quickly traded. Safetyman Glen Edwards went AWOL for one game in a similar dispute. He was traded. Bruce Van Dyke once hid an injury in order to get a day off and when Noll discovered it, the Pro Bowl guard was doomed and later traded.

All things were and are measured against a single yardstick: The good of the team. *All things*. A magazine writer once asked Noll to provide some general insights on how a game-plan is produced.

"I can't do that," he said.

"Why? I don't mean anything recent. Just one you used way back."

"No . . . it might let people get an idea on how we think."

That is part of the Noll system. Reveal nothing and no revelation will ever bring you harm. It is a system which inarguably works. In 1976, the Steelers lost four of their first five games and didn't escape last place in the AFC Central until the ninth week. Bradshaw was lost for six weeks with an injury and rookie Mike Kruczek won six straight. "Injuries are part of it, someone has to take up the slack," Noll insisted. The Steelers won 10 consecutive games as the defense yielded just 42 points, ran up one incredible string of 22 scoreless quarters, didn't allow a touchdown in eight of its last nine regular-season games, shut out six of its last eight opponents and lent new meaning to the term defensive excellence.

Routing Baltimore, 40-14, in the first round of the playoffs was expensive. The Steelers were reduced to a single healthy running back, Reggie Harrison, and with Franco Harris (ribs) and Rocky Bleier (foot) on the sidelines, lost to Oakland in the AFC championship game.

LYNN SWANN

The 1977 season was something of a puzzle. Some 49 turnovers and 122 penalties, parlayed with Bradshaw playing 10 games while wearing a cast on his fractured left wrist, the Steelers lost five times and needed a Houston win over Cincinnati on the final Sunday to lock up their fifth division championship in six years. But they turned the ball over five times and were mauled by Denver, 34-21, in the AFC championship game.

The system obviously wanted some tinkering and Noll did. Ten players, including such familiar names as Jim Clack, Jimmy Allen, Gordie Gravelle, Marv Kellum, Bobby Walden and Holmes, were dispatched by various means. Again, Noll's message was abundantly clear: The thirst for ultimate success had to be regained in 1978.

It was. In a season without tumult, they won 14 of 16 games and in the playoffs, they were indomitable, outscoring three opponents, 102-46, and dominating Denver, Houston and Dallas far beyond the dimensions of the scoring.

Super Bowl XIII brought immortality, as they throttled Dallas, 35-31, to become the first team to ever win three Super Bowl championships. The final score was an inaccurate barometer. Terry Bradshaw's passing, Lynn Swann's receiving and the defense of old smothered the Cowboys, who scored twice in the last two and a half minutes.

The game was rife with controversy. Veteran Dallas tight end Jackie Smith dropped a pass in the end zone which would've tied the game and a pass interference call against Cowboy cornerback Benny Barnes on Swann set up the pivotal touchdown. More importantly, though, it was a game with historic overtones. A dynasty to rival the Green Bay Packers' reign was born in Super Bowl XIII.

When it was over and he'd been vindicated for publicly predicting days before that "we're going to kick the Cowboys' ass," Joe Greene said quietly in the emptying lockerroom: "It all boils down to one person ... Charles Henry Noll. This is his team. He built it. He taught us how to win, how to keep winning. There aren't any indispensable Steelers, just Chuck."

It was as precise an assessment of all that had happened to the Steelers in the 1970s as could've been rendered. The Steelers *were* Chuck Noll. From the opening game of 1969 through the final one of 1979, they had been his creation.

No one questioned their dominance in the final year of the decade. To Noll's chagrin, no thoughtful person doubted they would win the AFC Central title and reach the playoffs for a record-tying eighth consecutive season; few even doubted they would not prevail in Super Bowl XIV and become the first team to collect four Vince Lombardi trophies.

They did, not effortlessly, but certainly inexorably. No NFL club lost as few games (4), none was so dominant in the playoffs. Miami's romantic resurgence ended in Three Rivers Stadium in the opening round, 34-14, and it was the measure of the game that the Dolphins' fine running game was humbled. A week later, Houston's glass slipper was shattered. The Cinderella Oilers, after a stirring upset of San Diego without quarterback Dan Pastorini and running back Earl Campbell, were dispatched, 27-13. For the sixth time against the Steelers, Campbell, the game's dominant runner, was shackled. The 12-point underdog Los Angeles Rams were resilient and gritty in Super Bowl XIV, but they lost, 31-19, in a game which classically defined the virtues of the Steelers of the '70s. Pressured by the plucky Rams, the running game shut down and the defense continually hard-pressed, the Steelers' survival was limited to a single weapon ... what Noll is wont to refer to as the big play. Bradshaw and John Stallworth and Jack Lambert made them.

"They are the National Football League team of the decade, no question," said the leading authority on the subject, Miami coach Don Shula, whose own team had been a candidate for that singular honor. "What it all comes down to in deciding which team was the best is how many Super Bowls you won. The Steelers won four, no one else could. That's the truest measure."

The decade ended, it was left for the Steeler who always seemed to have the best sense of the team to speak of the 1980s.

"We are still hungry," Joe Greene said. "We always will be ... that's what it means to be a Steeler."

And the man who had charted the heady success of the 1970s? He went to a party and got a little swozzled and the next day he said, "No, our football team won't be satisfied with just winning four Super Bowls."

**BIG HOPES FOR THE '80s:
QB Mark Malone and LB Bob Kohrs of Arizona St.**

PITTSBURGH STEELERS — SUPER BOWL XIV CHAMPIONS

Row 1:
Jack Hart (Field Manager), Craig Colquitt, Matt Bahr, Terry Bradshaw, Mike Kruczek, Cliff Stoudt, Rocky Bleier, Mike Wagner, J. T. Thomas, Greg Hawthorne, Tony Parisi (Equipment Manager).

Row 2:
Chuck Noll (Head Coach), Ron Johnson, Larry Anderson, Donnie Shell, Franco Harris, Anthony Anderson, Sidney Thornton, Rick Moser, Mel Blount, Dwayne Woodruff, Loren Toews, George Perles (Assistant Head Coach).

Row 3:
Dick Hoak (Offensive Backfield Coach), Mike Webster, Dennis Winston, Zack Valentine, Jon Kolb, Robin Cole, Sam Davis, Jack Lambert, Jack Ham, Willie Fry, Thom Dornbrook, Robert (Woody) Widenhofer (Defensive Coordinator).

Row 4:
Paul Uram (Administrative Assistant), Steve Furness, Tom Beasley, Ted Petersen, Gary Dunn, L. C. Greenwood, Fred Anderson, Gerry Mullins, Joe Greene, John Banaszak, Dick Walker (Defensive Backfield Coach).

Row 5:
Rollie Dotsch (Offensive Line Coach), Ralph Berlin (Trainer), Robert Milie (Assistant Trainer), Steve Courson, Dwight White, Larry Brown, John Stallworth, Theo Bell, Randy Grossman, Jim Smith, Lynn Swann, Bennie Cunningham, Tom Moore (Receiver Coach).

Steeler Scouting Department in mid '70s (l. to r.) TIM ROONEY, DICK HALEY and BILL NUNN, JR.

STEELER SKETCHES

Text By Jim O'Brien   **Illustrated By Marty Wolfson**

Photographs by Harry Homa, Bill Amatucci and George Gojkovich

95

"When you win, you have all the answers."
—Art Rooney

THE ROONEYS

'Twas two nights before Christmas, 1979, and all through the 130-year-old Victorian house of Art and Kathleen Rooney, not a creature was stirring. Until Art asked, "What's that?"

Singing could be heard, coming from outside. "Why don't you go see?" Kathleen suggested.

Mr. Rooney, the owner of the Steelers went to the door and, much to his surprise, he found three of his players—Terry Bradshaw, Lynn Swann and Gerry Mullins—standing on the doorstep, with their wives, singing Christmas carols.

Art and his wife were delighted, naturally.

Later, the Steeler carolers left the North Side house, where the Rooneys have lived nearly half a century, and moved on to Mt. Lebanon where they sang carols at the homes of Dan and Art Rooney Jr., and then to Upper St. Clair for more carols at the home of Chuck Noll.

Ask yourself how many pro sports owners and head coaches have been serenaded lately by players and you will see why the Pittsburgh Steelers are something special. The Rooneys are, that's for sure. They are elite citizens in the City of Champions. Mayor Caliguiri has given them more keys to the city than they could possibly need.

The Rooneys are Pittsburgh's answer to the Kennedy clan. They are Irish, rich, powerful and everywhere. Art is the patriarch of the pro franchise here, and the reason it stayed through many slim seasons. "I'm a Pittsburgh guy, that's why," he has often said.

He had the club for forty years before it ever played for a title.

His oldest son, Dan, who was 47 when the Steelers won their fourth Super Bowl, is the club president, and ran the business end of the operation during the '70s, when it was the most successful franchise in the National Football League.

Art Jr., the second son in the chain of command, is in charge of the scouting and player personnel department, and has contributed to the Steelers' success in the draft during the decade. "Chuck Noll has taught our scouts so that they know exactly what he's after," says Art Jr.

"When you win," says the father, one of the most famous sports figures in the country today, and certainly one of its most popular and endearing leaders, "you have all the answers.

DAN ROONEY   **ART ROONEY JR.**

ART ROONEY **ART ROONEY, JR.** **DAN ROONEY**

"Winning is it," The Chief continues. "It's everything. When you don't win, you're too dumb to come in out of the rain. When you win, you get smart in a hurry."

The elder Rooney is responsible for public relations these days; he greets everybody who visits the team's offices, offers them a firm and friendly handshake, a first-class cigar and the comfort of his company. The boys look after business.

"We have to pay full attention to it, and we do," says Dan Rooney, one of the NFL's most highly-respected executives. "My dad's different now, too. He's a legend. He comes up to people now, and he's a somebody. It wasn't always like that. He wasn't always like he is now. He wasn't that visible 20 years ago."

Everyone roots for the Rooneys these days. They're winners, that's why. And they're for real.

Steelers
NFL TEAM OF THE DECADE!

SUPER SHOT!
The prize-winning photo at right was taken by Albert M. Herrmann, Jr. of The Pittsburgh Press during the Super Bowl XIV celebration at Point State Park. An 11" x 14" copy of this unique photo may still be purchased at The Pittsburgh Press, Box 476, Pittsburgh, PA 15230.

"He knows so much about this game it gets scary."
—Rollie Dotsch

Chuck Noll was the No. 1 coach in the National Football League in the '70s.

His accomplishments as coach of the Steelers surpass those of his top peers, such as his one-time boss, Don Shula of the Miami Dolphins, and one of his chief championship rivals, Tom Landry of the Dallas Cowboys.

Only the coach of the Steelers can say his team won four Super Bowl titles during that time, though that fourth one, to be accurate, came in the first month of the '80s. The victory over the Los Angeles Rams in Super Bowl XIV did cap off the 1979 season.

The Steelers were 1-13 in Noll's first season back in 1969, one of the worst records ever posted by the Pittsburgh pros, but Noll knew what he wanted and where he was headed, and he had his team in the playoffs by the 1972 season. "There were a lot of question marks in those early years," said L. C. Greenwood whose arrival coincided with the coach's back then. "He got the kind of people he wanted. And he coached the ones he kept."

Starting in 1972, the Steelers made the playoffs eight straight seasons, tying Landry's NFL record (1966-73). At the end of the 1979 season, Noll notched his 100th regular

CHUCK NOLL

season victory as the Steeler coach. He became the 14th coach in pro football history to reach that milestone.

Following the Steelers' Super Bowl triumph over the Rams, Noll's post-season record was 14-4—only Vince Lombardi (9-1) did better in the playoffs—and Noll's overall record was 114-61-1.

Even with his success, Noll remains a private man in a public arena. Noll is an enigma of sorts, but seems to prefer to keep it that way. Charisma is something he grows in his garden. "Where it belongs," he says with a smile.

He thinks of himself and his staff as teachers. He knows something about a lot of things, and shares his thoughts on several subjects, but resists those who try to dig too deeply into his psyche.

"You can learn so much about life from football," notes Noll, "like how important basics are. You learn from so many people, and, if you have good teachers—and I think I have—what you learn is subtle."

One of his assistants said of Noll: "He knows so much about this game it gets scary. He knows what's going on all the time, and how to best employ his players to meet the occasion. Sometimes I just can't believe what he sees on those sidelines. He sees it all."

Steeler owner Art Rooney recalls that first year with Noll, and says, "He lost all those games, but he never lost the team. That's when I knew I had a coach."

THE NOLL YEARS

Going into the 1980 season, Chuck Noll had 100 regular-season victories to his credit in 11 years as coach of the Steelers. His record was 100-57-1, and since 1972, the first of eight straight playoff seasons for the Steelers, his record was 88-27-1—the best of any coach for that period in the National Football League.

As the Steelers seek another NFL title, it is reassuring to know that Noll's post-season record is 14-4, the best of any active coach and topped only by Vince Lombardi's 9-1 mark.

Mayor Richard Caliguiri signed an official proclamation in 1979 to acknowledge Noll's 100 victories.

Noll is not given, however, to reflecting on past achievements. He won't let his guard down to dwell on what has been done, but prefers to look ahead.

"My memory's not that good," he'll say to shun off inquiries into his feats as a football coach. Or, "I'm not that good a storyteller. I'd disappoint you."

It seems a shame.

"The spice of the business," he did say, "is that it's not exactly the same each season. The quotes may be the same, but the experiences are different."

Noll may not reflect on his accomplishment, but Steeler fans may wish to recall and savor some of the highlights of his first 100 regular-season victories. Playoff games are not included. It's the season for nostalgia:

1969 In their very first game with Noll as head coach, the Steelers surprised the Detroit Lions at Pitt Stadium, defeating them, 16-13, when Warren Bankston broke three tackles to score a TD from six yards out with 2:57 left.

"I thought we were on our way to the Super Bowl," recalls L. C. Greenwood. The Steelers lost their next 13 games. The Lions went on to post a 9-4-1 record and went to the Runner-Up Bowl. "He lost all those games, but he didn't lose the team," club owner Art Rooney is fond of saying. "That's when I knew I had a coach."

100 Wins
(Bold type indicates winning of Super Bowl)

SEASON	WON	LOST	TIED	DIVISION FINISH
1969	1	13	0	Fourth
1970	5	9	0	Third
1971	6	8	0	Second
1972	11	3	0	First*
1973	10	4	0	Second*
1974	10	3	1	**First***
1975	12	2	0	**First***
1976	10	4	0	First*
1977	9	5	0	First*
1978	14	2	0	**First***
1979	12	4	0	**First***
	100	57	1	

*Qualified for playoffs

1970 The Steelers lost their first three games—extending their losing streak to 16 games—before beating the Buffalo Bills, with O. J. Simpson, 23-10, here at Three Rivers Stadium. It was their first victory in the new stadium. They split in their next six games, then beat the Cleveland Browns here, 28-9, when beating the Browns was a big deal.

1971 In the third game, the Steelers defeated the San Diego Chargers here, 21-17, and that was significant because it was Noll's first victory over one of his former bosses. He first began coaching as an assistant to Sid Gillman at San Diego and was there six seasons. "Anybody who worked for Sid Gillman learned a lot of football," says Noll now. The Steelers stopped the Chargers several times when they were deep in the home team's territory.

1972 Beating the Oakland Raiders here in the opener, 34-28, was a big one. In the third game, at St. Louis, Terry Bradshaw threw a 43-yard TD pass to Frank Lewis in the final minute for the game-winning score in the Steelers' 25-19 victory. It was the first really come-from-behind victory for Bradshaw. They beat the Kansas City Chiefs, 16-7, and the Minnesota Vikings, 23-10, when both teams were only two years away from having been in the Super Bowl. Noll got his first shutout when Steelers beat his old team, the Browns, 30-0. The Steelers clinched their first divisional title in the final game, defeating the Chargers, 24-2, at San Diego.

1973 The Steelers started off with four victories, including a 33-6 victory over the Browns in the second game. They beat the Washington Redskins, 21-16, in a Monday night game here when George Allen, Larry Brown and Bill Kilmer and the Over-the-Hill Gang were going strong. In the next game, at Oakland, the Steelers beat the Raiders, 17-9, on a muddy field with Terry Hanratty at quarterback.

1974 In the sixth game, the Steelers beat the Browns, 20-16, for their first victory in Cleveland in 10 years. They clinched the divisional championship with a 21-17 victory at New England in the next-to-last game, after losing, 13-10, at Houston the previous week.

1975 The Steelers were so dominant that season. They overcame a 10-point deficit to defeat the Browns, 31-17, in the 12th game. The following week, they won their 11th straight game—still a Steeler record—when they beat the Cincinnati Bengals, 35-14.

1976 After defeating Dallas, 21-17, for their second Super Bowl triumph, the Steelers started poorly, posting a 1-4 mark. In the sixth game, against the Bengals, who were 4-1, Mike Kruczek started at quarterback in place of Bradshaw, who was injured the week before when Turkey Jones of the Browns "spiked" him in an 18-16 setback in Cleveland. Kruczek threw only 12 passes, but handed the ball off to Franco Harris an NFL record 41 times. The Steelers beat the Bengals, 23-6, for the first of nine straight victories.

During those nine games, Noll had his first win over another former mentor, Don Shula, when the Steelers defeated the Miami Dolphins, 14-3. There was also a big 7-3 win at Cincinnati, where Ernie Holmes recovered a fumble in the late going, and Harris scored a 4-yard TD to win it.

They won the division title in the season finale with a 21-0 victory at Houston, their fifth shutout in eight games. Harris and Rocky Bleier each gained 100 yards that day, and Bleier went over the 1,000-yard mark for the season to join Harris in that esteemed group. They were only the second pair on the same team to do it, after Larry Csonka and Mercury Morris of the Dolphins.

1977 In the 10th game, the Steelers defeated the Dallas Cowboys, 28-13, at Three Rivers. It was the local pro debut for Tony Dorsett, Pitt's Heisman Trophy winner on its national championship team of the previous season, and the game was billed as a showdown between Dorsett and Harris. Dorsett scored the game's first TD on a 13-yard run. On the first play of the following series, Franco replied with a 61-yard TD, and went on to gain a personal one-game high of 179 yards.

1978 In the third game, the Steelers went to Cincinnati and crushed the Bengals, 28-3, to set the tone for the rest of the season. Bradshaw had a big day, hitting 14 of 19 for 242 yards and two TDs, which triggered his great season. Another big win was the controversial 15-9 overtime victory here against the Browns the next week. The Steelers defeated the Oilers in Houston, 13-3, to clinch the division title in the 12th game. Donnie Shell knocked Earl Campbell out of the contest with a tremendous tackle in the first quarter. The Steelers won for the first time in Denver in the final game, beating the Broncos, 21-17, and stopping the opposition at the 1-foot line on the final play of the game.

1979 The Steelers began on a high note with a 16-13 overtime victory at New England in the Monday night opener. Penn State rookie Matt Bahr won it with a 41-yard field goal. They beat Houston, 38-7, in rematch of AFC championship game. They downed a familiar playoff foe, the Denver Broncos, here, 42-7, in a Monday night game. Then they defeated Dallas, 14-3, in a Super Bowl rematch.

The 33-30 overtime victory here against the Cleveland Browns on Bahr's field goals may have been the most exciting football game ever played at Three Rivers. The 28-0 win over the Buffalo Bills in the last game clinched a sixth straight divisional title, the seventh in eight years.

Reprinted from the Pittsburgh Press.

RAY MANSFIELD
"The Old Ranger"

Andy Russell and Ray Mansfield are reminders of what the Steelers once were and what they became. It's an update on the old Ugly Duckling tale.

They started their long and storied careers with the Steelers when the team was in its sorriest state, endured many frustrating days when it hardly seemed worthwhile to continue, and survived to enjoy the best of times, and wear Super Bowl rings, and be hailed as heroes here in Pittsburgh.

ANDY RUSSELL

RAY MANSFIELD AND ANDY RUSSELL

They got involved in the community while they were playing pro football, began business careers and found success as investment and financial counselors, and are partners in separate firms today. Andy is associated with Russell, Rea and Zappala in the Roosevelt Arms. And Ray with Puskar-Mansfield Associates in Gateway Center. They are still thought of as Steelers, and frequently make appearances at sports banquets about town.

They've got better stories to tell than the present-day Steelers. Russell started out with the Steelers in 1963—he was a 16th round draft choice, the same as Rocky Bleier who came later—missed the 1964 and 1965 seasons while serving as an officer in the U.S. Army—and returned to play 11 more seasons with the Steelers. Mansfield first played with the Philadelphia Eagles, for the 1963 season, and then came to Pittsburgh to play for 13 seasons. Only Ernie Stautner (14 seasons) played longer, and Sam Davis could pass him if he plays in 1980.

Mansfield and Russell are the Steelers' answer to Frick and Frack, Bob and Ray, Bud Abbott and Lou Costello. They play off one another, and can tell lots of jokes and funny stories about the old days. But the stories are only funny now because the Steelers have become the biggest of winners in the pro sports world.

Russell was an all-pro performer at outside linebacker for seven seasons before retiring after the 1976 season. But he was somewhat slow for his position. "He recovered a fumble once in a playoff game against the Baltimore Colts," recalls Mansfield, "and ran it back 93 yards for a touchdown. He set a record for time elapsed on one play."

Looking back on the bad old days, Russell recalls that Mansfield, who played offensive center, once made five tackles in a game to set an NFL record. "That gives you some idea of how bad our offense was," says Russell. "And Mansfield missed seven tackles in that same game.

"Our offense was so bad then that our coach used to tell the guys as they were going on the field, 'Now let's try to hold them, OK?' That tells you something."

Russell recalls his rookie season of 1963, and says they were the maddest, craziest moments he ever spent in football. Buddy Parker was the coach, and the playing cast included John Henry Johnson, Ed Brown, Lou Cordileone, Tom "The Bomb" Tracy, and Ernie Stautner.

The Steelers had a good team that year, though, and nearly made the playoffs, losing out with a 7-4-3 record on the final day of the regular season.

Russell missed the next two seasons, and Mansfield joined the team for the 1964 season, Parker's last before he quit, or got himself fired. Mike Nixon coached the club in 1965 when the team was 2-12.

Bill Austin came after him. He was the coach from 1966 through 1968 and those years were far from the fun season of 1963 for Russell. And, in 1969, present coach Chuck Noll's first season, the Steelers finished with a 1-13 record, their poorest since 1944 when they were 0-10.

"Although we were 1-13, there was never any panic under Noll," recalls Russell. "He was low key and said

"There was never any panic under Noll."

ANDY RUSSELL

we'd get the people and come out of it."

To which Mansfield adds, "The man kept his patience week after week, while we were blowing the games. I'd have lost my mind coaching a team like that."

During the '70s, Noll established a winning attitude which is a matter of sports history.

"He's an inspiration, a real-life hero."—Maury Gable, Movie Producer

Rocky Bleier best symbolizes the Steelers of the '70s, at least in the minds of most Pittsburgh fans.

Pirate great Dick Groat met Bleier for the first time, surprisingly enough, in October of 1979 at an affair in the downtown Duquesne Club, and told Rocky, "I've always rooted for you. When I came up in sports, I was always told I was too small, too slow, didn't have a strong enough arm, and you name it. So I sorta identify with you."

That's the way most fans view Bleier.

He is a legitimate hero. Bleier was told about all his shortcomings before he ever went off with the U. S. Army to Vietnam early in his stay with the Steelers. Then he had a part of his right foot blown off by a hand grenade. He was shot at and wounded during combat action in a rice paddy over there, and told by doctors that he could never play football again. They were hoping he'd be able to walk.

Rocky rehabilitated himself in a long and arduous, and often frustrating program. He was determined to play ball again, and his dedication, pain and sweat paid off. He just made the Steelers in the first place—as the 417th player to be taken in the 1968 draft—and it was even harder the second time around, when he came limping back from Vietnam, but he did it.

His is an inspiring story. It became a book, titled "Fight-

ROCKY BLEIER

ing Back," written by Terry O'Neill, and has since been made into a TV movie. It's a story that no Hollywood hack would dare to write, unless it were true.

Maury Gable of Upper St. Clair, who produced the film on Bleier's life, says this of his good friend: "He's the most inspiring man I know and people are just looking to be inspired. Here's the real McCoy. Anyone who knows Bleier has to admire his determination, his sensitivity. This is a beautiful person. I'm inspired by him."

Bleier grew up living over his father's saloon in Appleton, Wisc., led his high school team to state championships, and went off to Notre Dame—of course—and helped the Fighting Irish win battles on the football fields of the nation. Now he lives in a mansion in Fox Chapel.

He was a 16th round draft choice of the Steelers, and barely survived his first training camp. But after 11 seasons with the club, he ranked fourth on the team's all-time rushing list, behind Franco Harris, John Henry Johnson and Dick Hoak, and had a chance to pass Hoak and possibly Johnson in 1980 if he continued playing.

He's a big-game player, and considers playoff contests his special turf. "I've always had success, and I expect it," he says.

Bleier has always been available to his adoring public in Pittsburgh. Bleier is the banquet-going star of the Steelers, the team's most-polished speaker, and certainly one of Pittsburgh's most popular sports heroes.

Bleier is involved here in investment counselling and serves as a spokesman for First Federal Savings of Pittsburgh, among his many off-the-field enterprises.

He's gotten involved, along with his wife, Aleta, in many charitable causes, chiefly Multiple Sclerosis, United Way, Veterans Administration and retarded children. "I think there's a responsibility for athletes," remarks Rocky. "Athletes, historically, have always taken. It's part of their upbringing. I think we should be involved in the community, and give back some of what we've been given. Pittsburgh is an endearing city, and it's easy to get involved here."

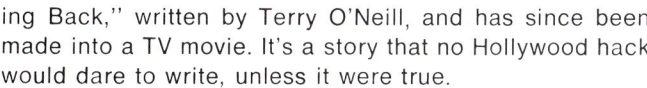

MEL BLOUNT

"I've never lost confidence in myself. I know I have the ability and the speed to stay with anybody."
—Mel Blount

Mel Blount may be the best cornerback in the history of the Steelers, and rates right up there with the Hall of Famers at his position in the annals of the National Football League.

Blount came to the Steelers in the same 1970 season as Terry Bradshaw, and has been just as much a stalwart of all those championship teams. Four times Blount was chosen to play in the Pro Bowl.

He gained top recognition for the first time in the 1975 season when he led the league with 11 interceptions—a Steeler standard—and picked off passes in six straight games, tying a league mark.

Three of the Steelers' defensive coaches, George Perles, Woody Widenhofer and Dick Walker, all love to boast about Blount, especially the way he lines up nose to nose on a wide receiver and dares him to beat him long, or the way he comes up to stop the run.

Blount best characterized the aggressive, hard-hitting Steelers' secondary in recent seasons. There have been some other standouts back there, such as Donnie Shell, Mike Wagner, Glen Edwards and J. T. Thomas, who've all been selected to play in the Pro Bowl, and younger top-notch defenders such as Jimmy Allen, Ron Johnson, and Dwayne Woodruff, but Blount has consistently been the best of the bunch.

Blount has been so good that some teams don't even throw in his direction. "I appreciate the respect, but I need the work to stay sharp," Blount said during the 1979 season. "I need to be tested.

"I've never lost confidence in myself. I know I have the ability and the speed to stay with anybody."

Blount is one of the best-conditioned athletes on the Steelers' squad, and reports to training camp as lean as a panther, and ready to deny his man the ball. Right from the start. He's always ready to play. He missed only one game in his first 10 seasons with the Steelers.

During the 1979 season, Blount also showed he's looking beyond his stay with the Steelers, where he's been one of the best paid players in his position in the NFL, to the future when football is behind him. He attended night school at Allegheny Community College to complete his credit requirements to graduate from Southern University.

This is a man much respected by his teammates. They named him the club's MVP after the 1975 season.

In his early days with the team, he returned kick-offs and averaged a fine 25.8 yards on 35 returns, bringing back 18 as a rookie for a sterling 29.7 yard average.

During the off-season he retreats to his family's farm in Vidalia, Georgia, where he raises quarter horses. He speaks with great pride of growing up on that farm, and the early values for hard work and dedication he acquired there.

TERRY BRADSHAW

"He's so great." —Art Rooney

When it comes to playing quarterback in the National Football League, and leading a team to a string of championships, nobody does it better than Terry Bradshaw of the Steelers.

Bradshaw joined the Steelers for the 1970 season, as the No. 1 pick in the entire pro draft, and, after a somewhat shaky start, came on to become the premier quarterback in the business.

Four times in those first ten years with the team, Bradshaw was calling the signals when the Steelers won Super Bowl championships. No one else can make such a claim. Bradshaw would never boast about his achievement, however, because that's not his style. He gave his first three Super Bowl rings to his dad and his two brothers.

Down-home, country-kitchen, fishin' 'n' huntin', that's Terry's style. Give him the simple life, and let him and his wife, ice skating star Jo Jo Starbuck, get off by themselves somewhere, away from the crowd. That's his idea of heaven. And heaven is something this earnest young man, who has a strong religious bent like so many of the Steelers, thinks about quite a bit.

The Steelers aren't Super Bowl champions by chance, as Bradshaw sees it. "I'm convinced," he says, "that a team of good characters—and by that I mean a bunch of guys who are morally sound and who really care about each other—will win the close games and come through in the clutch and perform well under adverse conditions. Basically, I think that's the makeup of our team."

Steeler owner Art Rooney raves about Bradshaw all the time. "As long as Terry's throwing the ball for us, we'll be up near the top," The Prez points out. "He's so great."

Rooney has a high regard for Bradshaw in every sense. "He's Pittsburgh all the way," remarks Rooney of the Louisiana-born and bred Bradshaw. "He's tough and durable. Nothing fancy. Nothing put on. Just right out in the open. And he plays hurt."

Bradshaw has come back from so many injuries, usually right smack in the middle of a big game, that Joe Greene kids him: "You deserve the Oscar and Emmy awards as well as the MVP award," says the giant defensive lineman with a big grin.

Awards come naturally to the big, blond athlete. He was named the MVP of the Super Bowl in 1979 and 1980. He's been named the MVP of the Steelers twice (1977 and 1978), the only one on the team to win the award more than once during the '70s.

Pat Livingston, the sports editor of the Pittsburgh Press, has covered the Steelers since the start of the franchise, and he's seen them all. "Let's face it," he wrote. "For pure craft and the tools that go into a man's craft, Bradshaw is without peer in the National Football League. Nobody throws the ball any better."

Bradshaw would smile and shrug about such suggestions. On the field, however, he's all business, and just goes out there and proves that Pat is right in his rating of him. "My world," Bradshaw says, "is brighter than I ever dreamed possible."

Have a Coke and a smile.

JOE GREENE PERFORMS CHAMPION TV COMMERCIAL IN '79

JOE GREENE

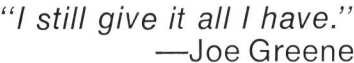

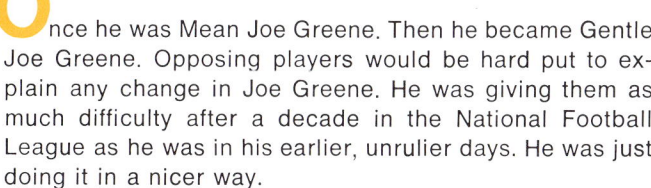

"I still give it all I have."
—Joe Greene

Once he was Mean Joe Greene. Then he became Gentle Joe Greene. Opposing players would be hard put to explain any change in Joe Greene. He was giving them as much difficulty after a decade in the National Football League as he was in his earlier, unrulier days. He was just doing it in a nicer way.

Greene was giving one rival quarterback a particularly bad day, knocking him to the ground at every opportunity, but then reaching down and pulling him back up to his feet again. "I think," said the quarterback, "he wanted to keep me in the game."

Greene has been in the game a long time. He was the No. 1 draft choice of the Steelers in 1969—Chuck Noll's initial season—and he has seen the Steelers rise from the ashes and ascend the mountain. Nobody talks about it any better on the ballclub. He has become the Steelers' senior statesman.

When Noll reached a milestone in his career during the 1979 season, marking his 100th regular season victory with the team, Greene gushed about the achievement: "You know, it never ceases to amaze me, the things this team has accomplished. Maybe it's because I've been through it all. One hundred victories . . . that's a helluva milestone when you consider what the man walked into," said Greene.

"And then he goes out and makes some defensive tackle from some little bitty school in Texas his first-round pick. Well, he deserves the success."

Noll knew what he was doing, right from the start. In Greene, a giant of a man in all respects, Noll had the beginning of a ballclub. The next year, he tabbed Terry Bradshaw as his No. 1 pick. Of Greene, Bradshaw says, "I can't see us being without him. He's like the last brick in the wall. Our foundation is not complete without Joe Greene. It'd be like going into battle without Patton."

Greene is the greatest defensive lineman in the history of the Steelers, and one of the NFL's all-time best, a sure-shot someday for the Pro Football Hall of Fame in Canton, Ohio. He was named to the Pro Bowl a team record 10 times in his first 11 seasons with the Steelers. "I'm not as good as I once was," says Greene, "but I still give it all I have. Just the thrill of the competition keeps me going."

Some say he's the single-most important person in the Steelers' success, but he defers to the front office. "You have to start at the top," he says, "with the decision-making process. Chuck Noll and Dan Rooney sit in the same seat. I've seen them form this championship team. I've been here when it wasn't so good. We're going to be championship calibre material as long as Dan Rooney and Chuck Noll are together."

Give Greene some credit, too. "He was our first real superstar," Bradshaw says.

L. C. GREENWOOD

"We lean on him a lot."
—Joe Greene

"When I was young and just getting started in football back in Canton, Miss.," says the Steelers' L. C. Greenwood, a giant of a defensive end, "somebody told me you hit or you get hit. I try to hit them harder than they can possibly hit me."

That's exactly what the powerfully-built 6-6½, 250-pound Greenwood has been doing ever since he started his career with the Steelers back in 1969. His coming coincided with that of Chuck Noll and Joe Greene and Jon Kolb, and they combined to help build a dynasty in Pittsburgh.

Greenwood and Greene were always the pillars in Pittsburgh's famed "Steel Curtain" defense. Greene was expected to be great, as the team's top draft pick out of North Texas State, but Greenwood was a pleasant surprise, as the team's 10th pick out of Arkansas AM & N.

Greenwood was at his peak in 1974 and 1975, when he gained more all-pro honors than any other defensive end. His height and quickness made him particularly tough on the pass rush, and his cross-field pursuit was such that he often made the tackle even when the opposition ran the ball around the other end.

In 1979 he started wearing glasses in the games for the first time, a concession to his advancing years, but the proud 33-year-old athlete still was named to the Pro Bowl for the sixth time in his 11 years with the Steelers.

Defensive line coach George Perles praises Greenwood all the time. "He's just a unique performer at his position," says Perles. "He plays it different from anyone else, and he's so elusive and cat-quick, and he can bat a ball out of the air because he comes in so high. He'll be tough to replace someday down the road."

His long-time partner, Greene, gives L.C. quite a pat on the back, too. "L.C. makes everybody go when he's healthy," said Greene. "He makes good penetration and he gets things confused back there. We mop up for him. We lean on him a lot."

Greene and Greenwood will often pause in the middle of a game, during a break in the action, and talk over their assignments, or pass-rushing techniques. "We've played together quite a while," Greenwood explained, "but you never really get it all down pat. We try to straighten out a few things, to get it right."

Greenwood wants to get it right, he wants to get the quarterback, and he doesn't want anybody beating him around his corner. In the 1979 season, in which the Steelers won their fourth Super Bowl title, Greenwood was the team leader in sacking the opposing quarterback, with seven.

He's always been a big play guy, and was the outstanding defensive player on the field when the Steelers beat the Minnesota Vikings in Super Bowl IX. He knocked down three of Fran Tarkenton's passes in that one, and the following year in Super Bowl X he sacked Roger Staubach three times. Greenwood's style is to stick out in a crowd, especially at the Super Bowl.

In Franco Harris, the Steelers have a shining star, a handsome hero, and one of the greatest big-game running backs in the history of the National Football League playoffs. He is to the Steelers what his good friend Willie Stargell is to the World Series champion Pirates, and they are pillars in what's now known as "The City of Champions."

Harris came out of Penn State in 1972 as the Steelers' No. 1 draft choice, and that was the start of the team's record-tying eight-year reign as playoff participants. Harris was selected to the Pro Bowl each of those sensational eight seasons, and was the only player in the American Football Conference to be selected every year during that span.

Harris was named to pro football's team of the '70s in a national magazine poll, and he certainly deserved such recognition. He's headed for the Pro Football Hall of Fame in Canton, Ohio. He's earned it just on what he's done in post-season competition.

Steeler coach Chuck Noll was asked before Super Bowl XIV why Harris always performed so well in the playoffs. Noll simply smiled and shrugged his round shoulders and responded, "I don't know why. I just accept it. And I'm grateful that he does."

As it turned out, Harris didn't have his usual vintage Super Bowl, running against the Los Angeles Rams at the Rose Bowl in Pasadena, but he did score two touchdowns on short runs to help the cause in a comeback 31-19 victory, and a fourth Super Bowl title for the Steelers.

Harris held two significant NFL post-season records, which he merely padded at Pasadena—most rushing yards gained, 1,484, and most touchdowns scored, 17. Furthermore, Harris was the leading rusher in 13 of the 17 playoff or championship games in which he played in the '70s.

"The playoffs are definitely different, no doubt about it," says Harris. "There's a whole new type of emotion. You only have one chance and you have to make the most of it."

FRANCO HARRIS

"I still consider O.J. *the* running back," says Franco. "I'd like to look at myself in the same light. O.J., to me, had so much natural ability. I know there's no way I can touch him.

"In some ways, though, I've been luckier than him. Being on a team that wins the Super Bowl, not just once but four times. I've had the good fortune to be with a winner, and not have anything bad—injury-wise—happen to me.

"I'm not that interested in individual goals. I've never won the rushing title, and that's all right. I just want to contribute my part—and that's what it is, a part—as best I can."

He is a quiet hero, seldom speaking above a whisper when he is interviewed in the locker room after a game. He is much more at ease, though still not outgoing, with his teammates, and with young fans. He is an obliging sports hero when it comes to kids. He has a special charisma with them, and is thought to have been the most looked-up-to and highly-regarded player in the NFL, with one exception, O. J. Simpson, among the other players in the league.

Harris weaved his way through so many holes in eight seasons in the '70s that he gained 8,563 yards in regularly scheduled games. He tied Jim Brown's career record of seven 1,000 yard seasons, and ranked fourth on the NFL's all-time rushing list. Jim Brown, O. J. Simpson and Jim Taylor were the only players in league history to run for more yards, and Franco figured to pass Taylor early in the 1980 season.

A child's smile and satisfaction provides a heart warming experience.

"I just want to contribute my part—as best I can."
—Franco Harris

"There's a lot of Lambert in Ham, and a lot of Ham in Lambert."
—George Perles

TWO GUYS NAMED JACK... LAMBERT AND HAM

Jack Ham and Jack Lambert have the same first name, dress in neighboring stalls in the Steelers' locker room, are perennial all-pro linebackers and the best of friends. Yet they seem so different, at least on the surface.

Lambert is the bad boy, and Ham is the good boy, but these are fuzzy images, and can be deceiving. Lambert is louder, Ham talks to himself a lot.

Chuck Noll's top assistant, George Perles, appreciates both players, and puts their roles and personalities in their proper perspective:

"Lambert has a reputation for being a mean, tough, rough football player, while Ham has a reputation for being so business-like, less emotional, and so forth. Lambert's the bad guy, and Ham has an altar boy image. That's not really, so, though. Ham is just as intense and hard-hitting as Lambert. Lambert knows his football as well as Ham, and is a very, very intelligent football player. I think more people ought to know that. There's a lot of Lambert in Ham, and a lot of Ham in Lambert."

That last line is true in more ways than one. Lambert is a bit of a put-on at times. He acts tough, but he enjoys a good laugh with the guys as much as anyone on the team. Seen with youngsters, signing autographs and such, it's obvious he's a good guy. Tell him that, however, and you better duck your head.

The soft side of Lambert is apparent to the players, too. Dennis Winston recalls that he was afraid of Lambert when he first joined the Steelers, but that Lambert looked after him, and two other rookies, Robin Cole and Sidney Thornton, right from the start. "He's a good guy deep inside," Winston said. "He just doesn't want anybody to know it."

Ham has a radar-like ability to get his job done at the outside linebacker position, where he's regarded as the best in the game, whereas it's still a toss-up as to whether Lambert, Denver's Randy Gradishar or Philadelphia's Bill Bergey is the best middle linebacker in the league.

"Ham is so good," said Joe Greene, the defensive captain along with Lambert, "that we sometimes take him for granted. We never gave him a game ball the entire 1979 season, for instance, and that's because he does his job so well without much fan-fare."

The 1979 season marked the seventh time Ham was selected to the Pro Bowl, and it was the fifth time for Lambert. At the same time, Lambert was named the best defensive player in the American Football Conference by United Press International. Ham joined the Steelers in 1971, as a second round choice out of Penn State, and Lambert came in 1974, as a second round choice out of Kent State.

Both have been big keys to the Steelers' long reign as champions, and both of these extraordinary athletes are at home in the City of Champions.

JACK LAMBERT

JACK HAM

"They make me look pretty good."
—Terry Bradshaw

LYNN SWANN AND JOHN STALLWORTH

The Super Bowl always seems to bring out the best in certain Steelers, especially the team's two wide receivers, John Stallworth and Lynn Swann.

Super Bowl XIV was no different in that respect. Both made sensational TD catches in the thrilling contest with the Los Angeles Rams, and enabled the Steelers to win their fourth NFL title, 31-19. Stallworth was so sensational, in fact, that many felt he should have been named the game's MVP rather than Terry Bradshaw.

Making big-game plays has become routine for these two gifted receivers. Swann was asked after the Super Bowl if they were, indeed, the best pass-catching combination in the league's history. He didn't drop that one, either.

"I believe John and I are the best pass receivers on one team," said Swann without a flinch. "If I didn't think we were the best, then we wouldn't be. We've proven over the years that we are. We have never been intimidated. I think John and I will catch the ball anywhere, under any circumstances, under any condition—wind, rain, or snow. There is no foundation for any other opinion, except that we are the best 1-2 pass-catching combination in pro football. John Stallworth and Lynn Swann are the complete receivers."

There's nothing shy about Swann, which is one area where he is different than Stallworth.

Both of them, however, are highly self-confident; Stallworth is simply not as extroverted, or as comfortable in front of a TV camera, as Swann. During the 1979 season, Swann was hurt in the early going, and missed several games and was sub-par in some others, and it gave Stallworth the opportunity to steal the spotlight from his more-publicized partner.

Stallworth was so good, in fact, that his teammates selected him as the Steelers' MVP for the 1979 season. "The greatest thing in a team sport," said Stallworth, "is the recognition of your peers. When they think you're good, it makes the work and the sacrifices even more gratifying."

Both superstars joined the Steelers in the 1974 season, Swann as the team's No. 1 draft choice from Southern Cal, and Stallworth as the fourth round choice from Alabama A & M. Swann had gained All-America attention in the big time, while Stallworth was less noticed on the small college circuit. Both had loads of ability, and Terry Bradshaw would get the ball to them to point up their pass-catching skills.

Speaking of Swann, Jack Butler, the former Steeler who heads up the Blesto scouting agency, said, "He's a great, gifted player, a real athlete. John Stallworth is a great wide receiver in his own right, but he's just that much better when Swann is out there, too. They're like home run hitters in baseball."

Stallworth set a Steeler record in 1979 for pass receptions with 70, and Swann padded his pass-catching records in the Super Bowl. "It's a nice situation," says quarterback Terry Bradshaw, "to be able to take your pick of those guys when you're going deep with a pass. They make me look pretty good."

JOHN STALLWORTH

LYNN SWANN

OFFENSIVE LINEMEN

MIKE WEBSTER

SAM DAVIS   **JON KOLB**

RAY PINNEY   **LARRY BROWN**

"An offensive lineman is like a blacksmith. At one time it might have been a good job."
—Anonymous

There aren't any anonymous members of the Steelers. After winning four Super Bowls in a six-year period, the Steelers have one of the most recognized lineups in pro sports. They have become Madison Avenue favorites.

Certainly in Pittsburgh all the Steelers were given due credit and recognition through the years. Steeler publicist Joe Gordon saw to it that no one was slighted, that everyone shared in the team's glory, and that everyone got a piece of the action when it came to personal appearances and autograph sessions and endorsements, whether it was at the opening of a local hardware store or a special promotion at a shopping mall.

Even so, some of the Steeler offensive linemen felt overlooked, or lost in the shuffle, and were often hailed as "The Unsung Heroes." But their praises were, in truth, often sung. Certainly line coach Rollie Dotsch does it, and so did Dan Radakovich before him.

Starting center Mike Webster, for instance, gained recognition as an All-Pro in the late '70s, and was considered peerless at his position.

Neither Jon Kolb nor Sam Davis was ever selected to the Pro Bowl, but no one took either of them for granted, certainly not opponents who had to confront them. They were fixtures in the Steelers' offensive line in the '70s.

Davis came to the Steelers as a free agent from tiny Allen University and made the grade in 1967. The 1979 season was Sam's 13th season, and only Ernie Stautner, with 14 years of service, played longer for the Black and Gold. Davis is the offensive captain of the club. During the off-season, he works in sales and marketing for the H. J. Heinz Co.

Kolb came to the Steelers in Coach Chuck Noll's first season of 1969. He was a center from Oklahoma State, but soon found a home at left tackle, and is regarded as the best ever to play that position in Pittsburgh history. He has a farm and meat packing business and ribs restaurant in Washington County.

Other stalwarts in the Steelers' offensive line in the '70s were Larry Brown, Gerry Mullins and Ray Pinney. In the 1979 season, Steve Courson and Ted Petersen broke into the lineup and showed great promise for the '80s. Thom Dornbrook of North Hills High School also made a good impression.

At the outset of the decade, the Steelers had several top interior linemen in Ray Mansfield, Jim Clack, Bruce Van Dyke and Gordon Gravelle. John Brown was another, as a stalwart tackle from 1967 to 1972, and is now a top executive with Pittsburgh National Bank.

GERRY MULLINS

JIM CLACK

STEVE COURSON

TED PETERSEN

BRUCE VAN DYKE

JOHN BROWN

THOM DORNBROOK

DAN RADAKOVICH

ROLLIE DOTSCH

Offensive Line Coaches of the '70s

TERRY HANRATTY

QUARTERBACKS

"Bradshaw's the best and he deserves to start. If I were Bob Griese, I wouldn't be starting on this team."
—Mike Kruczek

Fans sometimes forget that Terry Bradshaw had to battle against some pretty formidable competition to gain the starting job as the Steelers' quarterback.

There was Terry Hanratty, a hometown favorite as both an All-America high school performer in Butler and then an All-America at Notre Dame, and there was "Jefferson Street" Joe Gilliam, a gifted thrower from Tennessee State whose career was cut short by off-the-field shenanigans.

Terry has established himself as No. 1 now, but keeping him honest are two well-regarded reserves, Mike Kruczek and Cliff Stoudt. When Bradshaw was injured in 1976, Kruczek took over as a rookie and directed the Steelers to six straight victories.

JOE GILLIAM

MIKE KRUCZEK

CLIFF STOUDT

RECEIVERS

"I'm just glad I don't have to cover them."
—Mel Blount

Even before Lynn Swann and John Stallworth showed up on the Steeler scene in 1974 the club was blessed with gifted deep receivers in Frank Lewis (1971-78) and Ron Shanklin (1970-75). Those two still rate among the Steelers' all-time pass-catchers.

Behind Swann and Stallworth in recent seasons, Jim Smith and Theo Bell have both shown tremendous promise as pass-catchers and punt-returners, and give Terry Bradshaw one of the best group of targets in the game.

The Steelers are also twice-blessed at the tight end position where Bennie Cunningham and Randy Grossman have given outstanding clutch performances while dividing time at the position. The Steelers had some good ones here at the outset of the '70s with Warren Bankston, Dave Smith and John McMakin providing blocking and pass-catching ability in their well-built bodies. Larry Brown was a formidable figure there, too, until he switched to playing tackle in the offensive line.

Lionel Taylor and later Tom Moore got the most out of the receiving corps during their coaching stints.

BENNIE CUNNINGHAM   **RANDY GROSSMAN**

JIM SMITH   **THEO BELL**

FRANK LEWIS   **RON SHANKLIN**   **LIONEL TAYLOR**   **TOM MOORE**
Receiver Coaches of the '70s

"FRENCHY" FUQUA

RUNNING BACKS

"We are blessed with lots of good backs."
—Dick Hoak

Dick Hoak himself was one of the Steelers' finest running backs for 11 seasons until retiring after the 1970 season. He returned in 1972 to join Chuck Noll's staff and has worked with some good ones since then.

Two of the best were Preston Pearson, who picked up two Super Bowl rings while serving with the Steelers (1970-74) and two more later with the Dallas Cowboys, and John "Frenchy" Fuqua (1970-76), a classic and daring dresser who was also called "The Count."

Pearson, who continues to reside in Pittsburgh, and Fuqua remain among the team's all-time top ten rushers. Franco Harris and Rocky Bleier, of course, rate right at the top in that department along with such legendary alumni as John Henry Johnson, Fran Rogel and Hoak.

During the 1979 season, Sidney Thornton took over for the injured Bleier and started the first ten games and showed that he will be an offensive force in the '80s, and the Steeler coaches believe the same of their No. 1 draft choice in 1979, Greg Hawthorne, and a surprise free agent, Anthony Anderson, as well as special teams standout Rick Moser.

ANTHONY ANDERSON

PRESTON PEARSON

GREG HAWTHORNE

SIDNEY THORNTON

RICK MOSER

DICK HOAK
Offensive Backfield Coach

DWIGHT WHITE

DEFENSIVE LINEMEN

"I was a very large baby." —Ernie Holmes

The Steelers' famed "Steel Curtain" defense began with its front four—half a ton of defense. Joe Greene and L. C. Greenwood were there from the start and persevered. Ernie "Fats" Holmes and Dwight White were there for awhile, but have since given way to younger upstarts.

Defensive coordinator George Perles keeps all his people on their toes.

White was a Pro Bowl performer in 1974 and 1975, but split time with John Banaszak beginning with the 1978 season, and spelled Banaszak in the 1979 campaign. Steve Furness and Gary Dunn divided time at tackle in the 1978 and 1979 seasons. Tom Keating contributed to the cause here in 1973 after coming over late in his career from the Oakland Raiders.

Tom Beasley showed great promise on the defensive line in the late '70s, and he and Fred Anderson and rookie John Goodman were looked upon as outstanding prospects.

ERNIE HOLMES

GARY DUNN

STEVE FURNESS

JOHN BANASZAK

TOM BEASLEY

TOM KEATING

GEORGE PERLES
Head Assistant

LINEBACKERS

"It doesn't matter who's out there. We're so deep in talent."
—"Dirt" Winston

Loren Toews waited four years for Andy Russell to retire so he could start at the right linebacker slot. But he didn't get to stay there too long. Young candidates came along such as "Dirt" Winston and Robin Cole, to steal time there and establish themselves as future stars for the Steelers.

Looking farther down the road, the coaches can see newcomers such as Zack Valentine and Tom Graves getting time at linebacker, too, though the Steelers are pretty well set at the other two spots with perennial All-Pros Jack Ham and Jack Lambert. Should either get injured, as Ham was during the late stages of the 1979 season, Chuck Noll knows he has sound replacements.

Before Lambert arrived on the scene, the Steelers had a solid middle linebacker in Henry Davis from 1970 to 1973.

"DIRT" WINSTON

LOREN TOEWS

ZACK VALENTINE

ROBIN COLE

DEFENSIVE BACKS

"I have a basic philosophy in life—I can."
—J. T. Thomas

This philosophy was expressed by Thomas before the 1973 season. It served him in great stead when he made a comeback in 1979 after missing the entire 1978 season with a blood disorder.

A Pro Bowl performer in 1977, Thomas returned and started half the season at cornerback in place of the injured second-year star, Ron Johnson, and then at the end of the schedule and in the championship playoffs and Super Bowl at weak safety in place of the injured Mike Wagner, a much-respected nine-year veteran.

The Steelers' secondary is rated among the league's best, with Mel Blount and Donnie Shell, two All-Pro performers, showing the way, and Wagner, Johnson and youngsters Dwayne Woodruff and Larry Anderson following the veterans' lead. Shell sparks the group with his fierce hitting, and Johnson isn't far behind.

Earlier in the decade, the Steelers had some strong performers at the deep positions in Glen Edwards, John Rowser and Jimmy Allen. More recently, Tony Dungy was a versatile and popular performer back there.

Bud Carson coached this unit for many seasons, before Woody Widenhofer and Dick Walker took over.

DONNIE SHELL | MIKE WAGNER

 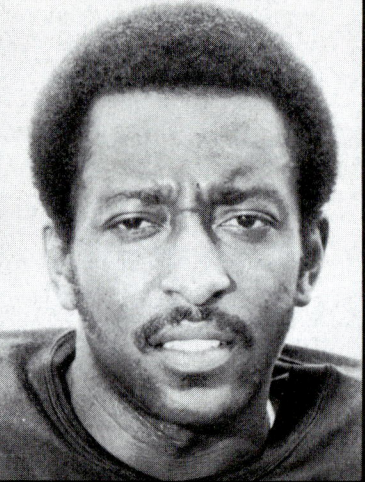  
RON JOHNSON | J. T. THOMAS | GLEN EDWARDS | DICK WALKER Ass'n't Coach

DWAYNE WOODRUFF | LARRY BANDERSON | BUD CARSON | WOODY WIDENHOFER
Defensive Coordinators of the '70s

KICKERS

"The biggest compliment you can give a kicker is to tell him he's helped the team."
—Matt Bahr

Matt Bahr became an instant success with the Steelers in the 1979 season opener, booting his first field goal in the National Football League from 41 yards out at 5:10 of sudden-death overtime to lift the Steelers to a 16-13 victory over the New England Patriots in a nationally-televised Monday Night Football Game.

The baby-faced soccer-style booter from Penn State also provided game-winning field goals in later contests with the St. Louis Cardinals and Cleveland Browns, tying the latter contest just before regulation time had expired, and then hitting another three-pointer to pull out the verdict in overtime.

He and second-year punter Craig Colquitt provided Pittsburgh with a solid and keenly accurate 1-2 kicking punch, and the team appeared set in this respect as the '80s began. Bahr and Colquitt replaced two grizzled veterans who had provided solid service to the Steelers over many seasons.

Bahr bumped off Roy Gerela, the team's all-time leading scorer, who handled the placement duties from 1971 through 1978, while Colquitt succeeded Bobby Walden, who handled the punting chores from 1968 through 1977.

MATT BAHR   CRAIG COLQUITT

ROY GERELA

BOBBY WALDEN

PAUL URAM Flexibility and Kicking Coach

 # BEHIND THE STEEL CURTAIN

JACK McGINLEY
Vice President

JIM BOSTON
Traveling Secretary

ED KIELY
Public Relations Director

JOE GORDON
Publicity Director

The Steelers have the No. 1 organization in pro football, but they don't believe in patting themselves on the back. They leave it up to other teams to come up with catchy slogans and such, and just continue winning championships in the National Football League. You won't find any of the team's front-office officials pictured in any of the Pittsburgh team's brochures or guides. They simply list the front-office personnel and their titles. "We like to put the players out front before the public," The Prez, Art Rooney, is fond of saying. The Steelers' behind-the-scenes people deserve recognition. Art's long-time friend and partner, Jack McGinley, is a congenial chap, but never seeks the spotlight. Jim Boston just looks after business, making all travel arrangements for the team and negotiating player contracts, while Joe Gordon and Ed Kiely combine to provide the Pittsburgh franchise with the finest publicity service in the pro ranks.

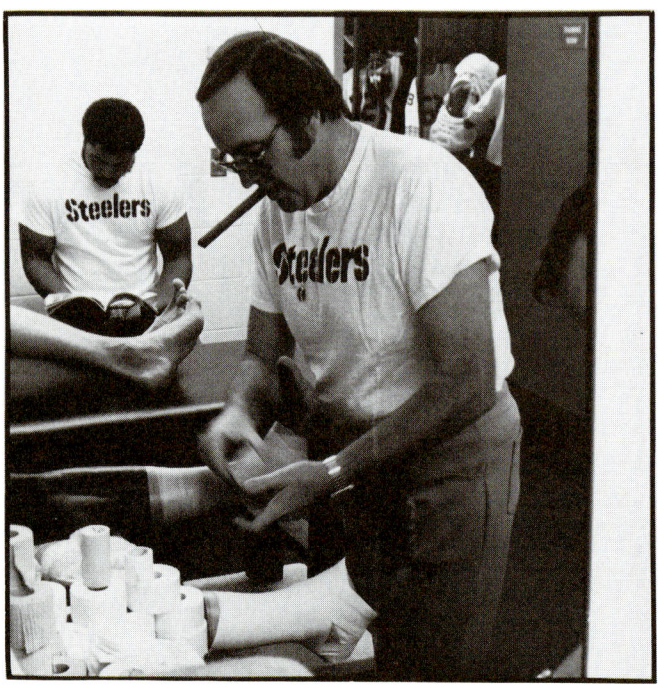
Head Trainer RALPH BERLIN tends to the players' needs.

Equipment Manager TONY PARISI is praised for his dedicated efforts.

WE'RE No. 1!

GORDON JONES and **TONY DORSETT** signal Pitt's national ranking after Sugar Bowl victory.

Pittsburghers could point with pride to many championship teams . . . the Steelers, Pitt, Carnegie-Mellon and Duquesne. They were all winners in the '70s.

PITT FOOTBALL — COMEBACK STORY OF THE '70s

By Jim O'Brien

"Coming up with a national championship at Pittsburgh was a rare thing. I may never have a national championship or go undefeated again. I'm not going to think that way, but one must face reality."

—Johnny Majors

"How'd I do it? Three things: excellent teammates, good coaching and The Good Lord."

—Tony Dorsett

"Coaches don't win football games. Players win games. Coaches don't go out there and line up."

—Jackie Sherrill

Those were the words of Johnny Majors upon leaving Pitt after a national championship season in 1976 and going home to become head coach at the University of Tennessee; of Tony Dorsett after the same sensational season when asked to explain how he had been the most productive runner in the history of college football and the winner of the Heisman Trophy, college football's most coveted award; of Jackie Sherrill upon being named to succeed Majors as the head coach of the Panthers.

Johnny Majors . . . Tony Dorsett . . . Jackie Sherrill. They are Pitt's answer to the Holy Trinity. They worked a miracle and saved college football in the City of Pittsburgh.

Who can forget Majors, the always-ebullient salesman with the penetrating hazel eyes? Or Dorsett, the effervescent, oh-so-confident kid who reminded you of the comedian Flip Wilson? They called him "The Hawk" because he could see out of the corners of both of his bright eyes at the same time. Or Sherrill, the slow-talking, low-talking coach with the long eyelids and thin lips who was the tough guy, the enforcer on Majors' staff, who went away for one year to become the head coach at Washington State University, and returned to Pitt to pick up where Dorsett and Majors left off?

They accomplished something that we may never see happen again. From the time Majors and Sherrill stood on Dorsett's doorstep at a housing project outside Aliquippa, where he had been a nationally-recognized running back at Hopewell High School, the Pitt program was on the upswing.

As John Pelusi, the starting center on the '76 team, said of Dorsett: "He's the sort of runner who comes along once in a lifetime and I'm so glad he came here in my lifetime."

Pitt won six games in Majors' first year, seven his second, eight his third, and went undefeated his fourth.

Majors, Dorsett and Sherrill put Pitt football on the map again, in the national rankings—the Panthers were No. 1 in all the polls in 1976—and made the Pitt football team a major part of the City of Champions.

"Sure we're part of it," said Sherrill as the Panthers prepared for the Fiesta Bowl at the close of the '70s, a decade in which Pitt went to a bowl game six times in the final seven years. "We use the 'City of Champions' in our recruiting pitch. We're close to the Steelers and Pirates, and our players know their players, and we share facilities from time to time. Young people like to come and play where there are winning teams, and a winning atmosphere."

Pitt pointed to the '80s with special pride, and the belief that another national championship was within its grasp. In 1979, the Panthers were led by a three-time All-America in defensive end Hugh Green, from Natchez, Miss., and Danny Marino, from Pittsburgh's Central Catholic High School, right down the street from the Pitt campus, who had a fabulous freshman season at quarterback. They posted an 11-1 record, and were ranked as high as sixth in the final national polls.

The Steelers still had their Joe Greene and Terry Bradshaw, but Pitt was holding its own with Hugh Green and Danny Marino.

The Pitt football program, four years after the departure of Majors and Dorsett, was still in outstanding shape. "It's tougher staying there," said Sherrill, "than getting there."

Well, Vince Lombardi said that, too, but Pitt is proving

OCTOBER 23, 1976 PITTSBURGH -VS- NAVY
THE DAY TONY DORSETT BROKE THE NCAA RUSHING RECORD

it can be done. It takes talent, hard work and dedication, and the people at Pitt have plenty of that.

Before Majors and Dorsett showed up at Pittsburgh, the Panthers had not played in a post-season bowl game in the previous 17 years. Sherrill was Majors' ace assistant back then, as he had been earlier at Iowa State University. Together, they wooed Dorsett to Pitt and away from Penn State and it was the start of a dynasty at the Oakland campus.

Russ Franke, a sports reporter for The Pittsburgh Press who covered the club during the period, offered this thought on the situation: "No single player ever carried a football team on his shoulders the way Dorsett did at the start of his career at Pitt. What happened here was one of the most dramatic comebacks ever seen in college football."

Majors, Dorsett and Sherrill gave college football a second chance in Pittsburgh. The three of them established and sustained—especially in Sherrill's case—one of the classiest and most successful football programs on a college level in this country.

Pitt's rise during Majors' four years as head coach was remarkable. The Panthers finished the 1976 season sitting atop the major-college polls for the first time since the Jock Sutherland era of the '30s.

They were the first Eastern team since the 1959 Syracuse team with Ernie Davis to be No. 1 in the nation. The odds against an independent other than Notre Dame winning a national championship are prohibitive, but Pitt pulled it off.

Pitt had endured nine losing seasons in a row prior to the arrival of Majors, Dorsett and Sherrill for the 1973 season. "I want to see guys with fire in their eyes," preached Majors. "Self-Image! Self-Image is so important!"

What is impressive about Pitt's rise to power was that it was sharing a city with the most successful pro football team in the land. There were many who believed the city wasn't big enough for both of them.

The pattern has been all too familiar in the last two decades. The growth of pro football has coincided with the decline of the college football game in big cities. New York, Chicago, Philadelphia, Miami, Detroit, Dallas, Atlanta and New Orleans have all been witness to the trend.

Apparently, Pitt was also suffering by comparison. It had not been so bad in the 1950s and early 1960s because the Steelers were such a pitiful football team themselves, never a legitimate contender and more often a basement-dweller and drawing below-par crowds by the National Football League's standards.

Chuck Noll was appointed head coach of the Steelers in 1969, the team was molded into a championship contender, and a new downtown stadium—Three Rivers Stadium, of course—was constructed at the confluence of the Allegheny, Monongahela and Ohio rivers. Suddenly, the Steelers were a hot item.

And that's where Majors came in. In 1972 the Steelers had reached the playoffs for the very first time; Pitt had lost 10 of its 11 games to reach an all-time low. The university chancellor, Wesley Posvar, had seen enough. He and Casimir Myslinski, the athletic director, were both West Point grads and they wanted a winning football program. They called for a new leader, a no-nonsense lieutenant—make that major—who could lead his troops to victory.

They brought in Johnny Majors—"We couldn't do any better than him," declared Myslinski—and Majors immediately let the local citizens know his approach to football. He compared football to war, and declared war on mediocrity as far as football at Pitt was concerned. "We want more guys who'll look you in the eye," he said.

During his first season, Majors was even moved to say, "We have the kind of schedule where if we recruit well enough and coach well enough, we can have a national championship at Pitt."

It seemed preposterous when he said it that first day of November, 1973, sitting in his office in Fitzgerald Field House alongside the 50-year-old concrete bowl where Marshall Goldberg and Bill Daddio and Curly Stebbins and John Chickerneo had led an earlier generation of Panthers to a Rose Bowl and national championship in 1936. Majors had some nerve then to talk about the possibility of returning Pittsburgh to that level of prominence, but confidence was one thing he didn't lack at the time.

On another November day, just three years later, Majors made good on his promise about Pitt football. Being No. 1 was not just an impossible dream. Those of us who were witness to the climax of the Majors-Dorsett era in Pittsburgh will never forget that fantastic Friday night, Nov. 26, 1976.

That was the night Pitt played Penn State in the final game of the regular season, under the lights at Three Rivers Stadium. It was a game that was changed from its originally scheduled time—the next afternoon at Pitt Stadium—so that it might be nationally televised. There were 50,360 in attendance for the finale.

It all began with the hiring of Johnny Majors as head coach in 1972: (l. to r.) the chancellor, Dr. Wesley Posvar, Majors and the athletic director, Casimir Myslinski.

JOHNNY MAJORS

It was a big game for my bunch, sitting in 40-yard line seats high in the stands. We were students at Pitt when the Panthers had their last outstanding football team prior to the arrival of Majors and Dorsett and Sherrill, back in 1963 when the Panthers posted a 9-1 record, losing only to Roger Staubach and a fine Navy team. Those were home-grown Panthers back then, such as Paul Martha of Wilkinsburg, Rick Leeson of Chartiers Valley, Fred Mazurek of Redstone, Ernie Borghetti from Youngstown, Al Grigaliunas of Cleveland. Even that team had a tough time against Penn State, winning the last game, 22-21.

The 1965 team was the last Pitt team to beat Penn State, and barely, by 30-27 at Pitt Stadium. That victory gave Pitt a 3-7 record that year, and was Johnny Michelosen's last game as head coach.

Pitt football was *so* depressed from 1963 to 1973. So it was with special pride that Pitt followers, alumni or anyone else, looked upon the Panthers against Penn State that Friday night at Three Rivers. None of the Pitt people were disappointed. Majors was more national in his recruiting missions, but his players, many with distant addresses, still represented Pitt.

At first, it was a struggle. Dorsett was limited to 58 yards in the first half—yes, that was a poor half for him—and the score was tied, 7-7.

At the start of the second half, Majors made a move. He put the Panthers in an unbalanced line, a formation he had used only 10 plays all season. Dorsett was the deep back in the I-formation. "I didn't think I'd see him at fullback," said Penn State coach Joe Paterno afterward.

The second half was all Dorsett and Pitt. Altogether, Tony gained 224 yards in 38 attempts—the seventh most productive outing of his star-spangled Pitt career—and the Panthers knocked off the Nittany Lions, 24-7.

With that victory, the Panthers blotted out ten years of bitter memories. During that spell, the Panthers had been whipped by Penn State by such scores as 48-24, 42-6, 65-9, 27-7, 35-15, 55-18, 49-27, 35-13, 31-10. Only once was it close, and Penn State outscored Pitt, 7-6, in that 1975 meeting.

"Beating Penn State was the biggest thrill of my life to date," said Majors afterward. "But right now there aren't enough words to express how I feel about Tony Dorsett."

Paterno expressed it even better than Majors that night. Talking about Dorsett, the Penn State coach commented, "He's the greatest football player we have ever played against at Penn State. In my 27 years here, we have played against some awfully good ones—Jimmy Brown, Archie Griffin, Bubba Smith and Greg Pruitt. But Tony Dorsett is the outstanding player in America; and it isn't even close."

It was the last time Dorsett and Majors would perform for the Pitt football team in Pittsburgh. They made it a memorable finale. For the record, this is what Dorsett accomplished:

• He finished with 6,082 yards to his credit, rushing for more yards in his career than anyone in the history of NCAA major college football. Near the end of the third quarter against State, he slipped free for 10 yards to become the first player ever to top the 6,000 yard mark.

• Became the first player in NCAA history to rush for 1,000 yards for four consecutive years.

• Scored 22 touchdowns his senior season to be the NCAA scoring leader, and 59 for his four-year career, tying him with Army's Glenn Davis in that department in the NCAA record book.

• Scored 356 points in his career for an all-time record.

• Established 12 NCAA records altogether, including a 5.8 rushing average in his senior season, and 29 Pitt records. He averaged 177 yards per game that last year. He ran for over 100 yards in every game and for at least 200 yards four times.

• He led the Panthers to the No. 1 national ranking and a berth against Georgia in the Sugar Bowl on New Year's Day.

No player in college football—at least in a long time—had turned a football program around like Dorsett.

Asked to assess his importance to the program, Majors said, "Could we have done what we did without Dorsett? I doubt it. This year, maybe. Over four years, never.

"As a freshman and sophomore, when we didn't have the help he has now, what Tony did for us then was unbelievable. He made Pitt a winner when, really, we didn't have the personnel to win."

Did he help recruiting?

"Yeah, he made it a little easier to recruit," said Majors. "High school kids like to play with a winner, and Tony showed them Pitt could win. That made it easier for some of the kids to decide to come to Pitt."

Three days after the victory over Penn State, it was announced that Dorsett has been named the winner of the Heisman Trophy as the outstanding college football player in the nation.

He was the first Pitt player to capture the award in its 41-year-old history. He had finished fourth in the voting the year before, which was the highest finish by a Pitt player since Mike Ditka—an Aliquippa area product like Dorsett—finished sixth in 1960.

One of Tony's teammates, Al Romano, a middle guard who gained All-America honors and finished runner-up to Notre Dame's Ross Browner for the Outland Trophy as college football's finest lineman, said of Dorsett, "Another thing that's important, he's a decent kid. And I'm awful proud to be on the same team with a Heisman Trophy winner. Week after week he gets all that ink and it doesn't affect him or us. We're all behind him."

Declared Majors: "He's the finest football player I've ever seen on the football field. I may never coach a player that good as long as I stay in the game."

Majors was named the College Football Coach of the Year after the 1976 season, repeating an achievement he had first attained after the 1973 season at Pitt.

A week after the victory over Penn State, Majors made an announcement most Pitt fans felt and feared was coming. He had accepted an invitation to return to his alma mater, the University of Tennessee, to rebuild its football team.

On Friday, Dec. 3, 1976, Majors resigned. He had two years to go on his contract at Pitt—it had been extended

ALL-AMERICA & HEISMAN TROPHY WINNER TONY DORSETT

after his first season—but he had to go. "I felt very comfortable here," he said. "I love Pittsburgh, and it's always hard to leave a place. But there are some roots I have there."

Majors had been an All-America tailback at Tennessee, leading the Volunteers to a 10-0 record in 1956, and finished second to Notre Dame's Paul Hornung in the Heisman Trophy balloting.

He became the Tennessee coach and athletic director in charge of football when he signed a six-year contract. It had a base salary of $50,000, and fringe benefits which brought his annual pay closer to $75,000.

His won-lost record at Pitt was 33-13-1. Only two previous Pitt coaches had fared as well. Sutherland's mark was 111-20-12, and Glenn "Pop" Warner was 59-11-4. Michelosen had been the only long-time coach with a winning record—56-49-7—before Majors made the scene.

"Very few people have experienced what I have these last four years," said the 41-year-old Majors. "I'd be an exceptional dreamer if I thought I could do it again, but I'm gonna give it my best shot. Heck, I'm young enough.

"Part of it is going back to where you were undefeated as a senior. That was Tennessee's last undefeated team.

"The people here have learned how to win—the players, the school, the boosters. I'm really pleased about that. I want to see them continue to win."

Myslinski made sure the Pitt people didn't look upon Major's departure as the signal to the end of an outstanding football program at the school. "We started with 15 Golden Panthers in 1971-72," said the athletic director, talking about the boosters' organization, "and now we're up in the thousands. Without them, we couldn't have got Johnny Majors or Tony Dorsett or what else we have. But we don't have to stop here."

Myslinski might also have mentioned that alumni contributions had quadrupled since 1972 to 1976.

Reflecting on his decision to leave Iowa State for Pitt, in the first place, Majors made this remark:

"I was coming to a city that I didn't think I would like, and it turned out that I loved it. When Mary Lynn (his wife) and I pulled out of our driveway at Ames for the last time, we didn't think we'd ever again experience the thrills of making a success out of something that had been in bad shape. But this, these four years in Pittsburgh, it beats it all."

Majors and Dorsett had finished their work in Pittsburgh, but they still had one more game to go, against Georgia in the Sugar Bowl in New Orleans on New Year's Day, 1977.

Dorsett had begun his four-year siege of the NCAA record books against Georgia in his first game as a freshman, when he exploded for his first 100-yard effort at Pitt. Now he was finishing up against the same Bulldogs, and he showed them he hadn't slowed up any in the four years he had been cracking college defenses.

Pitt beat Georgia, 27-3, and Dorsett set a Sugar Bowl record with 202 yards for a career total of 6,526 yards, if you count his post-season performances.

Georgia's Vince Dooley declared later, "The 1976 Pitt team was the most complete college football team I've seen. I knew they were good. But, until after they had manhandled us in the Sugar Bowl, I didn't realize how good."

Jack Butler, the Pittsburgh-born and bred head of the Blesto pro scouting firm, said of Dorsett that day, "He

Jackie Sherrill and Johnny Majors display Championship trophy after Pitt defeated Kansas in the Sun Bowl in December, 1975.

runs like water." Butler said Dorsett was the best running back prospect since O. J. Simpson.

"He's just a great, great football player," observed Butler, who was once a great defensive back for the Steelers. "He's got such great movement, such great acceleration. He accelerates two or three times in one run. People worry about his size, but he's durable. He's put together. And he's a good kid, too."

Back home, there were others who shared Butler's enthusiasm for Dorsett. He was named the Man of the Year for the Dapper Dan Sports Banquet, the first collegian and first amateur athlete to win the award since it began in 1939. Majors had won the same award earlier.

On a national basis, Dorsett, in addition to his Heisman Trophy, also claimed the Player of the Year awards from the Walter Camp Foundation, Football News, Maxwell Club, Washington Touchdown Club and numerous other organizations.

He went on to displace Preston Pearson in the backfield of the Dallas Cowboys, and that was quite an achievement for a rookie because Pearson had four Super Bowl rings to his credit, two each as a member of the Cowboys' and Steelers' championship teams.

Meanwhile at Pitt, Dorsett's No. 33 jersey was retired. It was the only time in the 90 years of football at Pitt that a jersey has been retired.

PRESIDENT GERALD FORD GREETS PITT ALL-AMERICA TONY DORSETT AND PANTHER HEAD FOOTBALL COACH JOHNNY MAJORS

There were some other things that occurred in Dorsett's senior season that are worthy of recall.

In the next to the last game of the schedule, for instance, in a 24-16 victory over West Virginia, Dorsett scored three touchdowns. He taunted and angered the WVU players by wagging his finger to indicate Pitt's national ranking, and gained 199 yards in his final appearance at Pitt Stadium. On a late hit in front of the Pitt bench late in the game, Dorsett came up swinging, and was ejected from the game; otherwise he would have topped 200 yards a total of five times in his senior season.

In the game before that, Pitt beat Army, 37-7, to become the top-ranked team in the country when Purdue upset Michigan, 16-14. Dorsett again led the way, rushing for 212 yards and scoring three touchdowns.

The week before, Dorsett overcame a bruised leg, jammed elbow and poked eye to rush for 241 yards and two touchdowns, leading Pitt to a 23-13 victory over Syracuse.

This came the week after Pitt had won at Navy, 45-0, in a game in which Dorsett became the NCAA all-time leading rusher, breaking Archie Griffin's record of 5,177 yards. Dorsett rushed for 180 yards and three touchdowns that day. He broke the record set by the Ohio State All-America on a 32-yard touchdown run in the fourth quarter

"Every time I do something that a lot of people recognize," Dorsett said, "I'm going to take pride in it. And no matter how long or how much I've been into this game, I'll take pride in every record I set. I want to be known as No. 1, and I want to be known as that as long as I live."

It all began with the hiring of Majors, at age 37, back in 1972. Majors had compiled a 24-30-1 record in six seasons at Iowa State and guided the Cyclones to the only two bowl appearances in the school's history. The best season was an 8-3 record in 1971.

His theme at Ames was "Football is for winning and winning is fun."

Pitt was sure hungry for some fun in its football program. The Panthers' fortunes had taken a dip following the 9-1 mark in 1963 and reached the low mark with a 1-10 record in 1972.

Johnny Michelosen had been moved out after the 1965 season (3-7) and replaced by Dave Hart, an enthusiastic charmer who had coached Johnstown High School to a string of glorious triumphs and was a well-thought-of assistant at Navy when Pitt hired him.

Hart fell flat on his handsome face. His much-ballyhooed ballclubs had three straight 1-9 seasons before Hart was fired with one year remaining on his contract at Pitt. To replace Hart, who went on to administrative success at Robert Morris, Louisville and Missouri, Myslinski had sought some of the best known coaches in the nation. He nearly snagged some of them, but they all changed their minds in the end—much to Pitt's embarrassment—and remained right where they were.

In desperation, Pitt turned to Carl DePasqua, a former Pitt player from Williamsport and a former assistant on Michelosen's staff, to fill the void.

DePasqua rallied Pitt from three straight 1-9 seasons to a 4-6 record in 1969 and gave promise of better things.

Many people have forgotten, but Pitt got off to a great start in football for 1970, winning five of its first six games. Injuries to key players crippled the club, however, and it lost the last four games of the season to finish at 5-5.

There were some outstanding players on the Pitt team back then. They included defensive tackle Lloyd Weston, who had gained national attention playing for Pete Dimperio's team at Westinghouse High in the City League, and Ralph Cindrich, an All-America caliber but injury-jinxed linebacker from Avella, who would advance to the National Football League.

Besides Cindrich, there were three other prospects who would later play in the NFL, namely defensive backs Bryant Salter of South Hills High and Charlie Hall of Bala-Cynwyd, and center Bob Kuziel of West Haven, Conn.

In addition, there were ace receiver Steve Moyer of Pennsbury, running back Dennis Ferris of North Catholic High, tight end Joel Klimek of Seanor and Jack Dykes of Apollo. These were fine players.

There were two top-flight players from McKees Rocks, quarterback Dave Havern and fullback Tony Esposito. Havern had a weekly aerial circus show, connecting with Klimek and Moyer.

All sorts of good things were predicted for DePasqua's Pitt teams, but nothing came of it. Passing records were posted, but, alas, not winning records. The 1971 team finished 3-8 and the 1972 team went 1-10. DePasqua was fired Nov. 27, two days after a 49-27 season-ending loss at Penn State.

Majors came in to pick up the pieces at Pitt. The Panthers had been 16-56 since Michelosen's departure. They were 3-27 under Hart and 13-29 under DePasqua.

"I don't believe in making quick promises," said Majors the day his hiring was announced. "My job is to make lemonade out of a lemon."

Several days later, on a tour of the campus, he told students, "I know why they've lost here. There are a lot of things here that haven't been touched. The rust hasn't been wiped off in 20 years. This school has an attitude of losing."

Dorsett was the first player Pitt went after, and it was a combination recruiting effort by Majors and his top aide, Sherrill. Dorsett had been named to many of the high school All-America teams and had been timed in 4.5 for the 40. "He is," said Sherrill after Dorsett signed a letter-of-intent to attend Pitt, "the most complete high school football player I've ever seen."

Dorsett had narrowed his many choices down to Pitt and Penn State. "The chances of playing at Penn State right away weren't as good as they were at Pitt," explained Dorsett.

Dorsett was the fourth son of Westley and Myrtle Dorsett. Wes worked in the J&L Steel Works in Aliquippa. He thought his first three sons, Ernest, Tyrone and Keith, were all faster than Tony.

The youngest Dorsett stood 5-10 and tipped the scales at less than 160 pounds then, but grew into 185 pounds of pure speed and surprising inside power during his stay at Pitt.

Majors inherited some solid players who helped him at the beginning. There was some quality in the offensive line talent left him by DePasqua, and Dorsett started in the backfield with three other leftovers from the DePasqua program: a tough redhead in Billy Daniels, another quarterback from McKees Rocks, a solid blocker in fullback Dave Janasek and an effective wingback, Bruce Murphy.

The best of the defensive players Majors inherited were linebacker Kelcy Daviston of Duquesne, and tackle Glenn Hyde, who would later play for the NFL's Denver Broncos.

In addition to Dorsett, Majors and his staff brought in over 80 recruits their first time out. Majors knew he had to do something in a hurry. His recruits included a junior college All-America, Gary Burley of Grove City, Ohio, who anchored the defensive unit at middle guard.

The freshman class oozed with talent. There was Carson Long, an ace kicker from Ashland, Pa. From Florida came Cecil Johnson, a linebacker and defensive end, Don Parrish, a defensive tackle, and Arnie Weatherington, another linebacker. Pitt also picked up Jim Corbett, a tight end from Erie, and Al Romano, a middle guard from Solvay, N.Y. There was also a fine future quarterback in Robert Haygood, from Georgia, who'd go great later on with Dorsett in the Veer-offense.

Burley, Hyde, Johnson, Parrish, Corbett and Romano all developed into pro prospects while at Pitt.

Majors still had his doubts. His favorite question for those who approached him in his early days at Pitt was: "Do you think we can win?"

Once, he got caught in a snowstorm and couldn't keep a date to speak at a YMCA meeting at the William Penn Hotel here. Sherrill subbed for him, and said on April 12, 1973, "It'll take time, but Pittsburgh's the greatest sports city in the country, and the people are hungry for victory."

Even then, he knew.

Pitt tied Georgia, 7-7, for openers. In the third game, against Northwestern, Dorsett gained a school-record 265 yards in a 21-14 victory. Six weeks later, Notre Dame drubbed Pitt, 31-10, but Dorsett showed his stuff that Saturday afternoon, and gained national notice.

As a 19-year-old freshman, Dorsett had gained 209 yards against Notre Dame. No one in the history of the game had ever gained 200 yards against Notre Dame. It came on Nov. 5, 1973, almost a year from when Dorsett had played his final high school game at Hopewell. He broke the record of 195 yards set in 1952 by Oklahoma's Heisman Trophy winner, Billy Vessels. Going into that game, Notre Dame had the second-best defensive rating against the rush in the collegiate ranks. Dorsett spoiled that in a hurry.

Pat Livingston, the sports editor of The Pittsburgh Press, was moved to write that day: "Dorsett has the fawn-like grace and hidden power of a Gale Sayers or a Hugh McElhenny in miniature."

Pitt fashioned a 6-4-1 record that first year, and gained a berth to the Fiesta Bowl—Pitt's first bowl in 17 years—where the Panthers lost to Arizona State, 28-7. It was a start.

Majors received national Coach of the Year recognition for his first-year accomplishment, and Dorsett became the first freshman to make first-team All-America in 29 years.

When Majors talked about Dorsett, his legs would swing like a puppy dog's tail, as writer Vince DiNardo once described it, and his voice would suddenly go soft. "I have a lot of respect for Tony," Majors said then. "He was the first player I visited after taking this job. I'm impressed with his pride in being a great football player. He takes a lot of pride in picking up things right away and doing things the way they should be done."

It was a mutual admiration society. "I think Coach Majors is the best coach in the country," said Dorsett. "Look at the job he's done here so far."

TROPHIES PITT WON IN '76

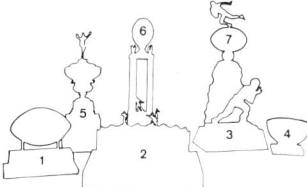

Trophies won by the 1976 National Champion Pitt football team: (1) Grantland Rice Trophy from the Football Writers of America, (2) MacArthur Bowl from the National Football Foundation and Hall of Fame, (3) Heisman Trophy awarded to Tony Dorsett, (4) Cool Ray Cup for the Eastern Championship among the major universities, (5) Sugar Bowl Championship Trophy, (6) United Press International National Championship, (7) Lambert Trophy for the Eastern Championship. Missing is the Associated Press National Championship Trophy.

The two of them had only just begun. Majors and his staff brought in some more blue-chippers for their second season. They brought in five future pros in quarterback Matt Cavanaugh, running back Elliott Walker, wide receiver Karl Farmer and, closer to home, defensive tackle Randy Holloway of Sharon and defensive back Bob Jury of Library.

In addition, they pulled in center Walt Brown of Allison Park, guard Tom Brzoza of New Castle, defensive back Dave DiCiccio of Midland, and defensive end Randy Cozens, to name some standouts.

Dorsett got off to a slow start in his sophomore season. He was limited by a groin pull and a bad ankle. Pitt was 1-2-1 after four games before everybody got in gear.

Late in the season, when Dorsett was hurting, freshman speedster Elliot Walker went wild against Temple, running for 169 yards and four touchdowns in a 35-24 victory over the Owls at Pitt Stadium.

Pitt finished the 1974 season with a 7-4 record, but again lost the big ones—to Southern Cal, to Notre Dame and Penn State—and Dorsett slipped somewhat and failed to make first-team All-America. Pitt stayed home for the holidays.

Pitt was making progress, though, and Majors was happy. "Tony has had a lot to do with what we've been able to accomplish here so far," he said. "But I'm not going to say he's been the only reason. That wouldn't be fair to all the other great athletes here and all the hard work and sleepless nights the whole coaching staff has put in.

"Football is bigger than one man, and Pitt football is bigger than me or Dorsett. Everyone's hard work has gone into it."

Dorsett had the two greatest games, statistically speaking anyhow, in his junior season. You had to be at Army's Michie Stadium that Saturday afternoon of Oct. 18, 1975, to realize how super Dorsett was that day. Doc Blanchard and Glenn Davis never ran as well when they were Mr. Inside and Mr. Outside at West Point.

Dorsett's family sat directly behind our alumni contingent, and you couldn't help but share their delight that day. Tony totaled 268 yards—the best at Pitt up till that point—in a 52-20 triumph.

A month later, Dorsett was even more sensational against his favorite opponent, Notre Dame. He ran for 303 yards—his best day ever—on 23 carries against Notre Dame and added 71 more on passes from Matt Cavanaugh to lead Pitt to its first victory over Notre Dame in 10 years, 34-20. It was the first major win in Johnny Majors' career at Pitt.

It was especially pleasing to Dorsett. "When you're young and growing up," Dorsett said, "Notre Dame is Football, U.S.A. Everybody has a dream to go there."

Thank heavens, he went to Pitt instead.

Dorsett broke his own record against Notre Dame in near-freezing weather before a sellout crowd of 56,480 at Pitt Stadium. Pitt was warmed that day when they accepted a bid to play in the Sun Bowl in El Paso, Tex. The victory over the Irish gave them a 7-3 record.

Joe Paterno of Penn State personally scouted that game because the Nittany Lions had a break in their schedule.

"We've always known Dorsett was great," he said. "He's always been great. Not just today."

The Panthers lost their season finale, 7-6, to Penn State at Three Rivers Stadium.

Pitt perked up for its Sun Bowl appearance and clipped Kansas, 33-19. It was December 25, 1975, in El Paso, and afterward Jackie Sherrill announced to the squad that he was leaving Pitt to accept the challenge of the head coaching position at Washington State University.

Dorsett gave Sherrill the game ball. Some shed tears.

When Majors moved on to Tennessee, Sherrill was called back to Pitt. "Pittsburgh is my home," Sherrill said at the announcement of his hiring. "When I came here in 1973, I didn't even know what pigs-in-a-blanket were. Now I know all about holupki, pierogi, and bakklava. I love Pittsburgh, with its people and rich culture. I hated to leave in 1975, but I really wanted a head coaching job.

"It's good to be back. I'm very ecstatic, honored, and very happy to be back. Pittsburgh is a big part of my life."

Sherrill signed a five-year contract with Pitt, saying that "coming to the number one team in the country and sustaining that program is a big challenge."

Sherrill had come a long way. He wasn't a smooth-talker to match Majors, and at the University of Alabama he was a solid, but not spectacular, performer who played several positions. He was a team man. Sincerity was his strength. That and a willingness to work hard, and get the job done. People were comfortable with Sherrill.

One of Sherrill's prize rookies was Mark May, a 6-5, 270-pound offensive tackle from Oneonta, N.Y. "I came in for a weekend at Pitt," he says now, "and spent one night each with Tony Dorsett, and his two best friends on the team, Don Parrish and Cecil Johnson, and enjoyed myself. I thought Pitt was for me."

Sherrill got lucky in a hurry. When his staff was recruiting a running back named Ray Charles "Rooster" Jones in Pascagoula, Miss., they also discovered a defensive lineman named Hugh Green of Natchez, Miss. Green turned out to be a great one, Pitt's most spectacular player since Dorsett.

Pitt looked promising, especially with a senior quarterback like Matt Cavanaugh coming back to lead the attack.

The opener was against Notre Dame, just to make sure Sherrill knew he was back in the big time. Before a national TV audience, the Panthers took a 7-0 lead but Cavanaugh suffered a broken left wrist in the first quarter. On the play that snapped Cavanaugh's wrist and Pitt's chances for another national championship, the All-America quarterback completed a 12-yard TD pass to Gordon Jones.

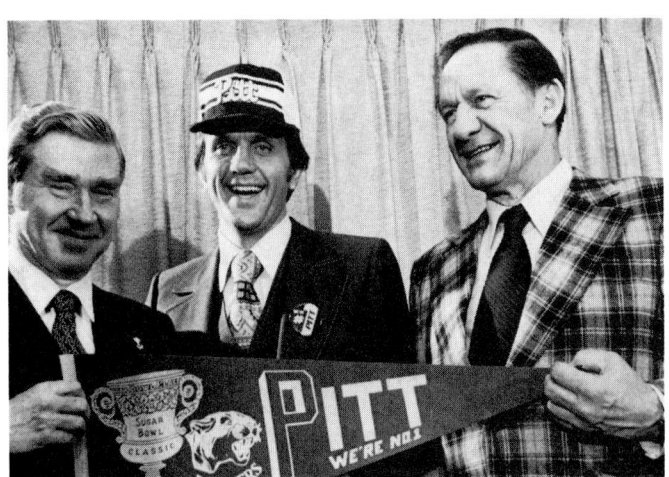

Chancellor Dr. Wesley Posvar (left) and athletic director Cas Myslinski welcome new head football coach Jackie Sherrill.

JACKIE SHERRILL

Pitt ended up losing that game, 19-9, despite heroic defensive performances by Randy Holloway, Al Chesley and Dave Logan.

Pitt bounced back to win the next three games, 28-6 over William & Mary, and 76-0 over Temple, and 45-7 over Boston College before Florida tied the Panthers, 17-17, at Gainesville.

Gordon Jones, Elliott Walker and Freddie Jacobs were the big offensive guns. Cavanaugh came back for the Florida game and played well, though turnovers cost Pitt dearly. With Cavanaugh at the controls again, replacing Rick Trocano, the Panthers put on a five-game winning streak, defeating Navy, 34-17, Syracuse, 28-21, Tulane, 48-0, West Virginia, 44-3, and Army, 52-26.

Pitt's streak was stopped on a snowy day by Penn State—who else?—in the season finale, 15-13. State's Matt Millen thwarted Elliott Walker's attempt to score a two-point conversion.

Pitt went to the Gator Bowl and beat Clemson, 34-3. So Sherrill's first slate showed a 9-2-1 record. Not bad.

Sherrill suffered major losses from that squad, however, with a half dozen moving on to the pros: Cavanaugh, Walker, Holloway, Gary Silvestri, Bob Jury and J. C. Wilson. The Panthers had four first-team All-Americas in Cavanaugh, Jury, Holloway and Brzoza, and eight players were picked in the NFL draft.

But Sherrill still had some good ones coming back for his second season, in Jones, an All-America flanker, Hugh Green, an All-America defensive end, Jeff Delaney, a senior strong safety from Upper St. Clair, and Matt Carroll, a senior offensive guard from Norwood. Other standouts returning were the mammoth May, an offensive tackle, Chesley, a senior linebacker, Logan, a senior middle guard from Pittsburgh's Peabody High, Steve Gaustad, a senior tight end from New Cumberland, and Dave DiCiccio, a senior defensive end from Midland.

Sherrill had a young team for 1978, but it registered a fine 8-4 record and accepted a Tangerine Bowl bid, where it lost to North Carolina State, 30-17.

Pitt won its first four games in 1978, defeating Tulane 24-6, in the opener as Trocano connected with Gordon Jones, while "Rooster" Jones, Larry Sims and Freddy Jacobs ran the ball well. The next time out, Trocano and Jacobs led the offense, and Chesley was a one-man gang on defense in a 20-12 victory over Temple.

Jacobs scored three second-half TDs in a 20-16 victory over North Carolina in the next contest. Pitt scored the first four times it had the ball to beat Boston College, 32-15, as Mark Schubert continued to boot field goals, and Trocano continued to find Gordon Jones open for passes.

Notre Dame interrupted Pitt, beating them 26-17 at South Bend, but the Panthers bounced back to beat Florida State, 7-3, the following week in a defensive struggle in which Green and Chesley starred.

Navy shocked Pitt in their next outing, 21-11, though Trocano threw for 275 yards, and Steve Gaustad grabbed 11 passes for 132 yards.

Pitt beat three long-time rivals in a row after that, edging Syracuse, 18-17, with Trocano coming through in the clutch; West Virginia, 52-7, with "Rooster" Jones running for 169 yards and two TDs, Trocano throwing for 146 yards and his backup, Lindsay Delaney, throwing for 72 more; and Army, 35-17, as Jeff Delaney picked off a fumble and ran 99 yards for six points, Trocano passing for 143 yards,

BIG HOPES FOR THE '80s

DAN MARINO
Whiz Kid QB From Oakland

and "Rooster" Jones running for 99.

Penn State stopped Pitt once again, 17-10, and the Panthers also came out on the short end in the Tangerine Bowl, bowing 30-17, to North Carolina State.

The record was 8-4, but Sherrill was hardly satisfied. He worked harder than ever, and he was a workaholic to begin with. "If you let him," said Jimmy Johnson, one of his former associates, "and if I didn't take him out once in a while and put a smile on his face, he'd work himself 24 hours a day and work himself into a grave."

Sherrill had to work hard because, from his second team, he was losing Gordon Jones, the best receiver in Pitt history, a dependable tight end in Gaustad; a starting center in Walt Brown; All-East offensive guard Matt Carroll; and five defensive stalwarts in Jeff Delaney, Logan, DiCiccio, Chesley and Mike Balzer.

Even so, Sherrill was looking forward to his third season. "I believe we will be a Top Ten team," he said at the outset of the 1979 season, and the Panthers played up to his expectations.

He came up with some fine freshmen, the best of whom was Danny Marino, perhaps the most sought-after prospect to come out of Western Pennsylvania since Dorsett. Marino, 6-4, 200, had been an all-everything quarterback at nearby Central Catholic.

Pitt opened at home against Kansas, and Trocano started at quarterback but split time with Marino. Sherrill was so anxious to get this great prospect some playing time. Marino's first pass was intercepted in the end zone, his second was nearly intercepted in the end zone, and, on his third try, he found Ralph Still in the end zone for a TD pass. Marino made things happen in a hurry. Pitt clobbered Kansas, 24-0, and another newcomer, fullback Randy McMillan, who'd been a great junior college rusher the year before, gained 82 yards in the first quarter and 141 yards altogether to give promise of big things to come.

The early euphoria for Pitt ended in a hurry, however, as North Carolina caught the Panthers napping the next week and won, 17-7. Pitt was still sleep-walking the week after and just managed to top Temple, 10-9, in Philadelphia.

Pitt beat Boston College, 28-7, with Marino coming off the bench and driving the Panthers to three of their four touchdowns. Trocano came back the next week and passed for 150 yards, and Marino came in and passed for an additional 120 yards, in a 35-0 victory over Cincinnati. Pitt had some 1-2 passing combination.

At Washington the week after, in a nationally-televised game, it was Trocano all the way in a hard-fought 26-14 win over the nationally-ranked Huskies. Anyone who watched that game won't soon forget the fabulous defensive showing of Hugh Green, or the running by McMillan, who gained 121 yards and scored two TDs.

The following Saturday at Pitt Stadium Pitt recovered from a slow start, and defeated Navy, 24-7. Trocano couldn't get anything going early against the Midshipmen, who had come into the game with the nation's top-ranked defensive unit. The Midshipmen had suffered many injuries to their ranks, but seemed capable of upsetting Pitt, especially when Trocano hurt an ankle on a quarterback keeper.

It took Marino, who had replaced Trocano, awhile to get going, and Pitt trailed Navy, 7-3, at the intermission. Marino drove Pitt to three TDs in the second half, and completed 22 of 30 passes for two of those touchdowns.

HUGH GREEN Goes After All-America Honors Again

With Marino calling the signals, and firing at will, Pitt overcame Syracuse, 28-21, West Virginia, 24-17, and Army, 40-0, with the fabulous freshman hitting 17 of 30 passes for 272 yards and a touchdown in that game at West Point.

At Penn State, Marino commanded the Panther forces in a hard-fought 29-14 victory. Marino was 17-for-32 in the air for 279 yards and a touchdown, while McMillan ran for 114 more yards, and caught a 52-yard TD pass. Marino showed so much poise against Penn State, a perennial nemesis for the best of Pitt teams.

So Pitt had put together a 10-1 record, with only that nightmare in North Carolina still nagging at them, and accepted a bid to play in the Fiesta Bowl once again. Sherrill also announced that Serafino "Foge" Fazio would be promoted to top assistant for the following season.

Marino and the Pitt offense were stymied most of the game by an aggressive and alert Arizona defense, but kept its poise and emerged with a 16-10 victory. Green had a great defensive game, and Marino passed for 172 yards and a touchdown, with McMillan picking up 81 more yards on the ground.

The three of them would all be back for 1980, and so would Sherrill. He said he intends to stay here.

"I can say it now and I'll say it again 10 years from now," he said. "I'll still be the coach. I'll still be in Pittsburgh. Even if I got fired, I'd probably open a hot dog stand here or something."

JOHNNY MAJORS

Johnny Majors is a modern-day "Music Man," college football's answer to Professor Harold Hill. Majors likes making the trumpets blare and the drums roll. He likes the TV shows and the media coverage. He likes getting into his twin-engine, phone-equipped Piper, and searching for new challenges.

He likes to build character, and instill discipline in his charges. In that respect, plus his penchant for flying his own plane—a zealousness also shared by Jackie Sherrill—he is a lot like Chuck Noll, the coach of the Steelers.

"A lot will depend," said Majors after his first few months at Pitt, "on the players' enthusiasm for our program."

Majors stood 5-10½, 180, but came across much bigger because of his boisterous, aggressive manner. He was more emotional and outgoing than Noll, but they both look at themselves as teachers.

"The fun of football is in the teaching," Majors once said. "I like to see a coach out there on his hands and knees, then jumping up to pat a guy on his back. As a football coach, I'm a Vince Lombardi fan.

"Lombardi had the two qualities that mean the most in coaching any football team. He was professionally tough, and he was personally emotional. And that's a heckuva combination.

"I was at Green Bay once when he was there and the thing that struck me was that they practiced like a good college team. Lombardi was a tough disciplinarian. His teams had to line up just so and run all their plays just so. But they ran them with the old man's emotion. It was very exciting to see how he stirred them up. You don't win football games with X's and O's. You win that way."

Coach Johnny Majors is flanked by his two top running backs— Elliott Walker (left) and Tony Dorsett.

JACKIE SHERRILL

Jackie Sherrill said he was glad to be back when he succeeded his old boss, Johnny Majors, after Pitt had won the national championship in 1976, but Sherrill felt he had some explaining to do about going away in the first place.

"I wouldn't have left Washington State for any other job except Pittsburgh," said Sherill upon his return. "Coming back to Pittsburgh was kind of special. My wife was from here, and I wasn't that far removed from the scene. I still had close feelings for the people here . . . Pittsburgh is what I consider to be my home."

His wife is the former Daryle Favro, who was a high school guidance counselor from Elizabeth, when they met soon after he arrived here the first time.

"The people in Pittsburgh are very honest people," said Sherrill, explaining his fondness for the place. "They're compassionate, yet they're tough, and I'm tough and like that, too. In five months, I probably met more people and became closer to them than I had in my whole time in organized sports. For a man just turning 29, it was a very important time. They gave me a home and they gave me a community involvement."

Johnny Majors, when asked to describe the role of a college coach, once remarked: "A coach has to be a salesman, a parent away from home, an academic adviser, a fund-raiser, a public relations man for the university . . . and a football coach."

Sherrill is all of those things, and then some. He not only sold Tony Dorsett on coming to Pitt in the first place, but he also talked Tony out of quitting school when he was a homesick freshman.

After three years on the job, Jackie Sherrill's record at Pitt was 28-7-1, and no other coach in the school's previous 89 years could claim that good a start in as many seasons.

"It hasn't been easy," said Sherrill: "There was a lot of pressure on me and my staff. What we have done the last three years has taken some of the pressure off.

"Though we haven't achieved the ultimate—winning the National Championship—it has been pleasing."

Coach Jackie Sherrill and Joe Pendry confer with QB Dan Marino.

TONY DORSETT

Tom Harmon looks on as Tony Dorsett receives Heisman Trophy.

Tony Dorsett always stood out in a crowd, even during those first few days at Pitt's football practices.

Johnny Majors, the new coach at Pitt, had gone out in 1973 and brought back players by the carload. He brought back in the neighborhood of 80 new players. That's about the size of some college teams—with four years of recruiting—and Majors brought them all in at once.

He believed there was quality in quantity.

One young man named John Hanhauser hardly knew anyone after the first week of practice when Majors held his first scrimmage.

"I was playing linebacker then," Hanhauser recalled, "and it was a screen pass. I went out to get this guy. It was easy. I'm not the fastest guy in the world, but I had this guy easy. I thought. When I got out there, he wasn't there. He was gone!

"I remember I went back to the bench and I said, 'Who in the hell was that? Who's 33?'"

Someone named Tony Dorsett, he was told.

"I'd never heard of Tony Dorsett myself," admitted Hanhauser. "I didn't know a thing about him."

He learned quickly, and so did the rest of his teammates. So did Pitt's opponents. Some of the coaches on the other side will tell you the rest:

• "I have not seen a running back like Tony Dorsett since O. J. Simpson," said Homer Smith, Army.

• "I don't know if I've ever seen a better running back," said Joe Paterno, Penn State.

• "It was (Dorsett's 303-yard day as a junior) as fine a performance as I've seen in 28 years of coaching," declared Dan Devine, Notre Dame.

Pitt's backfield coach at the time was Harry Jones. He had been a two-time All-America running back at Arkansas and a wingback for five years with the Philadelphia Eagles.

"I used to think Gale Sayers was the greatest runner I'd ever seen," said Jones, "until I saw Tony. He works harder than anyone I've coached. And he hasn't lost his modesty with all that exposure over the years."

PITT ALL-AMERICAS IN THE '70s

1973—1975—1976—TONY DORSETT

Tony Dorsett was hardly a one-man show at Pitt, though he received more publicity than anyone else. The Panthers may have put more talent on the field than anyone else in the country in 1976 when they won the national title under Coach Johnny Majors.

"After the material he had at Pittsburgh," opined Georgia coach Vince Dooley, whose team lost to Pitt in the Sugar Bowl at season's end, "there's not another school in the country where he could have gone and felt he had as good a team."

There were many members of that team who gained All-America recognition, and several who did not, but are now playing in the National Football League, like Cecil Johnson of the Tampa Bay Buccaneers, Don Parrish of the Kansas City Chiefs and J. C. Wilson of the Houston Oilers.

"We had a lot of great athletes," said Majors.

Pitt's first-team All-America honor roll during the '70s reads like this:

1973	Tony Dorsett
1974	Gary Burley
1975	Tony Dorsett
1976	Tony Dorsett
	Al Romano
1977	Matt Cavanaugh
	Randy Holloway
	Bob Jury
	Tom Brzoza
1978	Hugh Green
	Gordon Jones
1979	Hugh Green

1974—GARY BURLEY

1976—AL ROMANO

1977—MATT CAVANAUGH

1977—RANDY HOLLOWAY

1977—BOB JURY

1977—TOM BRZOZA

1978—1979—HUGH GREEN

1978—GORDON JONES

CARNEGIE-MELLON, CHUCK KLAUSING STAKE CLAIM TO LAMBERT BOWL

By Jim O'Brien

"To compete at a school like Carnegie-Mellon you have to have a great love of the game, and schoolwork must be taken seriously."
—Chuck Klausing

CHUCK KLAUSING
Head Coach—CMU

Coach Chuck Klausing poses with various "trinkets" he has accumulated over the years at CMU. The taller football trophy, nearest to Klausing, is the ABC-TV 1979 Small College Coach of the Year award; the shorter football trophy is the Lambert Bowl; the two wooden awards flanking Klausing are plaques received for advancing to the semi-final round of the NCAA Division III playoffs in 1978 and 1979. The three trophies topped with football players are the Presidents' Athletic Conference championship trophies for 1977, 1978 and 1979.

Chuck Klausing, the football coach at Carnegie-Mellon University, was on the same sports banquet dais as Dan McCann, the football coach at Duquesne University, during the winter of 1979. "Carnegie-Mellon and Duquesne will be playing football against each other again next season," said Klausing, "and it'll be for the city championship. The team that loses will play Pitt."

Klausing was kidding, of course, but he could afford to since he's been so successful at CMU, just as he has been at every school where he's worked. Klausing has built one of the best small college football programs in the country at CMU. He hasn't returned the school to its gridiron glory days of the '20s and '30s, but he has returned it to respectability. And that was the idea.

"We'd like to be the same thing in Division III that Pitt is in Division I," commented Klausing in reflecting on his objectives at the Oakland campus.

He's done just that. While next-door neighbor Pitt was picking up the Lambert Trophy, as the best Div. I football team in the East, in 1978 and 1979, Carnegie-Mellon was picking up the Lambert Bowl as the best team in Div. III in the East during the same seasons.

CMU became the first school in the 44-year history of the Lambert awards to be honored in two different categories. The 1938 Carnegie Tech squad won the Lambert Trophy as the top major college team in the East with a 7-1 record.

Under Klausing, CMU compiled a 10-1 record in 1979, going undefeated until it lost a last-minute 15-6 verdict at Ithaca in the NCAA Division III playoff semifinal. A victory would have put the Tartans in the Amos Alonzo Stagg Bowl in Phenix, Ala.

The year before, CMU had a 9-2 record. In Klausing's first two seasons, the team was 6-1-1 and 8-1. This represented quite a turnaround in the Tartan program. The best the team had done before that in the decade of the '70s was 5-3, which they achieved three times in six seasons under former coach Joe Gasparella.

A former Notre Dame and Steeler back, Gasparella guided the grid team at "Tech" for 13 seasons, compiling a 45-60-1 mark. He made his living as a much-respected architect, and "moonlighted" as a coach at CMU. There is more of a commitment now on the part of the school to field a fine team than there was back then.

The change in outlook came when Dr. Richard Cyert became president of the university in 1972. "I was unhappy with what I considered to be a loser's image at Carnegie-Mellon," recalls Dr. Cyert. "I didn't like the idea of our school to be identified with losing, whether it be in academics or athletics."

He brought in Jim Banner from Pitt to be the CMU athletic director, and Banner brought in Gary Meckley to coach track and cross-country, Dave Maloney for basket-

JOE GASPARELLA
Former CMU Head Coach

ball and Klausing for football. The programs all improved drastically, without, according to school officials, sacrificing the school's high academic standards.

Klausing was never connected with anything but winning programs. He had spent the first six years of the '70s as the assistant head football coach at West Virginia University. Before that he compiled a 47-7 record in six seasons as head coach at Indiana (Pa.) University and had served as an assistant before that at Army and Rutgers.

Originally from Wilmerding, and a Slippery Rock College grad, Klausing got his coaching start at Pitcairn High where he posted a 30-7-1 record, and then went to Braddock where his record was an incredible 54-0-1. He had six undefeated seasons and won six WPIAL titles there.

Bob Kennedy came to CMU when Klausing became the head coach. He was one of six starters on the 1979 squad who came from Central Catholic High School, whose campus runs smack up against the CMU campus. Pitt had its dandy freshman quarterback from Central Catholic in Danny Marino, and CMU had a senior quarterback from the same alma mater. "I've been called the forgotten Central quarterback, but I don't mind," said Kennedy. "I'm very much satisfied with my situation. I knew I wasn't good enough to make football my life, but I knew I wanted to make football part of my life.

"We've lost only five games in the four years I've been here. I think we take our football seriously."

Or as Klausing puts it, "To compete at a school like Carnegie-Mellon you have to have a great love of the game, and schoolwork must be taken seriously as well."

Part of the 1979 "Plaid Curtain" defense which led the nation in preventing scoring: Mike Fausti (66), Chip Miller (55), and Mark Demo (87).

Coach Klausing, the Lambert Bowl and Linebacker Coach Rich Lackner. Lackner, a graduate of Mt. Lebanon High School and 1978 CMU grad, was a standout linebacker for the Tartans. He joined the coaching staff in 1979. In 1978, he was All-PAC first team; Academic All-America second team; Pittsburgh Press All-District team; and a Post-Gazette Dapper Dan Awardee.

GUSTY SUNSERI

DON KAMINSKI

Kennedy was one of many stars on Klausing's clubs at CMU. His 1976 team produced the school's first academic All-America in Rick Lackner, a linebacker from Mt. Lebanon who went on to become one of Klausing's assistant coaches.

Last year's team had an especially good defensive unit. They were coached by Moe Smith and called "Moe's Maniacs." They were led by senior safety Gusty Sunseri, a Central Catholic grad, and Kerry Bove (North Catholic), Sal Fastuca (Burrell), Pat Olivo (Central Catholic), Pat Mechas (Penn Hills), Tom Frost (Butler) and Ken Murawski (Baldwin).

Offensively, the stars at the skill positions were Kennedy, Bob Gasior (Central Catholic), Rick Leaman (Thomas Jefferson), Greg Samsa (Turtle Creek) and Pete Recchia (Kiski Area).

The Tartans "unsung heroes" included Denny Postufka (Montour), Gene Marcink (Ambridge), Mark Rice (Carmichaels), Gary Matz (Elizabeth Forward), Joe Goldcamp (Central Catholic), Jim Prencipe (Ridgway) and Don Kaminski (Baldwin).

As Klausing looked to the '80s, he was excited about a six-year contract to duel with Duquesne University on an annual basis, and keeping CMU among the top small college football teams in the country.

BOB KENNEDY

BOB GASIOR was CMU's leading rusher in 1979.

BOB PRINCE
Radio Voice
of the Tartans

Views of the swarming CMU defense which had an outstanding season in '79.

IRON DUKES, DAN McCANN MOVE UP IN CLASS

By Jim O'Brien

DAN McCANN

Commissioner Tom Foerster presents 1972 trophy to Coach Dan McCann whose Duquesne team won the Eye Bowl—14-5 over St. Francis. Duquesne was 7-1 in 1972. Looking on (l. to r.) were Gary McHenry and Bob Mongillo.

"We always had a winning team, but there was a negative image to 'club' football. Now we're more accepted."

—Dan McCann

In his own inimitable manner, Duquesne University's Dan McCann has contributed to Pittsburgh's image as the City of Champions.

During his decade as coach of the Dukes' football team, the irrepressible, rosy-cheeked McCann compiled an enviable record, for nine years on a club basis, and in 1979 he turned out a winner when the Dukes moved up to the Division III level for the first time.

The Dukes never had a losing season in McCann's initial ten-year tour on The Bluff, and his 1973 team even won the national club football championship. The Dukes defeated Mattatuck Community College of Waterbury, Conn. in a title contest at Three Rivers Stadium. The Dukes were undefeated that year, posting a 10-0 record.

In 1970 Dan took over as head coach of the Dukes who were into their second season of club football. In nine years, he compiled an impressive 53-21-1 mark, and he pushed the school administrators to move up to Division III.

"We always had a winning team, but there was a negative image to 'club' football. Now we're more accepted," commented McCann.

No sooner had the school approved the move to Division III, than McCann was beating the drums—as only he can—for an annual contest with one-time cross-town rival Carnegie-Mellon University.

Chuck Klausing's Carnegie-Mellon team has been one of the best in the East in Division III. McCann could care less. "We're not to where they are now, but we're getting there," said McCann, soon after a six-year contract with Carnegie-Mellon was signed. "I think we can compete with them."

In their first season in Division III, where no athletic scholarships are permitted, the Dukes were 5-4. Only two seniors started, however, and ten freshmen were in the regular lineup, so McCann was confident about the future.

"We're getting good kids in here," he said. "I have to recruit rich kids and poor kids, but not in between. The rich kids can afford Duquesne, and the poor kids can get some financial aid based on need."

McCann recruits with great zealousness. He's an outstanding salesman. That's what he's been doing for a living during his stay at Duquesne. He's the assistant to the president at the Pittsburgh Brewing Company in Lawrenceville. His boss, company president Bill Smith, is a Duquesne grad and an engaging and enthusiastic sports fan.

Duquesne University's 1973 National Club Football champions had a 10-0 undefeated season.

He helps Dan whatever way he can, usually providing summer jobs at the brewery for the boys who need to work their way through school.

"I've got the best of two worlds, as far as I can see," said McCann. "I don't have a 9-to-5 job. We go out a lot in the evenings to banquets and sports dinners and such, to meet people, and push Iron City beer, but I still have time to coach the football team."

And he still finds time to run kids' basketball tournaments on his native North Side, usually at North Catholic, where he was once a star quarterback. As a young man from Manchester, he played at Pitt for two years under Johnny Michelosen, but two serious ankle fractures cut short his career. He did graduate from Pitt in 1955 with a degree in business administration.

His coaching career began in 1960 with a grade school team at St. Sebastian's in the North Hills. He coached there for seven seasons. He moved to North Catholic High School where he became freshman coach in 1967. In three seasons there, his teams were 20-0-1 and his 1967 team was unbeaten, untied and unscored-upon during a perfect 8-0 season. His overall coaching record, at the end of the 1979 season, was 122-31-3.

He was looking forward to the '80s, especially the opener at Carnegie-Mellon. His Dukes play their home games on the AstroTurf surface of South Side Stadium. A homecoming at a football game was in store at the school for the first time since 1950.

Football was discontinued at Duquesne after the 1950 season. Before then, the Dukes had a fine major college team that often went to post-season bowl games. The 1936 team, for instance, finished with an 8-1 record and went on to defeat Mississippi State in the Orange Bowl. Buff Donelli, Joe Bach, Elmer Layden and Mike Basrak—the first Duquesne All-America—were big names on The Bluff back then.

A return to those glory days is out of the question. But if anybody can bring back even a taste of those days, Dan McCann can.

Duquesne's 1973 Club Football All-Americas (l. to r.) Coach Dan McCann, linebacker John Stefanik (66), quarterback Jack Schroeffel (12), running back Steve Scherer (22), flanker Rod Hess (85), Assistant coach Jim Urbanic.

GOLF IN THE '70s
By Pat Livingston

For Arnold Palmer, the finest golfer ever to play in Western Pennsylvania, the decade of the '70s was an epitaph. It cried out the final hurrah to a brilliant career which saw the son of a simple Latrobe greenskeeper, an athlete who hob-nobbed with presidents and heads of state, put the cap on a career that will endure long in memory and rich in accomplishment.

The decade of the '70s wasn't that good to Arnie Palmer, not as good as it had been to the Pirates, the Steelers, the Panthers or the Triangles, each of which had brought a national championship to Pittsburgh.

Palmer's significant championships had come a decade earlier, when he had all but owned the Masters, when he might win seven tournaments a year and finish as runner-up in six others. Life begins at 40, they say, but whoever said that obviously wasn't thinking of golf.

Yet life didn't end for Arnold who reached that frustrating age by the time he had entered the '70s. There was life in those old bones yet, for Palmer greeted the new decade with a two-ball victory with Jack Nicklaus, enjoyed his most profitable campaign, and won his fourth and fifth Bob Hope Desert Classics at an age when lesser competitors are relaxing at the bank of a lake, casting for bass.

Palmer, in his 40s, won the Citrus at Orlando, and he won at West Chester. At Laurel Valley, he successfully defended his team title, pairing with Nicklaus again, while studs half his age shook their heads and wondered how he did it.

But the '70s were the decade of Arnie Palmer's greatest disappointment, the failure to win the one tournament he wanted most, the U. S. Open at Oakmont in 1973. It was, perhaps, the most heart-breaking defeat this bull-shouldered, heavily muscled golfer had ever experienced.

Palmer wanted that Open because, though Oakmont is one of his favorite courses—he joined the club that year, a couple of weeks before the Open—he never had been able to harness his remarkable skills, or acclimate his bricklayer's hands, there long enough to score a professional victory at the feared Hades of Hulton.

He came close, however. In 1962, he had shot a 283, an Oakmont record at the time, but the best he could get out of that was a tie with Jack Nicklaus, a rookie on the pro tour.

In the playoff, Palmer, whose putter had been behaving like a mischievous child throughout the week, never did solve Oakmont's fast, diabolical greens, while Nicklaus did. The young man from Ohio, poring intently over each putt before striking it, had only one three-putt green in 90 holes, an incredible demonstration of concentration on a course that is fraught with distractions. Palmer, no stranger to those greasy greens, three-putted 13 times over the five days of the tournament.

And that's how it was in the playoff. Three times Palmer three putted and those mistakes cost him the championship.

Twice more in the next five years, Palmer was to be a runner-up in the Open, a tournament which he had won in 1960 at Cherry Hills in Denver, beating a rallying 19-year-old amateur, this same Nicklaus, in a stirring duel to the final green. He lost an Open playoff to Billy Casper at Olympic in San Francisco in 1967, after having it locked up in his grasp with only nine holes to play, and at Baltusrol a year later, the persistent Nicklaus cropped up again to snatch still another triumph away from this unfortunate, star-crossed golfer.

And that, too, was why Palmer was so eager to win the 1973 Open.

He might have, too, for at the end of the third round, Palmer was three-under, a stroke ahead of Tom Weiskoff and even with John Schlee. The men who might beat him, Nicklaus and Lee Trevino, were over par and presumably out of contention.

Johnny Miller, who had been a factor after the second round, had skied to a five-over 76 on Saturday and, though he had been one of the stars of the tour that year, he didn't even draw a sizable gallery for his final record-

ARNOLD PALMER
Latrobe's Gift to Golf

shattering round, the 63 which had sorely embarrassed the proud members at Oakmont.

One thing Palmer wouldn't have to worry about, he told himself, were golfers like Miller on a day like this.

At the end of eight holes, Palmer could breathe easily. He was even par, level with Schlee, and Nicklaus had made up no ground on him. Palmer was all smiles, hitching at his unruly trousers, as he strode up the ninth fairway, a hole which comes back to the sprawling Victorian Clubhouse where Palmer's Sedentary Army, the Colonels and Brigadier Generals, followed the action from their chairs on the veranda. Palmer rewarded them with a birdie on the hole, going four under.

It wasn't until the 12th hole, after he had missed a four-foot putt for another birdie at 11, that Palmer learned there was trouble on the course. Miller, who had shot a 76 the day earlier, was going berserk shooting birdies.

Miller had started out six strokes behind Palmer, but after birdies on each of the first four holes, he had narrowed the margin to two. On the back side, Miller had birdied 11, 12, 13 and 15.

Although he still had a shot at winning the Open—Miller wasn't that far ahead at this time—Palmer drove down the middle on 12, but, on reaching the ball, found that it had bounced crazily into the deep rough. Trouble. Bogey. Psychologically shattered, he bogeyed 13 and 14. And now, Miller, instead of trailing by six, was up by four.

"I thought the only guys I had to worry about, Boros and Weiskoff, were behind me," said Palmer, recalling his missed putt on 11 and the erratic drive on 12. "I was shook. The bad lie might have caused the first bogey, but not the next two."

That Open was Palmer's last stand, his personal Waterloo. He appeared once more in Pittsburgh, playing the PGA Championship at Oakmont in 1975, but he was not a factor in that tournament, any more than he had been a factor in any tournament, really, since his victory at West Chester in 1973.

But no one can scoff at Palmer's achievements. His record of 61 tournament victories is fourth only to Sam Snead's 84, Nicklaus's 63, and Ben Hogan's 62. He won four Masters, two British Opens—at Royal Birkdale and Troon—and the U. S. Open at Cherry Hills. Although he never won the PGA, he finished second to Bob Nichols at Columbus, to Boros at Pecan Valley in San Antonio and to Dave Stockton—this one in 1970—at Southern Hills in Tulsa.

While Palmer may have lost his touch on the golf course, the years have been good to him. He owns condominiums from one side of the country to the other, and golf courses in places such as Japan and Bay Hill, Fla., and Palm Springs and Latrobe. He continues to make his home with his wife, Winnie, at Latrobe. The girls, Margaret and Amy, have married and gone.

Palmer maintains his old interests and hobbies, his flying and puttering around with his clubs in his golf shop. He has become more selective about his schedule, playing only in those events which strike his fancy or on courses which he enjoys.

In 1980, having reached 50, he agreed to play in The Legends, a $400,000 tournament at Austin, Tex., where he teamed with an old pal, Dow Finsterwald, one of his victims in a three-man playoff as he swept to a victory in the 1962 Masters.

Palmer has no plans to leave the Tour, and he shouldn't.

JIM SIMONS
The Pride of Butler

Even though he no longer is regarded as a favorite, he still derives a younger man's kick from tournament golf which, for a competitor such as Palmer has been, is understandable. It is understakable to those who believe that playing the game, not necessarily winning it, is important.

Arnie Palmer's era in professional golf, which bloomed when he won the Canadian Open in 1955, spanned two full decades. They were decades when he was one of the three most dominating figures in golf. What more could anybody ask of a lifetime.

Palmer wasn't the only Pittsburgh pro whose golf shots graced the pro tour in the '70s. He was merely the best of them, and, though his career was winding down while the youngsters' stars were ascending, none of them were to accomplish what this brawny shotmaker from Latrobe had done.

Like Palmer in his teens, the youngsters—Jim Simons of Butler, Pa., and Jim Masserio of Baldwin Borough—were the class of the field in Western Pennsylvania. If one wasn't beating the other, nobody else could do it, and it was natural that both of them would gravitate to the Tour.

Simons was the first to make it, getting his card in the fall of 1972, after he had finished college at Wake Forest. It took Masserio longer for he had failed to qualify in his first two attempts at the PGA School, quite a shock to those who felt that, of the two, the beagle-faced youngster from Baldwin would be more successful as a pro. Simons, many felt, hadn't the distance off the tee to make an impact on the pros.

Masserio, who learned his golf on the public course at South Park, spent four years on the tour, most of them in a constant, nerve-wracking hassle over money with a parade of sponsors. In his best year, 1976, his third on the tour, Masserio earned $29,376 which, considering that his family was traveling with him, left him with scarcely enough to make ends meet.

The following year, when his earnings dipped to the poverty level of $13,000, he decided to take a job as a club pro and signed on to teach the members and their wives at Canterbury, a prestigious club in Cleveland.

It was a comedown for Masserio, who had dreamed for years of winning on the tour, but he explained that his family meant more to him than golf, and, after all, he had some grand memories with which to retire.

While Masserio, 27 when he retired, never won a tournament, he had his moments on the tour. In the 1975 Kemper Open, for example, he was in the thick of the battle, fighting Ray Floyd tooth and nail for the first 11 holes of that final Sunday afternoon. But down by two with seven holes to go, Masserio's irons suddenly went limp and his putter, which had never been his most reliable stick, turned balky. He finished well out of the money.

Earlier that year, Masserio had played his most satisfying tournament. The PGA had started a new event, the Players Division Championship, and they held the initial event at Inverrary, a long, demanding course at Lauderhill, Fla. While Jack Nicklaus won it quite handily, Masserio and J. C. Snead battled it out for second. Once again, Masserio failed to come through, tying for third.

Masserio's most satisfying tournament came in 1979, after he had left the tour. As the Ohio PGA Champion, he had qualified for the PGA Championships which were held that year at Oakland Hills in Detroit. Starting with a 69—which included a double-bogey six on the 18th hole—Masserio was tied for third after two rounds. But the problems which plagued him his entire hitch on the tour struck again, and after skying to a bad third round, a 78, he saw another golden opportunity turn sour.

Simons, who had lost consistently to Masserio as an amateur, was a striking success on the tour. Despite the fact that he didn't hit the ball as far, or strike it as crisply, as most of his contemporaries. But he had a short game, chipping and putting, that made him the envy of many of the pros with whom he was paired.

While he struggled for the better part of five years, Simons, the son of a Butler County manufacturer, finally hit it big in his fifth year, 1977, when he won his first tournament. Putting marvelously, Simons won the New Orleans Open, which was hardly a total surprise for a week earlier he had finished fourth in the Tallahassee Open. Simons' first win was a big victory, for it took him out of the ranks of the rabbits. But it was not to be his last score on the tour.

The following year, he won an even richer and more appealing tournament, the Muirfield Memorial, for which he received the princely purse of $50,000—the largest prize won by a Western Pennsylvania golfer other than Palmer.

It should not have been such a surprise that Simons did so well on the tour, however. From his days at Knoch High School in Saxonburg, he had been a very skilled shotmaker and a very competitive player. Once, in the state amateur, he won the tournament by a stroke, holing a wedge from 40 yards out on the 18th fairway.

Before he ever joined the tour, when he was a baby-

**JIM MASSERIO
The Pride of Point Park**

sion, but neither one looked as the decade ended as if she would leave a mark on the girls who follow the sun, often in a mobile housekeeping van, making a living.

Pittsburgh's most accomplished female golfer, actually, was an amateur, an amateur who flatly refused to consider turning pro.

That was Carol Semple of Sewickley, whose parents, Harton S. (Bud) Semple and Phyllis, had been prominent local golfers and administrators of the game for years. In 1973, when Carol, 24, won the U. S. Amateur, she accepted the prize from her beaming father, Vice-President of the United States Golf Association. The following year, Semple was installed as President of the USGA, the first Pittsburgher to hold that prestigious office since Frederick A. Byers was named to it a half century ago.

In addition to the National Amateur, Carol Semple, who annually competes on a demanding national tour of her own—the North-South, Broadmoor, the Trans-National, the Canadian Open, the Western and Curtis Cup Matches—added the British Open to her list of accomplishments. The spring after winning the Amateur, Carol beat Angela Bonallack in the final at Royal Porthcawl in Wales, 2-and-1.

Later that year, Carol was to lose a heart-breaking match in the Western, 2 and 1, to a promising young golfer from Roswell, N. M., 16-year-old Nancy Lopez, who was to dominate the women's tour as nobody else had done in a matter of years.

faced 20-year-old collegian, he had served notice on the pros that he was a comer. Although an amateur, he had led the 1971 U. S. Open at Merion through the third round, taking the lead in that round as he cooly shot a casual Saturday afternoon 65 while playing with Jack Nicklaus.

But, despite his youth, that was not Simon's first Open. Actually, it was his third, for the youngster from Butler had qualified first as a 17-year-old high school junior, and he had qualified again as a student at Wake Forest. Prior to turning pro, he had finished third in the 1970 U. S. Amateur, and he was named that year to the Walker Cup Team.

Later Pittsburghers who tried the tour, Ron Milanovich of Rimersburg, Pa., and Mike Nicolette of Mt. Pleasant, earned their tour cards too late in the decade to make any final appraisals of their careers. But Milanovich, a former state champion, didn't make a cent in his first two years on the tour and, in desperation, he finally tried his luck on the less demanding Asian Tour, where he didn't do much better.

While Palmer and Simons were able to win on the tour, a couple of district women had no such luck. Jan Anderson Alex and Sandy Burns tried their hand at golf as a profes-

**CAROL SEMPLE
A Winner from Sewickley**

HOCKEY

PENGUINS SKATE FROM THIN ICE TOWARD STANLEY CUP IN THE '80s

By Norm Vargo

"The league always felt Pittsburgh was a good sports town."
—Clarence Campbell
Former NHL President

The City of Champions. Do the Penguins fit in?

No, the Penguins haven't won a Stanley Cup to display in the Civic Arena offices. And the team has never come close to winning the coveted National Hockey League trophy of supremacy, really.

But the club that brought the exciting NHL to Pittsburgh must be considered a champion in its own right.

Any professional team, or any other organization for that matter which can endure a decade of turmoil and uncertainty and survive is a champion of sorts.

Hope. Enthusiasm. Tragedy. Frustration. Disappointment. Elation. Uncertainty.

The Penguins ran the whole gamut of human emotions through the hectic 1970s. And they're still around.

"There were often times during the last 10 years that I wondered if this hockey team would make it. But it's still here..." says club Director of Player Personnel Ken Schinkel, the only person in the organization today that can claim the distinction of being around in some capacity since the team first hit the ice against the Montreal Canadiens back on October 11, 1967.

There was reason for uncertainty.

During the '70s, the club experienced four ownership combinations, saw four coaches—including Schinkel who had the job twice—death and bankruptcy.

Somehow the Penguins managed to weather the storm, although often the battle for mere existence bordered on chaos.

There was little doubt that the NHL wanted a viable franchise in Pittsburgh. Often during the club's trying times, the league helped out, both with money and advice.

"The league always felt Pittsburgh was a good sports town," says retired NHL President Clarence Campbell. "They have always managed to come up with a good, competitive hockey team down there. That's why we wanted to locate a club there."

Campbell and the NHL soon found out that the Penguin situation at times would get downright impossible. "There was always some sort of problems with the ownership," remembers Campbell. "I feel the club is on solid footing now, but it took years just to get this far..."

MOMENTS TO REMEMBER
There were triumphs to savor in '70s

PIERRE LAROUCHE, at left, may have been the most gifted hockey player in the Penguins history, but he wasn't happy here.

Indeed, it did take a bit of doing just to survive the chaotic '70s.

A smooth-skating, rugged Frenchman named Michel Briere was the Pens' hope for the 1970s. Coach "Red" Kelly's club made the Stanley Cup playoffs for the first time in 1969-70 after a second place finish in the NHL's expansion Western Division.

Briere played superbly as the Pens eliminated Oakland in the quarterfinals. And the flamboyant youngster dominated the action as the Pens lost to St. Louis in six games in a semifinal series that was punctuated when the gregarious Kelly had club officials draw enough money out of the bank to total the players' winning playoff share.

Kelly, in fact, came into the Pens' dressing room one night just before the team prepared to skate onto the ice to face the Blues and threw the money down, then walked out. Kelly's ploy worked for that game, which the Pens won.

Kelly's Pens lost in their bid to challenge for the Stanley Cup. But Briere's effort was reason enough for optimism.

Then fate stepped in. Briere was injured in an automobile accident in Northern Canada. Fans were shocked. Briere lay in a coma for months. He died. The Pens knew tragedy...

Briere's death has to be the blackest hour in Penguin history.

The blackest day was yet to come...the day that Pittsburgh almost lost its hockey team.

Ironically, the club's darkest day would come after the Pens enjoyed what most observers feel was the team's best season ever. It was on June 12, 1975, that agents from the United States Internal Revenue Service padlocked the doors to the club's Civic Arena offices.

A day later—while workmen were outside installing seats in the arena's expansion to the current 16,033 capacity—then owner Thayer R. "Tad" Potter called a press conference to confirm that the Pens were mired in voluntary receivership under the bankruptcy act.

Even while the press quizzed Potter after his announcement, a few blocks away in Allegheny County Court of Common Pleas, Equibank, the club's largest single creditor, was filing 10 separate judgment claims totaling an incredible $5 million.

That action brought the club's known debt to more than $6.5 million, including $527,346 owed the IRS and at least $1 million to the NHL, which attempted to bail the club out of its financial difficulties.

Schinkel remembers that June 13. So does Campbell.

"It was a shock. We heard rumors for sometime. And we knew the club was having trouble meeting its financial commitments. But all of us hoped things would work out...," sighed Schinkel. "And it happened on Friday, the 13th, too..."

While it was a shock to Schinkel that the Pens were indeed in dire financial straits and in danger of folding, it was not a shock to Campbell.

"We advised the Penguin ownership to go the course they finally did early in the season when it became evident that the club would have money problems," recalled Campbell. "But the ownership chose to attempt to work out their own financial problems..."

A month later, the Penguins were saved.

This time it was ruddy-faced Indianapolis financier Albert A. Savill who headed a combine which included Wren

RED KELLY **KEN SCHINKEL**

JACK RILEY **JACK BUTTON**

Lowell MacDonald Led "The Century Line"

GOAL-GETTERS: Syl Apps and Jean Pronovost put lots of points on the scoreboard for Penguins.

Blair and Banker Otto N. "Nick" Frenzel. Two years later—after sustaining losses rumored to be almost $3 million—Savill sold his interests to current owner Edward J. DeBartolo, Sr., a Youngstown, Ohio, construction magnate.

So, midway through the decade, the Pens endured a severe and shocking loss of a bright star in Briere and managed to survive a financial mess that threatened the organization's very existence.

"Briere's death was a shock. But we got over that," says Schinkel. "But it was a rather traumatic experience when the club almost went under . . . I don't want to go through that again."

Helping Penguin fans forget Briere—whose No. 21 jersey holds a place of respect encased in a frame on a wall in the Igloo Club—was another young Frenchman named Pierre Larouche.

A brash, young 18-year-old with a brilliant NHL future on the horizon, Larouche took Pittsburgh—and his Penguin teammates—by storm. Instantly, Larouche became the darling of the fans, especially the women who began flocking to Penguin games.

One night, Larouche was the prize in a contest run by the club for a date and night on the town. Larouche complied happily. Pittsburgh was his "town."

Two seasons later, Larouche and another lantern-jawed Frenchman named Jean Pronovost would make Penguin history by scoring over 50 goals and breaking the coveted 100-point scoring mark in the same campaign.

In fact, Larouche and Pronovost combined for probably the greatest night in Penguin history on March 25, 1976.

During a 5-5 tie with Boston, Pronovost became the first player in Penguin history to score 50 goals. And Larouche chipped in with his 45th goal and an assist to become the first Pen to eclipse the magic 100-point mark.

It was an emotional night. Penguin fans went wild cheering first Pronovost, then Larouche. Their cheering and tossing of hats onto the ice delayed the game for almost 10 minutes.

Schinkel happened to be the coach. He remembers the game, saying "Yes, it was very emotional. The fans were really charged up anticipating Prony's 50th goal. When Pierre scored his 100th point, that was a bonus . . .

"And it was a game that we had to come from behind just to gain a tie. That added to the emotion. I don't think I'll see that kind of emotion unless the team wins the Stanley Cup," suggested Schinkel.

"People forget that Syl Apps almost made 100, too," noted Pronovost, now with the Atlanta Flames. "Syl finished with 99 points that season. If he would've scored in Detroit the last game of the season, Syl would have got a hundred."

"We tried to set Syl up, but he passed off," recalled the unselfish Pronovost. "Too bad Syl didn't get a point. We would have made history. Three players on the same team

TOWER OF STRENGTH
Ron Stackhouse held fort for Pens.

scoring 100 points was unheard of at that time..."

Just a few seasons before, in an obvious effort to entice fans to see the Pens play, publicist Terry Schiffhauer dubbed the line of Apps, Pronovost and Lowell MacDonald the "Century Line" because they combined to score 101 goals for the 1973-74 campaign.

The Apps, Pronovost, MacDonald line was the first "big" line the Penguins would have, and so far, the only one that has produced goals with such frequency. And the smooth-skating trio, especially the soft-spoken MacDonald, would be fan favorites for years to come.

"Apps, Prony and Lowell gave the fans something to cheer," reasoned Schinkel. "Back then, the team was still struggling for respectability. Now they're scoring 50 goals and 100 points all the time. When the Century Line was working, a hundred goals from three people was something to brag about..."

Down through the decade, there were plenty of other fan favorites.

When the club owned by a combine headed by midwest banker Donald H. Parsons entered the 1970s, fans cheered for players like 38-year-old Andy Bathgate, Dean Prentice, Glen Sather, Duane Rupp, Bryan "Buggsy" Watson, Dunc McCallum, Keith McCreary, Les Binkley, Ken Schinkel, Val Fonteyne and Bob Woytowich.

Bathgate was the Pens' first established NHL star. Coach "Red" Sullivan plucked Bathgate off the Detroit roster during the expansion stocking draft when the Red Wings took a gamble and left the scoring sensation unprotected.

Watson, McCallum and Woytowich were rugged, rock 'em, sock 'em type defensemen who delighted fans with their on-the-ice efforts.

"Fans wanted to see fights, back then," Schinkel recalls. "Hockey was still new to this town. Oh, the Hornets used to play here, but that wasn't the type of hockey we played in the NHL."

Woytowich became an instant hero to the city's strong ethnic-oriented population. The rugged blue line picket can claim the first bonafide fan club—"Woytowich's Polish Army"—which used to clan up in the D Sections around the arena.

"That's what we needed, a hero for the fans to identify with. Woytowich filled the bill perfectly," said Schinkel.

A season later, former Pittsburgh Hornet star Tim Horton came to the Pens via the inter-league draft. Horton spent almost 18 seasons with the Toronto Maple Leafs before being traded to the New York Rangers.

The Rangers chose to leave Horton unprotected and coach and general manager "Red" Kelly picked the veteran defenseman. Kelly realized full well that Horton would be popular with the hardcore hockey fans.

Horton was the second of several established veterans NHL teams would ship to the Penguins in obvious efforts to dump off fat contracts. Jack Riley, the executive officer during those early years, knew what was happening.

"It was good business," reasoned Riley. "We wanted to build interest as fast as possible. And the fastest way to do that was to sign a star or two."

Schinkel reasoned: "I guess management and Kelly hoped that established veterans like Horton and Bathgate would help us get going on the right foot. I know it was a thrill to play with people I read about in the newspapers. There wasn't the extensive hockey coverage then, but people knew who the stars were."

In 1974, the Pens would sign still another fading veteran.

Vic Hadfield—despite a knee injury which limited his playing capacity at times—came in a trade from the New York Rangers.

Hadfield was a hot property. New York lost to the upstart Philadelphia Flyers in the Stanley Cup finals the previous season. Hadfield was the captain of the Rangers with a reputation as a "digger" in the corners.

Hadfield could've been the answer to some critical problems had he been healthy. Instead, the veteran played a couple of seasons until the knee worsened to the point that it just wasn't practical to play anymore.

Jack Button, who was the general manager then, defended the Hadfield acquisition.

"Vic helped us more than people think," recalls Button, now an executive with the Washington Capitals hockey team. "When Vic played, we were a heck of a team. He was a major reason we went as far as we did in the playoffs in 1974-75.

"Hadfield's aggressive play was infectious. He set the tempo for younger guys, and some of the veterans, too.

"Everybody on our club knew that Hadfield had been through the pressures of the Stanley Cup playoffs. They looked to him as a leader," added Button.

There was no doubting Hadfield's leadership qualities—both on and off the ice.

"Vic Hadfield helped people like Larouche and Prony and Rick Kehoe find themselves," said former coach Marc Boileau. "Vic's value in the dressing room was another thing. He did those little things to settle us down when we needed it, or make us laugh when we were down. You don't put a dollar value on a man like that."

But those "established" aging veterans commanded rather lucrative salaries, which the Pens assumed when they came to Pittsburgh. In fact, one of the major reasons,

MARC BOILEAU   **JOHNNY WILSON**
Penguin Leaders

some observers feel, that the club got into financial difficulties in the first place was the commitment to back the financial obligations of people the caliber of Bathgate, Horton and Hadfield.

"Yes, we paid some big salaries in the middle 1970s," admitted Button, who was appointed receiver when the team went the bankruptcy route. "People might not realize, but we had a few players making big money even then. Add Larouche and Jacques Cossette to that bunch and you know we paid out a bundle."

The Pens drafted Larouche and Cossette, the two hottest prospects in Canada at the time, during the 1974 amateur lottery. Both rookies reportedly were signed to long-term contracts calling for six-figure annual salaries.

Larouche was the No. 1 pick. He stayed with the team, never spending time in the minor leagues.

| BOB WOYTOWICH | VIC HADFIELD | GARY INNESS | DENIS HERRON | STAN GILBERTSON |
| LES BINKLEY | BRYAN WATSON | BOB KELLY | TIM HORTON | RON SCHOCK |

Cossette, reputed to be the better player of the young pair, never quite made it in the NHL. Sent to Hershey when it became evident that he couldn't make the jump from Sorel in the juniors to the NHL, Cossette continued to collect his fat salary.

Some of the veterans openly resented Larouche and Cossette for being paid so handsomely.

"My years in Pittsburgh were good, but most of the time bad," uniquely recalls Larouche, who is coming into his own as a scorer with the Montreal Canadiens.

"I came to the Penguins with high hopes. Maybe I grew up too fast, I don't know. But some players didn't like it that I was making big money. You can tell when people resent you . . .," added Larouche.

Some observers feel that resentment by his teammates led to Larouche's disenchantment with the Pens. "I don't think Larouche was ever really happy with Pittsburgh," says Boileau. "Pierre always wanted to play for Montreal. Now he's there and you see how he's playing. Larouche is where he belongs."

Larouche, Pronovost, Apps, MacDonald, Kehoe and a burly defenseman named Ron Stackhouse made the Pens offensive-minded under Boileau, the gregarious French-Canadian who led the team to within a game of the Stanley Cup semifinals in his first full season as coach.

The fans were coming to see the Pens unleash their firepower. Larouche and Pronovost were scoring. Stackhouse was setting his teammates up and wound up putting his name in the NHL record book for the most assists by a defenseman for a season, 71.

DAVE BURROWS WAS A REAL DIGGER

Finesse was taking over. But the fans still yearned to see fights.

When Button brought in Boileau to replace Schinkel during the late stages of the 1974 campaign, he also had on hand in a trade from St. Louis some pretty rough guys in Bob "Battleship" Kelly and Steve Durbano, two of the acknowledged ice ruffians of their day.

Fans swarmed to games hoping to see Kelly or Durbano drop the gloves with an opponent. It happened often enough to keep the turnstiles clicking.

"We gave the fans what they wanted to see, action," offered Button. "Interest certainly picked up when we got Kelly and Durbano."

Some fans feel Button was smart enough to remember the days of Watson and McCallum. Whatever, Kelly became a favorite until he gave up being a "goon" to concentrate on becoming the "complete" player in his last two seasons with the club.

"When the 'Battleship' stopped firing his firsts, they wanted to get rid of him," contends Larouche. "Bobby did a lot to bring in the fans."

Durbano never lasted. A freak injury in a collision with Philadelphia's Andre DuPont left the Penguin roughneck with a badly shattered wrist which never healed properly. That injury cheated Penguin fans out of some great action.

Toward the end of the '70s, wily Aldege "Baz" Bastien would resort to a similar tactics—bringing in a fighter—to hype attendance. In this case, Bastien lured rugged Dave Schultz from Philadelphia.

Bastien, Mr. Pittsburgh Hockey to the fans because of the many years he spent with the old Hornets as both a player and coach, knew what Pittsburgh fans wanted. Fans wanted action and Bastien figured Schultz would fit nicely.

Schultz, though, became somewhat of a liability. Fans soured on Schultz, who was spending more time in the penalty box than he was on the ice.

Realizing that the Pens couldn't win playing shorthanded so much, Bastien dealt Schultz to Buffalo.

"Yes, we've had some colorful players here," laughed Bastien. Watson, McCallum, Schultz, Durbano, Kelly, Horton. That's an understatement if there ever was one.

Bastien is playing a key role in keeping the Penguins as contenders. In fact, some observers feel the Penguin owners who allowed the former goaltender to go to Kansas City as assistant general manager instead of keeping him with the team after it was reorganized, contributed to the rough beginning of the team.

"Baz Bastien is a shrewd trader," said veteran hockey writer Leo Monahan last spring when the Pens were in Boston to face the Bruins in the Stanley Cup quarterfinals. "Baz would've been a great horsetrader in another era."

Bastien laughed then. And he laughs now.

He hardly fits the mold of an architect, his role with the Penguins. It's Bastien's duty to build a competitive team, contends Paul Martha, the former Pitt and Steeler football star who runs the Penguin operation for DeBartolo.

"In Baz, we feel we have a very capable hockey man," said Martha. "When Baz has traded, he's shown he knows talent. In fact, one of the reasons this team is so competitive is the deals he made a year ago."

Bastien traded away popular defenseman Dave Burrows to the Toronto Maple Leafs in exchange for forward George Ferguson and defenseman Randy Carlyle. Both have played major parts in the Pens' success.

DENIS HERRON had his highs and lows as Penguins' popular goaltender. Photo by George Gojkovich

Prior to that, Bastien shocked the hockey world by getting center Orest Kindrachuk, wing Ross Lonsberry and defenseman Tom Bladon from Philadelphia. Kindrachuk was the key. His leadership qualities have earned him election as team captain.

Bastien gambled that the Philadelphia trio would influence the Pens to play their style. To a point, Kindrachuk and Lonsberry have done just that.

"That was an important deal for us," agrees Bastien. "We got three fine players to build around."

A year before, Bastien stunned Penguin fans by trading Larouche to Montreal for veteran Pete Mahovlich and untested rookie Peter Lee. Mahovlich settled the young Pens while Lee showed he can play in the NHL, adding to a bright future for the Pens.

And Baz doesn't play favorites. A guy named Denis Herron found that out.

Looking for more scoring power, Bastien dealt the established Herron—the Pen's No. 1 goaltender—to Montreal for forward Pat Hughes and young netminder Rob Holland. It was a gamble.

Bastien's decision to put young Greg Millen into the nets over Herron stunned hockey observers. The goalkeeper is a club's last line of defense. What was Baz doing, people wondered?

One thing Baz recognizes is trouble. And the best way to prevent trouble is to nip it before it can get started.

"Herron's contract was coming up," explained Bastien, who traded for the veteran netminder twice, once when he was with Kansas City and again when he came to the Pens. "Denis didn't like the contract we had. He wanted to talk. I don't think he could've been happy here."

Martha's mandate to Bastien: "Give us the best hockey team you can find."

Coaches have always come under fire during their stints with the Pens. Kelly took over for Sullivan. Then Schinkel was called out of the playing ranks to take over for Kelly on Jan. 13, 1973.

Just about a year later, Feb. 6, 1974, Button brought in Boileau from the International League Fort Wayne Komets. In the Pens' scheme of playing musical chairs, Schinkel replaced Boileau on Jan. 17, 1976.

Schinkel coached a season, then relinquished the reins to former NHL star Johnny Wilson for three seasons.

Building a solid hockey club is no easy task. Bastien has been criticized as much as he's been complimented.

"Fans have their favorites," reasons Bastien. "I got a lot of flak when I traded Pronovost for Greg Sheppard. And people didn't like it when I sent Herron to Montreal.

"But those are the things we must do. I have to give my coach the players. That's my prime objective in this job," suggested Bastien, a man who had a promising pro hockey career cut short when he was hit in the eye by a puck during a Hornet training camp.

Teams have personalities. Usually, a club reflects the

personality of its coach and general manager, who are often one and the same.

In the early seasons of the decade, the Pens were struggling to gain identity on two fronts—with the rest of the NHL and with Pittsburgh fans. They were a happy-go-lucky lot. And they played that way.

During the mid-'70s, a different Penguin image emerged.

Watson was traded. So was McCallum. They were replaced by Burrows, a smooth-working defenseman who won fans by his rugged, yet flamboyant style of blocking shots.

Burrows, Apps, Pronovost, Hadfield, they dressed in vested conservative suits. In a lounge on the road, Penguins appeared more like young businessmen or lawyers than hockey players. Privacy was their goal.

Then came more young players. Again the team complexion changed, thanks to a pair of rugged players named Greg Malone and Russ Anderson, the American-born icer who later married a Miss America.

Malone was a tough center who has developed into one of the NHL's premier forwards. Anderson, too, is developing into a rugged customer around the nets.

Martha likes to think about the future.

"There's room for the Penguins in Pittsburgh," says the young corporate attorney confidently. "Our players are developing more each season. And we have a good blend of veterans to mix in.

"Baz is always looking for players to help us. When he finds a guy we can use, he goes after him. We could be a player or two away from being a genuine Stanley Cup contender."

Martha looks at Lee, young Paul Marshall, Rod Schutt, Millen, Hughes, Holland, and he sees the future.

But Martha is cautious in overseeing DeBartolo's Penguin interests. The Penguins have been burned, both in the draft and by other NHL teams.

"We are committed to a positive future," maintains Martha. "But we don't intend to allow people to take advantage of the organization. We'd like to think we can belong up there with the Steelers and Pirates before too long."

The Pens are on the brink of being a good hockey team. They weren't that bad of a club during the 1970s, really.

Martha played with the Steelers when the team was just beginning to pick itself up. He knows, better than most, that patience must be a virtue when somebody is building a champion.

During the last decade, the Pens made the playoffs six times. That's not a bad record at all. Some teams haven't made it at all.

But Martha, Bastien and DeBartolo aren't people to take things for granted. Unforeseen circumstances can throw a monkeywrench into a bright future and destroy it.

"Yes, injuries play a big part in success," agrees Wilson. "Over the years, the team that stays away from injuries winds up playing for the Cup."

Briere is an example. He was a player whom the Pens figured they could build a high-scoring line around. A season of promise, then disaster. When Briere died, he delayed success in the early '70s.

There was another tragedy that would stall the Penguins' drive toward the top. Midway through the decade, the Pens acquired veteran Stan Gilbertson from Washington.

Gilbertson was a happy-go-lucky sort who was invaluable in the dressing room. He was witty. And he was a rugged player when he hit the ice.

One night Gilbertson was returning to the club's training headquarters near Belle Vernon when the jeep he was driving went out of control and overturned. Gilbertson was pinned in the wreckage. When rescuers finally removed him, the gutsy forward's left leg was shattered.

Attempts to save the leg failed. A few weeks later, the limb was amputated to save Gilbertson's life.

"Those things happen," sighed Bastien. "You never know. That's why it's not always good to plan too far ahead. The club lost Briere at a time when he was about ready to help.

"Then Gilbertson's injury hurt. It left a void."

One thing Bastien is committed to is finding a standout netminder for the Pens. Through the 1970s, those chores were handled by Binkley, Jimmy Rutherford, Andy Brown, Gary Inness, Herron, Dunc Wilson and Michele Plasse.

Somehow, goaltending was always a Penguin weakness. Bastien realized that when he came to the club. He's made a search for a top-flight goalie a top priority.

"People don't realize, though, that a good goaltender comes along once in a lifetime. You have to be there when

BIG HOPE FOR '80s
Olympic hero Mark Johnson

he does...," says the genial general manager.

Martha is excited about the club's future. So is Bastien.

But Schinkel has seen enthusiasm develop before, only to be later tempered by frustration when things didn't work out.

"We must be cautious and build firmly," says the veteran scout, who also possesses a keen eye for young talent. "It's good to get excited, but we can't get overconfident. We're building a solid team, but so are many others..."

Schinkel has been through it all. He's watched the Pens grow. He suffered through the early growing pains. He rode the crest of success and endured the frustration of disappointment.

But Schinkel sees a future that could come this decade, in fact.

"I think the rough part is over. The ownership is solid, more solid than it ever has been. That itself is a plus. When you have good management, things tend to take care of themselves on the ice..."

Who knows? Perhaps the Penguins will put it all together in the '80s.

They began this decade by changing their team colors from blue and white to black and gold—"We're jumping on the bandwagon," admitted Martha, "and we want to be a vital part of the City of Champions."

In that direction, the Penguins signed Mark Johnson, one of the heroes of the U. S. hockey team that upset Russia and several more experienced European teams to grab the gold medal in the Winter Olympics at Lake Placid, N.Y. In Johnson, they hoped to have the Mark of a champion.

79/80 PITTSBURGH PENGUINS

Greg Millen—G

Bob Holland—G

Dale Tallon—D

Orest Kindrachuk—C

Gregg Sheppard—C

Greg Malone—C

Paul Marshall—LW

Rod Schutt—LW

Ross Lonsberry—LW

Gary McAdam—LW

Nick Libett—LW

Bob Stewart—D

Peter Lee—RW

George Ferguson—RW

Randy Carlyle—D

Pat Hughes—RW

Rick Kehoe—RW

Tom Bladon—D

Ron Stackhouse—D

Mario Faubert—D

Kim Clackson—D

Russ Anderson—D

John Wilson
Coach

Steve Thomas
Trainer

John Doolan
Equipment Manager

DeBARTOLO & CO.
By Jim O'Brien

"If everyone gives a hundred percent, winning the Stanley Cup is not beyond the realm of possibility."
—Edward J. DeBartolo, Sr.

"We want to jump on the bandwagon in the City of Champions. It's our turn."
—Paul Martha

If Edward J. DeBartolo, Sr. wants to own this town, all he has to do is develop an honest-to-goodness contender for the Stanley Cup. His Penguins don't have to win it all—that's asking for an awful lot considering the current state of competition in the National Hockey League—but just be a serious challenger, from start to finish, and sports fans in this city would climb aboard their bandwagon.

"They'd go crazy," says Paul Martha, the former Pitt and Steelers' football player turned attorney and front-office boss of DeBartolo's hockey team. "It's Pittsburgh, that's why. They're waiting for us to win."

DeBartolo is a builder, a developer and he may be just the man to put the Penguins on the top, or at least near it in the NHL. This is a man who made his money in the real estate business, developing magnificent shopping centers round the country from his office in Youngstown.

Here's a man, whose dark eyes burn with wonderful visions, who turned a slag heap in nearby West Mifflin into Century III, the crown jewel of all his shopping malls. Perhaps he can turn the Penguins into beautiful swans, or Stanley Cup contenders, anyhow.

He placed Paul Martha in charge here, along with Baz Bastien, Ken Schinkel and Johnny Wilson to build a winner, and turn the franchise into a financial success. His son, Eddie Jr., looks after the San Francisco 49ers, another sports franchise DeBartolo bought in the late '70s. Father and son are both graduates of Notre Dame University, and they want winners in the grand tradition of the campus under the Golden Dome in South Bend, Ind.

Like the Rooneys, the DeBartolos are also big on the national sports scene with racing interests in Cleveland, Chicago and Shreveport, Louisiana. Vincent J. Bartimo is DeBartolo's top aide, looking after many of his interests, and serving as president and chairman of the board of the Penguins.

ED DeBARTOLO

"Pittsburgh has unusually knowledgeable and enthusiastic sports fans," observed Bartimo. "They are entitled to be given the best performance a club can produce. This is what we believe in, and this is what we are here to do in Pittsburgh for the Penguin fans."

DeBartolo is interested in building a winning team with the Penguins, but also in improving the operation of the Civic Arena, bringing more and better sports promotions to Pittsburgh, and developing the area surrounding the Arena. He could turn out to be the catalyst Mayor Richard Caliguiri needs to complete his Renaissance II program for improving Pittsburgh.

In Martha, DeBartolo has a man with solid connections in Pittsburgh. An All-America running back at the University of Pittsburgh, later a No. 1 draft choice and six-year performer for the Steelers, and a Duquesne Law School grad, Martha is a man for all seasons. He's equally at ease with the well-heeled corporate types he needs on his side, say in the board room at Dollar Savings Bank, as well as the critical fans he finds and chats with in a hockey hangout such as the Pleasure Bar in Bloomfield, where hockey sticks hang from the rafters and pictures of the Penguins paper the walls. Martha is a mover and a shaker and, with DeBartolo behind him, all goals are possible.

Just before Christmas in 1978, DeBartolo paid a visit to the Civic Arena, disclosed plans to take over the operation of the building, and delivered a pep talk to the Penguins in their clubhouse. "I know what it is to work your way from the bottom to the top," he told them. "All I want from you is a hundred percent. All the time. If everyone gives a hundred percent, winning the Stanley Cup is not beyond the realm of possibility."

PAUL MARTHA

VINCE BARTIMO

BAZ BASTIEN

FRANK FUHRER

By Pat Livingston

"The name of any game is winning."
—Frank Fuhrer

In any recorded documentation of the City of Champions, peripatetic Frank Fuhrer cannot be overlooked. He was as much a part of Pittsburgh's sport scene in the feverish '70s as any other figure in town.

In a decade when entrepreneurs flinched at bringing basketball to Pittsburgh, in an inflationary era when wise investors put their money in bonds, Fuhrer brought two professional franchises to the Civic Arena, the Triangles of the short-lived World Team Tennis League in 1974, and the Spirit, a team in the Major Indoor Soccer League, four years later.

They were minor sports it's true, but the flamboyant Fuhrer, the son of the proprietor of a men's clothing store in East Brady, brought a certain class to these franchises which made them big league all the way.

Badgering, cajoling, pleading, Fuhrer, a hard-nosed businessman, who is revulsed by failure, made a temporary success of both of them. The Triangles didn't last long, but the jury is still out on the Spirit.

It wasn't Fuhrer's fault that the Triangles folded. In a league where other owners weren't as dedicated as the self-made insurance executive from Fox Chapel, and where few of his players shared his enthusiasm, the Triangles survived three seasons, and won more matches than any team in the league. They also won the league championship. In 1975, the year the Steelers won their first Super Bowl, the Triangles charged through World Team Tennis and won that league's second championship.

To do it, Fuhrer had dug deeply into his pocket, paying $150,000 to Evonne Goolagong, a young Australian star who had won the women's singles title at Wimbledon. The key to the men's unit was a 19-year-old Vitas Gerulaitis of New York City, a spoiled, colorful young man who was to make a much greater impact on the game after the Triangles had folded.

Despite winning the title, Fuhrer wasn't happy, either with the league or its players. He was disturbed that too many other owners, for one reason or another, weren't going about forming their tennis teams with the same zeal, or the same sense of purpose, that he was.

"And if they don't get damn good teams," said the short fused Fuhrer, "the league's not going to work. The only way we're going to succeed is to give the people the best damn tennis it's possible to see."

Well, Fuhrer couldn't swing it. And as the years went by, the well-heeled man who paid millions in cash for Life Assurance Company of Pennsylvania, a Philadelphia firm, and moved it lock, stock and premiums to Pittsburgh, grew more and more disenchanted with both the league and the ingratitude of its players.

He was appalled that Goolagong, despite her generous salary, was thoroughly uncooperative in making personal appearances and trying to sell the city on Team Tennis. He raged when Gerulaitis, in a talk with the press, had blamed the Triangles' slide on management.

While Fuhrer revealed he had held a meeting with the players, Gerulaitis insisted there had been several, and further, he had said, Fuhrer had threatened the players with fines for losing.

FRANK FUHRER Owner and President

"That's a plain outright lie. I can't tolerate it," raged Fuhrer angrily, bothered that, considering the salaries he was paying these stars, he was getting less cooperation from them than he might have expected from one of his adjusters. Later Vitas apologized. "What good does that do me?" asked Fuhrer through lips that trembled with rage. "You told the lie to 300,000 people!"

When he finally folded the Triangles in 1976, Fuhrer made it plain that he was finished with today's spoiled, over-paid athletes. He had built his winner by being generous with his players; he had created the game's credibility by being fair with his fans.

In 1976, when the Triangles struggled through one of their rare losing streaks, Fuhrer decided that the fans who had loyally supported the Triangles deserved more than lackadaisical tennis. In an absolutely remarkable concession to those who pay the freight, Fuhrer instituted an exciting new policy, one which had been previously unheard of in professional sports.

If the Triangles lost, decreed Fuhrer, the fans, by merely using their ticket stub, would get a free admission to the next match.

Fuhrer, an open, out-going man who doted on the attention which had been bestowed on him as owner of the Triangles, wasn't to stay out of sports long. In 1978, upon hearing that a group in Philadelphia was setting up an Indoor Soccer League, Fuhrer's ears perked up. Because of the growing interest in soccer, Fuhrer became involved in it, although his was a passive interest in the Spirit of 1978, its initial year in the Major Indoor Soccer League.

But anyone who knew Fuhrer knew that he would never sit back and let a team he was involved in turn out to be anything but a winner. It wasn't long until he proved it.

A year later, in the summer of 1979, Fuhrer informed Jim Mihalke, his managing partner, that he would take a more active interest in running the team. A couple of months later Fuhrer abruptly fired the coach, Alex Pringle who was in his second month of his contract, and replaced him with a man who had been recommended to him by someone whose opinion this impulsive owner respected.

As he introduced his new coach, Len Bilous, to the press, Fuhrer reiterated a sentiment that has governed his life, his business and his fling at sports.

"I will not tolerate losing," declared Fuhrer, "the name of any game is winning. The fans deserve that. If Bilous can't be a winner, we'll keep trying until we find someone who is."

Len Bilous, to the delight of Frank Fuhrer, suddenly led the Spirit on a 13-game winning streak that had crowds streaming to the Civic Arena as the decade ended.

While Fuhrer certainly is pleased with his forays into professional sports, he is most dedicated to an amateur event which he runs as a labor of love, the Frank Fuhrer Memorial Challenge Cup, a golf tournament which honors the memory of his father. It matches the 12 best professionals in Western Pennsylvania against a field of amateurs. One of those amateurs is his son, Frank III, a student at North Carolina, who, at the end of the decade, was the dominating figure in amateur golf in Western Pennsylvania, another champion.

TRIANGLES — WORLD TEAM TENNIS CHAMPIONS IN '75

By Jim O'Brien

"The world championship means more to me than any money I've made or lost on this team. It's the winning that counts."
—Triangles' owner Frank Fuhrer
August 25, 1975

Frank Fuhrer will never forget the championship season of his Pittsburgh Triangles in World Team Tennis.

Whenever he sits behind his big desk in his sparkling office building complex in O'Hara Township—the base of his multi-million dollar insurance business—the sometimes smiling, sometimes stern, but never-in-between face of Fuhrer is framed by two glittering reminders of the best of times for the Triangles in the too-short history of WTT.

There is the beautiful Bancroft Cup, symbolic of the WTT championship the Triangles seized in the summer of '75, the second season of the league that lasted five years, two more years than the Triangles.

Then, too, there is a trophy won by the Triangles when they traveled to New York before the start of the '76 season and finished first in a round-robin showcase tournament involving all the WTT teams which was held in Madison Square Garden's Felt Forum.

Those trophies cost Fuhrer $1.3 million, which is how much this self-made millionaire from Fox Chapel—or East Brady, if you want to go back a little further—forked out during his stormy three-year involvement with WTT. To see Fuhrer fondle them, however, it was worth it.

"The world championship means more to me than any money I've made or lost on this team," offered Fuhrer after the Triangles defeated the San Francisco Gaters in a best-of-three WTT championship series on August 25, 1975. "The money's immaterial. It's the winning that counts. That comes first with me."

Fuhrer is an interesting figure on the local sports scene, a fine golfer in his day, a hard-working, iron-willed individual who demands performance from his troops, and perhaps the most aptly-named nabob in the history of sports. Twice in the '70s he financed new and risky sports concepts in Pittsburgh, in team tennis in the mid '70s and in the Major Indoor Soccer League at the end of the '70s.

It's too bad the Triangles are no longer on the scene in the City of Champions, but perhaps his Spirit soccer team will succeed where the Triangles failed—at the box office.

After the Triangles had beaten the Boston Lobsters in two straight contests to win the Eastern Division playoffs and advance to the finals that memorable summer of '75, Fuhrer offered these thoughts before the showdown with the San Francisco Gaters:

"You know it sounds corny, but I'd like to do something for the city that's been so good to me over the years."

That is exactly what the Triangles did. Their triumph, or even their existence, did not affect as many fans as the successes of the Steelers and Pirates and the Pitt football team in the '70s, but for those of us who were involved in WTT, and watched the league from its origin to its untimely end after the 1977 season, the Triangles and World Team Tennis were something special.

The Triangles... think of them. They included some of the greats of the game of tennis, starting with those Australian aces, Kenny Rosewall and Evonne Goolagong, and then the golden boy, Vitas Gerulaitis, who grew up before our very eyes to become an international star. Wherever they go the rest of their life, each of those globe-trotting superstars will carry a piece of Pittsburgh with them.

Only Peggy Michel remains on the scene. She and Goolagong, look-alikes with their short, curly hair and bouncy manner, were great as a doubles team that championship season. Michel stayed behind, curiously enough, when the Triangles split for other parts, and, as the '70s drew to a close, was providing tennis instruction at South Park.

Gone, too, were Mark Cox, Bernie Mitton, Sue Stap, Carole Graebner, Kim Warwick, Vic Edwards, Gerald Battrick, JoAnne Russell, Nancy Richey Gunter, Roger Cawley, Danny McGibbeny, Lowell Lubic and others in the supporting and always interesting cast of characters in the Triangles' road company.

Winning the WTT title, though, is something they can never take away from Fuhrer or this town's tennis afficianados. The Triangles took on the best in big-time tennis and beat them. For too brief a time, Pittsburgh was the capital of pro tennis.

From the start, the Triangles were the team to beat in World Team Tennis. "They were clearly the league's dominant franchise," wrote Bill Heufelder in The Pittsburgh Press, but he might have gotten an argument from New York on that note. Twice, in their first and third years, the Triangles were eliminated from the playoffs by the New York entry.

The Triangles were the first team to sign a big-name international star when Fuhrer and one of the team's founders, Chuck Reichblum, signed Evonne Goolagong to a three-year contract. That was a significant breakthrough in WTT's recruitment of players.

Then they signed the legendary Ken Rosewall, a 5-7, 150-pound one time U.S. Open champion and Davis Cup star whose backhand was the envy of everyone on the tour. Rosewall was the Triangles' top choice in the first draft of players, and was signed as the player-coach of the club.

Another original member of the Triangles was the golden-haired Gerulaitis, a lithe Lithuanian from Long Island who was just getting started as a pro and, with Rosewall's tutoring, became the best player ever developed within the WTT ranks. Today, Gerulaitis earns more than a million dollars a year, all things considered, and has a fantastic future.

At age 21, the frisky and fun-loving Gerulaitis was named the MVP of the playoffs when the green-and-yellow smartly-clad Triangles took the league's title. Earlier that season, Gerulaitis had thousands of fans—they called themselves G-Men—celebrate his birthday with him at a hotel party in suburban Pittsburgh.

Oh, there were many magic moments, big nights with big crowds at the Civic Arena, times when Rosewall and Goolagong and Gerulaitis were at the top of their game, and gave the fans and Fuhrer more than their money's worth.

These were the best of times:

• On May 6, 1974 at the Spectrum in Philadelphia, the Triangles played in the first match ever played in World Team Tennis. The Philadelphia Freedoms, led by player-coach Billie Jean King and cheered on by owner Elton John, topped the Triangles before 10,611 spectators.

• The following night, over 9,000 came to the Civic Arena to see King in a rematch against Goolagong in the local opener as the Triangles turned the table on their Philadelphia foe.

• On August 16, 1975 at the Civic Arena, with the Eastern Division title at stake in the final game of the schedule, a WTT record crowd of 10,859 turned out to see the Triangles defeat the New York Sets, 26-22. The Triangles finished the season with the league's best mark of 36-8.

• On August 25, 1975, a vocal crowd of 6,882 at the Civic Arena saw the Triangles rout the San Francisco Gaters, 21-14, in an abbreviated program to win the WTT title in the third game of a best-of-three series to claim the Bancroft Cup. San Francisco had won the opening match of that series.

• On July 8, 1976, following the WTT break for Wimbledon, a WTT record crowd of 13,492 at the Civic Arena cheered Goolagong to a sensational comeback victory over Wimbledon queen Chris Evert and the Triangles to a 24-23 win over the Phoenix Racquets, who had been the hottest team in WTT.

There weren't enough of those times, however.

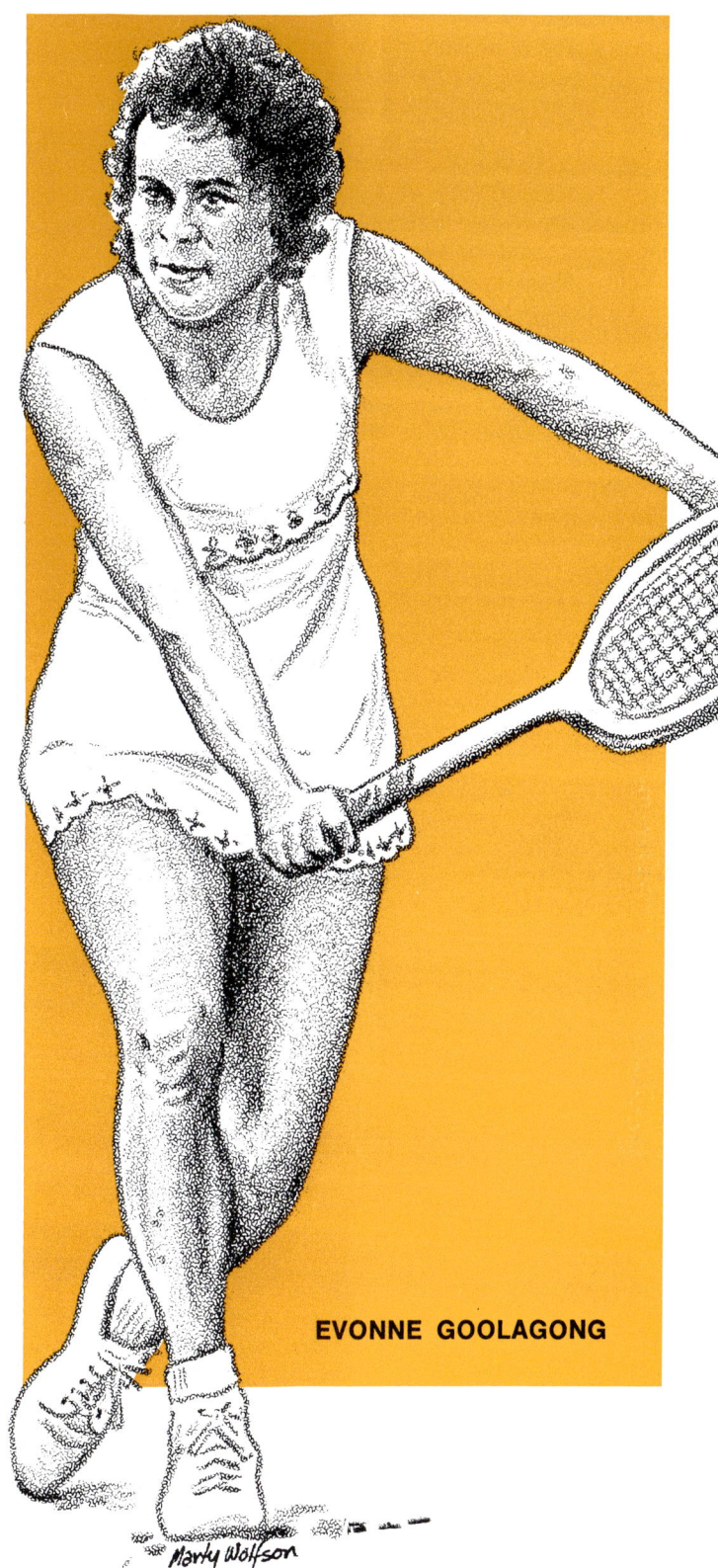

EVONNE GOOLAGONG

"There were too many nights when we had 2500," said Fuhrer, who felt the WTT was not catching on in Pittsburgh, or any place else for that matter. It lacked commitment on the part of the players and the owners, he thought.

There were highs and lows, when champagne was hoisted high, or when voices were raised too high in bitter arguments. Fuhrer was an iron-fisted sports boss in the mold of another insurance magnate, Charles O. Finley, and pushed his players hard.

Winning the WTT title was the biggest high.

The death of Danny McGibbeny, the team's first-rate publicist and good-natured ambassador, was the deepest low.

McGibbeny was a great kid—he was the son of the executive sports editor of the Pittsburgh Post-Gazette—and young Danny even coached the club in a token effort for a few matches when the job was more than Mark Cox could handle in the team's third season. McGibbeny got sick that last season, and died in the fall—from cancer—at age 24.

Fuhrer chose to fold the team after its third year of operation because he didn't think the league was headed in the right direction.

He had gone first class, but felt the rest of the WTT wasn't as dedicated to the same goals which he held for the league. "We had the best team in the league as long as I owned the team," he said. For the record, the Triangles won more matches than any other team in the three years they competed.

It was an expensive proposition. Goolagong was getting $150,000 a year during her three-year stay; Rosewall was paid $105,000 the year he was the team's player-coach, and Gerulaitis got $75,000 in his final year of his three-year involvement.

"Of course, you're in it to make money," said Fuhrer. "In sports, your team's record is in the paper every day. You do foolish things. You mortgage your soul."

Looking back, he concluded, "I loved tennis, but there weren't enough people who appreciated it."

Team tennis was an interesting concept, though the format may have had a few flaws. It consisted of five sets of tennis in which there was one set each of men's and women's singles, then men's, women's and mixed doubles. The home team picked the order in which those events would be held, which was part of the strategy.

There was no "love" in WTT, the league boasted. The scoring was simplified—1, 2, 3, 4 instead of 15, 30, 40 and game—and streamlined to produce quicker and more dramatic results. Each game counted toward the team's total and, of course, the team that won the most games would win the event.

It was quick and put pressure on the players right from the start. It wasn't for slow starters. It improved the play of most of its members, especially their concentration and killer-instinct.

When it was formed in 1964, there were 16 franchises, from New York to Hawaii and from Canada to Florida and Texas.

The players were well paid, but there was never really the commitment from them that their salaries should have assured. Self-interest came first; that's what tennis players were accustomed to, and they were reluctant to extend themselves to help promote their respective teams. It was strictly a fast buck for the majority of them.

The fans were encouraged to cheer and shout, to root for their team and to react to the play, while the ball was going back and forth. They were not to sit on their hands as tennis crowds had traditionally done. No one was to hush them. "It's against all my tennis training," said Goolagong at the beginning. "I have to get used to it."

The most magic night of all, as far as the Triangles and their fans were concerned, had to be the night of July 8, 1976 when 13,492 turned out at the Civic Arena to see the Triangles take on Chris Evert and the Phoenix Racquets.

The timing was perfect. It was the start of the second half of the WTT season, following a break so the players could compete at Wimbledon. Evert had won the women's title at Wimbledon, and defeated Goolagong in a three-set showdown. Goolagong and Gerulaitis had both done wonderfully at Wimbledon.

In WTT competition in the first half of that season, Chris had compiled a 19-1 record in singles, while Goolagong was 15-1. The attendance that night was the second largest for an indoor tennis event in the U.S., topped only by the crowd which saw Billie Jean King and Bobby Riggs fight the Battle of the Sexes three years earlier at the Astrodome in Houston.

"We didn't discount any tickets that night," Fuhrer pointed out. "Our gross was something like $80,000, which was the highest for any one match in World Team Tennis."

The Civic Arena crowd was provided with a real treat, and they, in turn, provided a real circus atmosphere. Chris took a 3-0 and 4-1 lead over Evonne. But Evonne got her game together and, with a little help from the boisterous crowd—mounted a miraculous comeback. The 25-year-old Aussie beat Chris, 6-4.

"I felt somewhere along the line I'd start playing well," said Goolagong later in her usual nonchalant manner.

Even more important, Goolagong teamed up with player-coach Mark Cox to conquer Kris Shaw and Tony Roche, another Wimbledon champion, in mixed doubles, 6-3. Cox and Goolagong produced the decisive point in the final game for a dramatic 24-23 victory.

The Civic Arena crowd outdid itself and then some that special night. Not only did they boo Chris Evert every so often, but they booed the Triangles' own Sue Stap at one point when they felt she wasn't putting forth her best effort.

Chris didn't care for the crowd's behavior. "I think tennis is a very classy sport," she said. "I don't like to hear people boo. I wouldn't like the fans to be like that at Forest Hills or Wimbledon. Then it might affect me."

Gerulaitis liked the crowd, of course. After all, this was a young man who thrived on the din of disco joints. He liked commotion. Vitas used to telephone Myron Cope during his sports talk show, just for the hell of it, to talk about tennis and the Triangles, the G-Men or the Bee-Gees, or whatever else Cope wanted to chat about.

"Pittsburgh is an exciting city to play tennis in," said Gerulaitis. "The fans get so involved. It's the only city in the league where the crowd does that. In other cities, where people are more oriented to tennis, you get the same polite applause for both sides. Here, they boo the visitors and cheer for the Triangles. Until you start to lose. When you start losing, everybody gets booed."

No, Pittsburgh was not a normal stop on the pro tennis tour, not before or since the rise and fall of the WTT, but thanks to WTT the game's biggest names came to play in Pittsburgh.

They included Billie Jean King, of course, who helped get World Team Tennis off the ground along with her husband, Larry, who bankrolled several of the franchises, and John Newcombe, Jimmy Connors, Bjorn Borg, Rod Laver, Chris Evert, Virginia Wade, Diane Fromholtz, Martina Navratilova and Marty Reissen, among others.

The first club president of the Triangles and one of the league founders who nurtured the WTT concept was Chuck Reichblum, a former newspaperman turned promoter who owned Century Features, Inc., in Pittsburgh. He and local attorney Bill Sutton received the WTT franchise for nothing. They, in turn, got John Hillman to invest in the new venture.

Soon after Fuhrer entered the picture, he bought every-

KEN ROSEWALL

body else out. "I actually made money in the WTT," Reichblum boasts.

Before Fuhrer took over, he and Reichblum ran the show together. "Reichblum represented us at the first draft of players in New York," recalled Fuhrer. He was hot to draft Ken Rosewall because he felt he could sign him. I thought Rosewall was too old (at 39) to build a ballteam around. Reichblum took Rosewall in the first round. I wanted to get Goolagong. But she said she wouldn't play in World Team Tennis. I'm in Pittsburgh and I'm talking over the telephone to Reichblum in New York. I told him, "If you don't draft Goolagong in the second round, I won't put any more money into this. If you don't have a strong woman' you're not going anywhere."

Fuhrer was right on one count, and wrong on the other, though he would surely insist he was only half-wrong. The teams with the strong women players—Billie Jean King, at first with Philadelphia and then three years in New York, Virginia Wade in New York, Chris Evert in Phoenix—dominated the WTT. Mixed doubles, it developed, often was the pivotal match in WTT competition.

Reichblum and Fuhrer traveled to Australia and signed Rosewall. He was approaching his 40th birthday, but that same year he would reach the finals of both Wimbledon and Forest Hills. It was something, having him and Goolagong, one of Australia's Wimbledon champions, on stage together.

Goolagong was a shy girl. She was just 22 when she signed a multi-year contract with the Triangles. At 19, she had captured the 1971 Wimbledon title. It didn't take her long to capture the hearts of tennis fans in Pittsburgh, either.

When she first arrived, she was asked what she knew about Pittsburgh. "I know it from that song . . . the pawn shop on the corner in Pittsburgh, Pennsylvania," she said with her charming Australian accent.

"You can tell what a city is like by what the people are like," she continued. "And the people I've met here are just great. In traveling, I've discovered the first impression you get about a place is the correct one. I like the feel of Pittsburgh."

She enhanced the local sports scene, that's for sure. "She's the ballerina of the tennis court," cooed John Felman, the director of operations for the Triangles. "Her stroke is so natural, so beautiful. She kisses the ball."

She was enchanting. She was looked after, at first, by Vic Edwards, who had discovered her at age nine, nurtured her game, became her legal guardian at a later date, and doted over her. Later, Roger Cawley, a British chap, came on the scene, and stole her affection, and to hear Fuhrer talk about it, her attention to tennis and the Triangles.

She had a falling out with Edwards, and dismissed him. "I wish we had kept him as coach for the third season," Fuhrer says now. "We would have won it again."

Coaches were always a problem for Fuhrer. His first, Rosewall, was a poker-faced competitor and a defender of tradition, quiet and concentration. He could never get used to the circus atmosphere of World Team Tennis. Even so, he and Goolagong teamed up to lead the Triangles to a successful first season before the New York Sets stopped them in the playoffs.

If you were at Forest Hills after that first season you could have seen how Pittsburghers adopted this pair. All of a sudden, Goolagong and Rosewall weren't just representing Australia at the U.S. Open. They were representing Pittsburgh as well.

They were dye-in-the-wool Pittsburghers now as much as Vee Toner, who could be heard, in her inimitable scratchy voice, umpiring an important match inside the stadium of the West Side Tennis Club, involving Chris Evert.

"There were a lot of things about team tennis that I liked," Goolagong told us at Forest Hills, "and some that I didn't like. I made a lot of friends in Pittsburgh. In fact, a lot of people come up to me here, and tell me they're from Pittsburgh. They say things like, 'Let's go, Triangles.' I've gotten a lot of letters from people from Pittsburgh, saying they hope I come back."

Goolagong came back, but Rosewall refused. Vic Edwards was named the new coach. Fuhrer was named the president of the league for 1975, and it signaled the start of something big for the Triangles.

They finished the season with the league's best mark of 36-8, and had to win on the final night to clinch first place in the East Division. They set an attendance record when 10,859 turned out at the Civic Arena to see them beat the Sets, 26-22, with Evonne beating Billie Jean King, 6-2, in a key victory.

The Sets were then shocked in a one-game playoff, getting beaten by the Boston Lobsters, 25-24, and were eliminated from contention. The Lobsters, led by Ion Tiriac, Bob Hewitt, Cat Stevens and Wendy Turnbull, were no match for the Triangles and bowed out in two straight playoff matches.

The Triangles got off to a bad start in the best-of-three championship series, losing the opener, 26-25, before 2,160 in San Francisco. The Gaters had a good women's doubles team in Ann Kiyomura and Llana Kloss, a strong singles performer in Betty Stove, two good men in Tom Okker and Frew McMillan and were a formidable foe. But the Triangles bounced back to beat them in the second outing, 28-25, before 2,182 at the Civic Arena.

"It's like playing a Davis Cup match every night," said the Triangles' Mark Cox. "There's an added sense of responsibility, whether you're playing for a team, your country . . . or Pittsburgh."

Peggy Michel said there was more pressure than being at center court at Wimbledon.

Fuhrer showed up for the final, wearing a green G-Man shirt and softball cap. He was "up," that was certain. So were the Triangles, even though they got off to a slow start. Stove and Kloss clipped Goolagong and Michel in the opening women's doubles, 6-2. But Goolagong came back to beat Stove, 6-2, in singles.

Gerulaitis and Cox defeated McMillan and Okker, 7-5, and then, in the deciding matchup, Vitas defeated Okker, 6-1, and drew the third standing ovation of the night from the crowd of 6,882. He was named the MVP of the playoffs.

There were problems the next season, the final one for the Triangles. Edwards was replaced as coach by Cox, who was never comfortable in the role. Cox later gave way to McGibbeny, until he became ill, and, in the final stage of the season, the team doctor, Lowell Lubic, a 49-year-old neurologist, sat in the coach's chair.

When the Triangles struggled at the start, Fuhrer told the fans that whenever the Triangles lost a home match they could use their ticket stubs for admission to the next home match. "If we can't do any better than we've done," he said, "I don't want to take anybody's money.

"People shouldn't have to pay to see a bunch of losers."

Fuhrer was fighting with his players, and Goolagong's boyfriend, Roger Cawley, on a regular basis that 1976 season.

Cox, a bright and conscientious and well-traveled 33-year-old competitor, defended Fuhrer in the press. "He does pay well," said Cox, "and he does send the team first class."

"Most of the players feel very, very intensely about playing for this team," continued Cox. "They have a tremendous loyalty to Pittsburgh by comparison to the other teams in the league."

VITAS GERULAITIS

Gerulaitis didn't get along too famously with Fuhrer, but he explained why he stayed. "Because Fuhrer's fair, generous and the most competent owner in the league. That's why we win. I can live with his temper."

At the mid-season break for Wimbledon, Gerulaitis went to England and excelled. He reached the quarter-finals in men's singles by defeating the defending champion, Arthur Ashe, and teamed up with Sandy Mayer, a New York friend who also emerged from WTT play, to win the men's doubles title.

The Triangles resumed their season with new vigor, but once again, for the second time in three years, they were bounced from the playoffs by the New York Sets.

Fuhrer had gone far enough. In December of 1976, he tossed in the towel. It was the end for the Triangles, and for all intents and purposes, the beginning of the end for World Team Tennis, which folded after two more seasons.

ALLEGHENY COMMUNITY COLLEGE OUTDISTANCED EVERYBODY IN THE '70s

By Jim O'Brien

"If you talk with any distance runner and you say 'Allegheny,' they'll know. We've left our mark. Nobody will ever forget us."
—Neil Cohen

Nobody won more championships in Pittsburgh during the '70s than the distance running teams at the Allegheny Campus of Community College of Allegheny County. Credit Neil Cohen and Sam Bair for building and maintaining, respectively, one of the nation's outstanding cross-country and marathon teams during that period.

Allegheny's "Run For Fun" teams won national junior college titles in cross-country in 1973, 1976 and 1977, team marathon championships in 1974, 1975, 1976, 1977 and 1978, the national junior college women's cross-country championship in 1976, and the JC indoor track championship in 1978.

"At our peak, we had the outstanding college distance-running teams in the country," says Cohen, who was the coach and athletic director in his early days at Allegheny, before giving way as coach to Sam Bair, a sub-four-minute miler from Scottdale, Pa. who'd starred as a collegian at Kent State. "We could have beaten Texas-El Paso, or Oregon, Tennessee, Penn State or Villanova, who were regarded as the best among the four-year schools. There's no doubt in my mind we'd have beaten the U.S. Olympic team in long distance events."

There are track people who will argue loud and long about that statement, especially since Cohen is known to get carried away with ACC teams.

It was incredible that the Allegheny Campus achieved what it did in the sport, but mounting costs made it impossible to continue the program, at least at the level of excellence Cohen and Bair had established.

Allegheny Community College compiled a record of 110-0-1 against two-year schools during an 11-year period, and a mark of 51-5-3 against four-year colleges and universities. "If you talk with any distance runner and you say 'Allegheny,' they'll know," says Cohen. "We've left our mark. Nobody will ever forget us."

Economics forced the abandonment of the program after the 1978 season. "We really had no competition, and it got to the point where it wasn't fun for anyone," says Cohen. "Also, we had budget problems. We had to decide whether to keep track and cross-country and drop our basketball team and women's programs or go the other

Members of 1976 NJCAA Cross Country Championship Team. Coach Sam Bair is the middle man in the first row.

way, and that's what we decided to do."

There was a void in the closing years of the decade, but Cohen had a vicarious thrill by seeing what Allegheny alumni were doing at some of the top collegiate programs in the nation.

The honor roll of long-distance running greats at Allegheny include Tim McMullen of Rochester, N. Y., Robin Holland of Johannesburg, South Africa—the first of the foreign imports and really super athletes to attend Allegheny—J. J. Rotich and Amos Korir of Kenya, Malcolm East of Britain, Wayne Coffman, J. Tim Frye and Matt Leddy.

With a mixture of American and international talent, Cohen and Bair combined to make Pittsburgh the capital of junior college distance-running in the '70s. "One of the secrets of our program," confides Cohen, "is that we took a sport like distance-running and we made it important."

Cohen has been the catalyst for sports activity at Allegheny Community College since the school opened in 1966. He converted a bathroom into the A.D.'s office, tapped his own bank account too many times to make ends meet in his pursuit of sports excellence, and put the school on the map. A new physical education facility opened in October of 1973, and it is a showcase on the North Side campus. Looking southward from the City of Champions, it can be seen above Three Rivers Stadium on the horizon.

ACC champions included (l. to r.) Britain's Malcolm East and Kenya's Amos "Kip" Korir.

Allegheny's Amos "Kip" Korir was NJAA Steeple Chase Champion and Record Holder.

Sam Bair, left, and Neil Cohen, right, flank Allegheny's 1976 National Championship Cross Country Team.

OTHER HEROES, OTHER FACES POPULARIZE PITTSBURGH IN MANY DISTANT PLACES

By Jim O'Brien

KINER AND KUHN AT COOPERSTOWN

"He used to be Ralph Kiner. No kid in Pittsburgh ever used to want to be anybody else."
—Maury Allen

The sun came out when it was supposed to, burning up the moisture on the grass at Doubleday Field, and in the surrounding area at the Baseball Hall of Fame in Cooperstown, N.Y. It would be a nice day after all, as the rain gave way to the sun. Bowie Kuhn beamed as brightly as the sun, for the Commissioner of Baseball welcomed an appropriate day for induction ceremonies at the sports shrine in upstate New York.

August 18, 1975 was a special day in the baseball business, especially if you had been a young boy back in Pittsburgh in the '40s and '50s when Ralph McPherran Kiner came from Alhambra, California and put peerless punch in the Pirates' hitting attack.

If you had been a member of the Knot-Hole Gang, and could get into Forbes Field for 50 cents and sit in the right field stands, or if you had sat in the left field bleachers, close to Kiner, this was, indeed, a special day.

Kiner was the Willie Stargell of those long-gone summers, only his teammates weren't as good as those who played for the Pirates in the '70s. Kiner was a hero in Pittsburgh, when it had little else to cheer about.

He looked good and well-tanned at the Hall of Fame ceremonies, moving among other greats of the game such as Stan "The Man" Musial, the pride of Donora and the St. Louis Cardinals, Yogi Berra, Hank Greenberg, and countless other heroes from the past.

Kiner played for the Pirates from 1946 to 1953, and put in stints with the Chicago Cubs and Cleveland Indians in 1954 and 1955 before injuries cut short his career after ten major league seasons.

He hit 369 home runs in that period, and averaged better than 100 runs batted in per season. He was the only player to lead his league or share the lead in homers seven years in a row (1946-1952). He twice hit more than 50 homers, and he set a National League mark with 101 home runs in two successive seasons, with 54 in 1949 and 47 in 1950. He led the NL in slugging percentage three times.

No. 4 was something else. Writing about Kiner's selection to the Hall of Fame, Maury Allen of the New York Post put it this way: "He played a lot of baseball and hit a lot of home runs. He used to be Ralph Kiner. No kid in Pittsburgh ever used to want to be anybody else."

JOHN UNITAS
At Canton, Ohio Shrine Ceremonies

"We won't see anyone quite like him again."
—Hall of Fame Selector

Every kid in Pittsburgh, in truth, didn't want to be Ralph Kiner. If you are a football fan, and you played quarterback on the sandlot fields of Pittsburgh, especially the fields in Bloomfield and Mt. Washington and the South Side, and you wore No. 19, well, then you wanted to be the next Johnny Unitas.

And you wanted to be in Canton, Ohio on July 28, 1979 when Johnny U. was inducted into the Pro Football Hall of Fame.

As one writer observed at the time Johnny retired before the 1974 season: "Superstars are constantly making the scene, but Johnny Unitas was maybe the last of the real sports heroes. He was the kind of athlete little kids could admire and copy and whose stories were the kind you could read with your breakfast cereal. We won't see anyone quite like him again!"

They called him "Mr. Clutch," and the 6-1, 195-pound field general of the Baltimore Colts came through time after time in the big games.

In 1969 the Board of Selectors of the Pro Football Hall of Fame, when asked to name an all-time team from the National Football League's first 50 years, picked Unitas as the quarterback. Exactly one decade later, that same group unanimously voted pro football's highest honor—Hall of Fame membership—to Johnny in his first year of eligibility following the mandatory five-year retirement period.

Game after game, season after season from his rookie 1956 season until a final year with the San Diego Chargers in 1973, Unitas was a legendary figure.

His last-second heroics in the 1958 NFL title game with the New York Giants, the first overtime championship contest in the league's history and commonly called "The Greatest Game Ever Played," turned Unitas into a household name among American sports buffs. Unitas cooly quarterbacked Baltimore to a 23-17 victory.

Unitas' career statistics are awesome—5,186 attempts, 2,830 completions, 40,239 yards gained and 290 touchdown passes!

He was all-NFL five times and he was named the NFL Player of the Year three times. He played in 10 Pro Bowl games and won MVP honors a record-tying three times. He guided the Colts to two championships. His top feat was throwing touchdown passes in 47 straight games.

He was born May 7, 1933 into a Lithuanian family in Pittsburgh. He knew hardship early in life as his father died when he was only five, and throughout his childhood he had to help his widowed mother make ends meet during those late-depression years. He credits his mother for instilling in him the traits of courage and determination that served him so well in pro football.

He was all-Catholic League two years while playing at St. Justin's High School, and then was a starting quarterback for almost four years at the University of Louisville. The Pittsburgh Steelers drafted Johnny in the ninth round of the 1955 draft, but cut him before he could even throw one pass in a pre-season game.

What happened next is already American sports folklore. Unitas turned to semi-pro football where he played with the Bloomfield Rams for $6 a game. He performed well and caught the attention of some scouts. When the Baltimore Colts needed a backup quarterback, Weeb Ewbank gave Unitas a chance, signing him to a $7,000 contract on a make-it basis.

Johnny U. made good on that second chance.

JOE SCHMIDT
At Canton, Ohio Shrine Ceremonies

"Joe is the best linebacker in the league."
—Paul Hornung

Joe Schmidt grew up in Mt. Oliver, not far from Mt. Washington, and played sandlot football with older fellows when he was a youngster. Then he played at Brentwood High School, and went from there to the University of Pittsburgh.

He was a fine football player at Pitt, but his career there was hindered by injuries. He was not drafted by the Detroit Lions until the seventh round in 1963, and the Lions were a lot more interested in another Western Pennsylvania product, Gene Gedman, who came out of Duquesne, Pa., to star at Indiana University, and was the Lions' second pick.

Schmidt turned out to be one of the greatest middle linebackers in the history of the game. He was voted to the NFL all-star team eight times, and was named to the Pro Bowl nine straight years from 1955 through 1963, and he was named the MVP of the Lions by his teammates in four of those years.

"Joe is the best linebacker in the league," said Green Bay's Paul Hornung.

"He's always in the way," said John Henry Johnson, one of the NFL's all-time great backs who resides in Shadyside these days.

Schmidt was a 1973 inductee into Pro Football's Hall of Fame.

BRUNO SAMMARTINO

"He's a legend in the sport."
—"Main Event"

Still active, and an even bigger rags-to-riches story than Unitas or Schmidt is Bruno Sammartino. As a 16-year-old, Sammartino immigrated with his family to America from Abruzzi, Italy in 1951, and settled in Oakland. He attended Schenley High School, and from there he went on to worldwide fame and popularity as a professional wrestling champion.

Sammartino made more money than any Pittsburgh-based athlete, drawing over $100,000 in the late '60s, over $200,000 in the mid-'70s and as much as $300,000 annually by the late '70s. He was known to more people around the world than Terry Bradshaw, Willie Stargell, Joe Greene, Dave Parker or even Arnold Palmer. He owned a Rolls Royce in 1971, long before any other local athletes.

He did more for wrestling, according to a recently-published book entitled "Main Event" than any other individual. "He's a legend in the sport," it said. He was the proverbial 95-pound weakling when he arrived in town, but built himself up by lifting weights at the YM&YWHA in Oakland, and soon the word was out among the Schenley students: "Don't mess with Sam!" Al Quaill tried to turn him into a boxer, but he chose wrestling as a way to the top.

Bruno turned pro in 1959. In 1963 he defeated Buddy Rogers in a celebrated 48-second bout at New York's Madison Square Garden to win the world's championship.

He was unseated on Jan. 18, 1971 by Ivan Koloff, but regained the title by defeating Stan Stasiak in New York on Dec. 9, 1973, and retained it till April 30, 1977, when he lost it to Billy Graham in Baltimore.

All together, Bruno held the title more than 11 years.

During that period, Sammartino wrestled all over the world, pulling in crowds over 22,000 in Australia, over 45,000 in Brazil, and over 50,000 in Venezuela and Japan. All the time, he maintained a residence in suburban Pittsburgh—Ross Township—with his wife, Carol, and their three sons. He sold out Madison Square Garden (over 22,000) more than any other single performer.

The 5-11, 260-pound Sammartino received a real scare in April of 1976 when, at age 37, he suffered a fractured vertebrae in his neck, otherwise referred to as a broken neck, when he was slammed to the mat by Stan Hensen, a 375-pound Swede.

"It was a very frightening experience," recalls Sammartino. "I came within inches of being paralyzed for life."

His wrestling career certainly appeared to be over. But Bruno came back, with a more limited schedule, and wrestled again. He talked about retirement, but never kept his word. He was enjoying it too much, and making too much money to walk away from it.

Proof of his continuing popularity was offered in March of 1980 when, at age 41, he wrestled Larry Zybisco and drew a record crowd of 16,661 to the Civic Arena and, a week later, he and Zybisco drew the largest wrestling crowd of all time at Madison Square Garden—26,102 including 4,000 in the Felt Forum. As far as his fans are concerned, Bruno will always be the world's champion.

DANNY AND RICK SEEMILLER
Crack Carrick Doubles Duo

"My goal is to be world champion."
—Danny Seemiller

Danny Seemiller hasn't made the sort of money Sammartino has, but he's also made his mark on the international sports scene. The kid from Carrick became the No. 1 ranked table tennis player in America in 1974, and still held the title going into the '80s.

At age 24 in 1979, Danny headed the first U.S. sports team to compete in Korea, and he was seeded in world championships in a sport dominated by Chinese, Japanese and East Bloc European countries.

He's competed in China, Japan, Russia, Yugoslavia, Czechoslovakia, Hungary, Saudi Arabia, Iran, Germany, France, Italy, Sweden and Denmark. In early 1980, he returned from winning the Western Open in Japan to dominate a tournament he and his father helped organize and promote at Robert Morris College in Pittsburgh.

Danny and his younger brother, Ricky, are the No. 1 ranked doubles team in the U.S. In singles, Ricky is ranked No. 3. An even younger brother, Randy, has been a top-notch junior competitor. So it's a real family affair. The best competition they get in this country is in their own Carrick home.

Dan's biggest purse has been $2,500, and that was for winning a "Challenge of the Sexes" match in 1977. Usually, the total prize money in a tournament is $1,000. Once, he won a total of $10,000 by sweeping through 30 U.S.-based tournaments. "When it comes to money, I guess I'm in the wrong sport," says the lightning-fast lefthander who looks like and competes like Jimmy Connors. "If I'd get to be a world champion, then maybe I can get the recognition and make some real money. That's still my goal."

SAM McDOWELL
...with Indians

GEORGE MEDICH
...with Yankees

"I had Sam first and he had more ability than anybody."
—Birdie Tebbetts

Two tall, hard-throwing pitchers from Pittsburgh made their mark in Major League Baseball during this period. The first was Sam McDowell, a skinny 6-6 left-hander who signed as a bonus baby with the Cleveland Indians upon graduation from Central Catholic High School in 1960, and the second was George Medich, a solidly-built 6-5 right-hander who signed with the New York Yankees upon graduation from the University of Pittsburgh in 1970.

There was more than just a decade that separated these two pitchers. McDowell, from Morningside, was known as "Sudden Sam," and had every major league baseball scout drooling over him while he was firing no-hitters at Central. Medich, who preceded Tony Dorsett as a football player at both Hopewell High outside Aliquippa and at Pitt, proved a surprise to many. The Neville Island native was recruited to Pitt to play tight end on the football team, which he did, and his playing baseball for the Panthers was strictly a bonus. He wasn't even the best pitcher on the Pitt nine. He became known as "Doc" Medich because he attended medical school at Pitt while also pursuing a professional sports career. Medich managed to combine both, and became a proficient pitcher and doctor during the decade.

In 1970, McDowell won 20 and lost 12 with a 2.92 earned run average for the Indians, and led the American League in strikeouts (304 in 305 innings) for the third straight year and fifth time in six seasons.

"I had Sam first and he had more ability than anybody," said Birdie Tebbetts, who managed McDowell from 1963 to 1966. "He had a fastball, a curveball, a change, a slider, and he could throw them all for nine innings."

Somehow, though, Sam never quite pitched to his potential. He wasn't satisfied to strike out batters with his fast ball, and he made it more difficult than it had to be—for everybody. In 15 seasons, he posted a record of 141-134 while pitching with Cleveland, the San Francisco Giants, New York Yankees and Pittsburgh Pirates. He was named to the American League All-Stars six times.

He made it as a non-roster candidate with the Pirates in 1975. He was a standout in spring training, but something less when the season started. Even so, he posted a winning record—2-1—in 16 games at age 32 before the Pirates wrote him off. He still resides in Monroeville.

After three years of minor league seasoning, Medich made it with the Yankees in 1973. He was 14-9 and runner-up for the American League's rookie pitcher of the year award. In his second season, Medich had a 19-15 record and proved to be one of the most durable and dependable pitchers on the Yankees' staff.

He was 16-16 in 1974 and was traded after that season to the Pirates in exchange for Ken Brett, Dock Ellis and Willie Randolph. It was a terrific trade for the Yankees. Medich slipped to 8-11 in 1976 with the Pirates, and was traded away at the end of the season. As the '80s began, he was pitching, and doing a fine job of it, with the Texas Rangers. And he was a full-fledged medical doctor.

LARRY BROWN

MERCURY MORRIS

"What makes life interesting is that everyone is different. Every runner has a different style."
—Chuck Noll

This area produced three of the greatest running backs in the National Football League during the past decade: Eugene "Mercury" Morris of the Miami Dolphins, Larry Brown of the Washington Redskins and Tony Dorsett of the Dallas Cowboys.

Morris emerged from Avonworth, Brown from Schenley High here in Pittsburgh, and Dorsett from Hopewell High and the University of Pittsburgh. Morris played his college ball at West Texas State and Brown at Kansas State. None of them were big, but they could run with a football.

A vibrant, happy-go-lucky sort, Morris broke NCAA rushing records established by O. J. Simpson, and joined the Dolphins in 1969. He and Larry Csonka and Jim Kiick combined to give Coach Don Shula a smashing ground game. Morris was the game-breaker, always a threat to go all the way whether he was returning kicks or following Csonka around the corner.

He gained 1,000 yards on the nose in 1972 and he and Csonka were the first backs on the same team to break the barrier in the same season. Mercury averaged 5.3 yards per carry and scored 12 TDs that year.

The Dolphins went to three straight Super Bowls—VI, VII, VIII—and won in their second and third tries. They won 17 games without a loss in that 1972 season.

A three-time all-pro choice, Morris remains the Dolphins' leader in combined yardage for a career. He gained 3,877 yards rushing, and was their all-time top kick-returner. He returned three kicks for TDs, going 105, 96 and 94 yards. He returned 43 kicks for a 26.4 yard average in 1969.

One of Mercury's best efforts came against the New England Patriots in 1973 when he carried the ball 15 times for 197 yards, including a 70-yarder, and scored three touchdowns. One of his blockers back then was tackle Doug Crusan of Monessen.

Brown was even better than Morris, certainly more reliable. He was with the Redskins from 1969—breaking in under Vince Lombardi in his first and last season as coach with the Washington team—and lasted through 1976—being used the rest of his career as a workhorse by George Allen.

He led the Redskins in rushing for six seasons, and at the end of the 1979 season he ranked as the Redskins' all-time top rusher and fifth among their all-time receivers. He ranked 18th on the NFL's all-time rushing list. In eight years, he gained 5,875 yards on 1,530 carries for a 3.8 yard average and 35 touchdowns. He caught 238 passes for 2,485 yards and 20 touchdowns for a career total of 55 touchdowns.

The Steelers' Franco Harris said he was amazed by how hard Brown hit every time he carried the ball. "He always fought for that extra yard," offered Franco.

On Dec. 13, 1970, Brown became the first Redskin in history to rush for 1,000 yards. He was the top rusher in the NFL that season with a total of 1,125 yards on 237 attempts for a 4.7 average. He was the first Redskin to ever win a rushing title.

The Redskins won the NFC title in 1972, and Brown won the NFC rushing title that year with 1,216 yards. Brown was honored as the NFL Player of the Year in 1972. Willard Fisher's fullback at Schenley High had soared the heights, that's for sure.

Dorsett broke into the pro ranks in a more spectacular manner than either Morris or Brown and was still going strong at the start of the '80s. He still held the record for most yards gained in a college career, eclipsing totals set by Simpson, Morris and Archie Griffin of Ohio State.

Dallas made a deal with the Seattle Seahawks in order to draft Dorsett on the first round. The 5-11, 190-pound back won Rookie of the Year honors in 1977 and set three club rushing records. "I think I've come a long way," he said. He was a starter in his first Pro Bowl game.

He rushed for over 1,000 yards in each of his first three seasons, though he didn't break into the starting lineup as a rookie until his tenth game when he finally pushed former Steeler Preston Pearson out of the lineup. In his second pro season, Dorsett set a Dallas record by rushing for 1,325 yards.

He's been a spectacular performer in the playoffs. Dorsett helped the Cowboys claim the Super Bowl title in his rookie season, and then was a big contributor as they made it back to the NFL title game in 1978, only to lose to the Steelers, 35-31, in a real barn-burner.

As the '80s began, Dorsett had his burning eyes set on several goals, and hoped to get to carry the ball more for the Cowboys in the coming seasons. "His potential still hasn't been scratched," says Blesto scouting service head Jack Butler.

TONY DORSETT **JOE NAMATH**

"Playing pro football for a living sure beats the blast furnaces."

—Joe Namath

Joe Namath of Beaver Falls, the best-known pro football player of his generation, closed out his storied career in the mid-'70s, but he's still with us because of his many TV commercials and appearances. Broadway Joe wasn't just another football player. He was a personality, a sports-showbiz celebrity, "Broadway Joe" Namath.

Namath quarterbacked the New York Jets from 1965 through 1976 and closed out his career with the Los Angeles Rams in 1977.

Namath made big news when he went from being an All-America at Alabama to being a $400,000 quarterback with Sonny Werblin's Jets. Namath made the American Football League a living entity, and was the single-most important force for its popularity on TV and for the eventual merger of the AFL with the National Football League.

He was at his peak when he made good on a boast that the Jets would beat the Baltimore Colts in the 1969 Super Bowl. His AFL team was tabbed 17-point underdogs by Jimmy "The Greek" Snyder, but Namath made the Steubenville-born odds-maker look silly.

Namath put his name in the record books by passing for 4,007 yards in the 1967 season, and passing for over 400 yards in three games in 1972, topped by his 496-yard total at Baltimore on Sept. 24, 1972.

That was his finest day as a pro. He passed for six touchdowns in a 44-34 triumph over the Colts. Namath and John Unitas set an NFL record for combined passing yardage (872) that day. And both of those quarterbacks, of course, trace their roots to this area. There may never be another Namath or a Unitas. But Bradshaw ain't bad.

Another all-pro performer was Ted Kwalick of McKees Rocks who became the best tight end in the National Football League from these parts since Aliquippa's Mike Ditka.

Kwalick had an All-America career playing for Joe Paterno at Penn State and was the No. 1 draft choice, along with Gene Washington, of the San Francisco 49ers in 1969. Kwalick was chosen for the Pro Bowl in 1971, 1972 and 1973 and was all-NFL in 1972.

He twice led the 49ers in receiving, with 52 catches in 1971, ranking second in the National Football Conference and fourth in the NFL, and in 1973 with 47. He played from 1975 through 1977 with the Oakland Raiders.

McKees Rocks also turned out several fine quarterbacks, including Davey Havern and Billy Daniels of Pitt, and Chuck Burkhart and Chuck Fusina of Penn State, but the best was Tommy Clements who came out of Canevin High—where he was an all-around athletic star—to become a national coverboy hero at Notre Dame. He went on to stardom with the Hamilton Tiger-Cats in the Canadian Football League and, after five years there, signed with the Kansas City Chiefs of the NFL for the 1980 season.

TED KWALICK   **CANDY YOUNG**

"We don't set our sights unless we set them high."
—Butch Ryan, coach of Candy Young

Beaver Falls turned out some more outstanding football players, namely Kevin Scanlon, whom Coach Larry Bruno tabbed as his best quarterback since Namath and looked good on the boast when Scanlon gained All-America honorable mention in his senior season in 1979 at Arkansas, and Dwight Collins, a speedster who's sure to be heard from as a running back or flanker at Pitt in the '80s.

But Beaver Falls turned out another speedster who gained even more national attention than Dwight Collins in Candy Young, a world-class hurdler. At 16, Candy set a world's record for women of 7.5 seconds in winning the 60-yard high hurdles in the AAU National track and field championships, and later in the summer she finished second to Deby LaPlante who set a new American record time of 12.86 seconds in the 100 meter hurdle event at Mt. San Antonio College in Walnut, Calif. Miss Young established a world junior record time of 12.95 while finishing runner-up. She and LaPlante are the only American women ever to run the distance in less than 13 seconds.

At 17, Candy Young was one of the most celebrated Olympic Games candidates in the world of track and field. She was a four-time state champ in the 100-meter hurdles, and twice broke the world's record for the 60-yard indoor hurdles. At graduation time, she held every national high school and AAU junior record in four hurdles events. She twice was voted an All-America by *Track and Field News* and as Female High School Athlete of the Year.

There were many young women in this area who distinguished themselves in sports in the '70s and better things loomed on the horizon for the '80s.

Bethel Park's Linda Kardos competed in the Pan American Games in Puerto Rico in the summer of '79, and was ranked among the top gymnasts in the U.S.

Berta McCallum of Mt. Lebanon is a fast-rising star on the women's tennis tour. She was a three-time national junior champion.

At Pitt, there are presently two outstanding young women athletes. There's Pam Miklasevich, who was super in the 1979-80 basketball season, her freshman campaign for the Pantherettes. She tied a Pitt Field House single-game record with 31 points. Then, too, there's Amy Jackson, an 18-year-old star for the Pitt swimming team. She went undefeated in college competition in 1979-80. She was a four-time high school All-America and a past AAU national finalist.

She was an All-America in ten events at the end of her sophomore season (1979-80), so she's right in stride with the super standards established at Pitt by Kathy Stetler.

"Pittsburgh has produced a lot of world-class swimmers."
—Dick Bradshaw

Kathy Stetler is a name synonymous with Pitt swimming and to excellence in women's swimming. In her four-year career at Pitt, Kathy received 18 All-America awards, and she and football player Tony Dorsett are the only athletes in Pitt history to earn All-America status for four years.

Kathy, who comes from Oakmont, was the national champion in the 50-yard butterfly in 1978 and earned All-America honors in the 1979 National Championships at Pitt in the 50 free-style, 800 free-style relay, 200 free-style relay and 400 free-style relay.

She was one of Pitt's most popular athletes, and the pride of swim coach Dick Bradshaw, who began developing her skills with the Pitt Aquatic Club. She won the Panther Award as the top female athlete at Pitt in 1979.

Two other outstanding products of the Pitt Aquatic Club are Jan Ujevich of Aliquippa, who was a freshman at the University of Florida for 1979-80, and Janis Hape.

Ujevich placed in the finals in ten national championship events over a five-year period, and qualified for the Olympic Trials for Montreal and Moscow. Janis Hape, a North Allegheny High School graduate, made the Olympic team for Montreal in the 200 breaststroke event.

Dr. Dick Rydze of Mt. Lebanon, who competed for the swim team at the University of Michigan and graduated from Pitt's medical school, won the silver medal as the second place finisher in tower diving in the Olympic Games in Mexico City in 1968.

One of the two best local male swimmers during the

'70s was Melvin Nash of Gateway High who was the top high school backstroker in the nation, competed in the Pan American Games in Columbia, starred for the swim team at Indiana University, where he was a member of national championship relay teams, and currently coaches the swim team at Texas A&M.

The other local product was Rick Hoffstetter of the Greater Pitt Swim Club who was an outstanding breaststroker and also went on to Indiana U., and qualified for the Olympic Trials. He's presently at the Duke University Law School.

"Pittsburgh has produced lots of world class swimmers," says Pitt's Dick Bradshaw with more than a hint of pride in his voice.

KATHY STETLER   JERRY RICHEY

He's a lawyer now, and sometimes he can be seen jogging on the streets of downtown Pittsburgh. It's not something new with him. Jerry Richey is a real runner and always has been. Pitt has never produced a better long-distance runner in its history. The young man from North Allegheny High School became the first Pittsburgher to break the four-minute mile barrier when he ran a 3:58.6 in the IC4A Indoor Championships on June 1, 1968.

Richey was a two-time track All-America (in four events) and a two-time cross-country All-America. He paved the way for the Pitt distance medley relay team to set a new indoor world record on Feb. 27, 1971 at the Delaware Invitational.

WORLD RECORD HOLDERS
Pitt's distance medley team, coached by Jim Banner (r.), consisted of (l. to r.) Jerry Richey, Mike Schurko, Smittie Brown and Ken Silay.

The record time was 9:39.7. Richey led off with a mile leg of 3:59.7; Mike Schurko of Bethel Park ran the three-quarter mile leg in 2:57.3; Smittie Brown of Coraopolis ran the quarter-mile in 48.2; and Ken Silay of Avalon ran the half-mile in 1:54.5. They were coached by Jim Banner, who is now the athletic director at Carnegie-Mellon.

FRANK FUHRER, III   ANDY URBANIC

This area's next great golfer could be Frank Fuhrer III, who presently competes for the University of North Carolina. Son of the Pittsburgh insurance magnate and sports entrepreneur of the same name, young Frank is a future bet for greatness.

He may not approach Arnold Palmer's accomplishments on the tour, but he could surpass Jim Simons, the second-best local golfer during the '70s.

This young man learned the game from his father and was tutored by Pete Snead, the head pro at the Pittsburgh Field Club, when Frank first took up the sport. Nowadays, he goes to Gardner Dickinson for instruction.

He won the West Penn Boys' title in 1973 and the West Penn Juniors in 1976. Representing Fox Chapel High School, Frank won the WPIAL golf title three times ('75-'76-'77), and won the state high school championship and state amateur titles in 1977. He also won the West Penn Amateur in 1978 and 1979. He's also won several college titles, and he was just 21 years old in 1980.

The most successful high school football coach in the area during the '70s was Andy Urbanic of Penn Hills. His Indians won the WPIAL title outright in 1976, 1978 and 1979 and tied Butler for the championship in 1977.

Andy's 12-year record at Penn Hills, counting 15 play-off games, was 100-28-2 going into the 1980 fall schedule. And you thought Chuck Noll was the only one to win 100 games during that period! During a six-year period from the 1974 through the 1979 season, Andy's teams posted a record of 66-4-1. His 1976 team posted a perfect 13-0 record, beating Beaver Falls, Gateway and Butler in the WPIAL playoffs.

Another area coach who distinguished himself was Pete Antimarino, the football coach at Gateway High School in Monroeville. His team beat Altoona to win the WPIAL grid championship in 1969, topped Jeannette to take the title in 1972 and tied Upper St. Clair in the championship contest in 1974. Antimarino's squad was 11-0-1 that season.

Gateway won the tough West Penn Conference eight

times in a ten-year period to qualify for the playoffs. In 1979, they beat Mt. Lebanon in post-season competition, but bowed to Penn Hills, 3-0, in the finals, leaving them with an 11-2 record. Antimarino's career record at Gateway going into the '80s was 153-42-10.

Joe Moore won a WPIAL title and tied for another in consecutive seasons at Upper St. Clair before moving on to Pitt, where he's an assistant to Jackie Sherrill. Lindy Lauro continued to do a great coaching job with the football team at New Castle.

1976 WORLD MARBLE-SHOOTING CHAMPS
With Walter T. Lease, Jr., their coach, behind them the 1976 championship team consisted of (l. to r.) Larry Kokos, Susan Regan, Ray Morgano, Ray Jarrell, Jerry Mages and Ricky Usner.

"We skunked them."
—Walter T. Lease Jr.

If Pittsburgh is, indeed, The City of Champions, then Lawrenceville must be looked upon as the world capital of marble shooters. In 1975 and again in 1976, a U.S. marble-shooting squad of six, five from Lawrenceville and a "ringer" named Ray Jarrel of Whitesville, West Virginia, claimed the world's championship by defeating England's Toucan Terribles in a championship series in Sussex County, England.

Gulf Oil Corp. sponsored the team two years running, and they came home victorious both times. The British team, whose members averaged 53 years of age, had claimed the world championship for 19 straight years until they got their comeuppance by the local youngsters, all 14 years old or less.

The first time didn't count, for one reason or another; it wasn't the traditional date to determine a championship. Even so, the U.S. team's coach, Walter T. Lease Jr. of Pittsburgh, said, "We skunked them. They claimed to be the world's champs for 19 years and today they got a lesson on how to shoot marbles."

In 1976, with the help of Gulf president James Lee and County Commissioner Thomas Foerster, the kids went back to England, going without sleep for 36 hours, and they still prevailed, beating the British team, 25-0, 25-0.

It was quite a triumph for the team's coach. Lease hails from the South Side, works for the City Department of Parks and Recreation, and teaches math at North Catholic High School. He coached nine national marble champions over a 12-year period.

The honor roll of national champions lists Ray Morgano (1970), Ray Jarrell (1972), Larry Kokos (1974), Ricky Usner (1975), Walt Morgano (1977). Matt Joyce and Chuckie Bosiljevac were twice runners-up, Mark Zupsic also finished second. Another fine shooter from Lawrenceville was Jerry Mages, the 1975 Allegheny County champion.

Girls' national champions were Karen Yurkovich of Troy Hill (1970), and several young ladies from Lawrenceville, Kathy Pazkowski (1972), Susan Regan (1974), Judy Bosiljevac (1976), Denise Ricci of the South Side (1977), and Diane Bertosh of Lawrenceville (1978).

The local youngsters were sponsored in the national finals at Wildwood, N.J. by the Sarah Mellon Scaife Foundation, with a big boost always coming from Commissioner Foerster, long a supporter of neighborhood sports teams.

MY RECALL OF THE '70s

If the calendar didn't tell me so, I would never believe that I have lived and worked in Pittsburgh for ten years, and what better decade could any man ask for.

I began at WIIC-TV in March of 1970, and ten years and a month later, I resigned, to move on to a greater challenge with NBC Sports, but in between, were the most glorious years of my life.

Enough to thrill any man, were the births of my two daughters, Dana and Molly. But four Steeler Super Bowls, two Pirate World Series, a World Team Tennis title for the Triangles, a National Football Championship for Pitt, and a frustrated love affair with the Penguins, provided a lifetime of fulfillment.

The events are indelibly etched in my mind, but it's the *people* who are truly unforgettable.

Roberto Clemente and Michel Briere . . . the man and the boy, both so beautifully graceful in what they did, and both forced to leave us, so tragically.

Willie Stargell and Joe Greene . . . cut from the identical mold . . . warm and caring, and possessors of that truly rare quality of leadership.

Terry Bradshaw and Tony Dorsett . . . God saw fit to bless them with an inordinate amount of talent, and luckily for us, they utilized every bit of it.

Chuck Noll and Johnny Majors . . . as contrasting as two personalities could be, with differing styles, but two extraordinary motivators of men.

Pierre Larouche and Norm Nixon . . . one crazy mixed up kid, and another as reliable as the Rock of Gibraltar.

And Dave Parker . . . his success story began in the seventies, but the final chaper will not be written until another decade has passed.

It is an endless stream that time and space doesn't permit me to follow, but to them and to the hundreds of other athletes, coaches and management, I offer my appreciation and gratitude.

They have not only given pride and prestige to our wonderful City of Pittsburgh, but they have helped bring to fruition, a life long dream of this sportscaster.
—Sam Nover

TESTIMONIAL TO CHET

Chet Smith was a wit, humorist and talented craftsman who wrote with exceptional poise. His rare gift of the written and spoken word fascinated everyone whom he touched. Chet still lives in the thousands of written words he created. Grantland Rice said it best in declaring Chet Smith the "best sportswriter of them all". We shall all miss him.

M.W.

In 1969 at the end of another decade at another time, Chet Smith, former sports editor of the Pittsburgh Press, and I produced a book called "Greater Pittsburgh History of Sports." It was a *veritable* bible of names, places, facts and faces. It was the first effort by anyone to document Pittsburgh district sports from Fort Pitt to Three Rivers Stadium.

Produced by Wolfson Publishing, the book was written by my dear friend, Chet Smith, who is now gone, while I was responsible for editing and illustrating it. We told a story of Pittsburgh's sports heroes, sung and unsung, in fields large and small . . . in terms of real people who had contributed to the growth of a great city.

"Greater Pittsburgh History of Sports" was the first book of its kind in the entire nation. No other sports city has ever attempted to publish such a complete compilation of its sports greats. It was a book long overdue.

In 1970 it was the first book to receive the Golden Quill Award for journalistic excellence in the field of sports.

Now that the decade of the '70s has passed, the timing was right to do another book on Pittsburgh sports. I am proud that "Pittsburgh: The Story of the City of Champions" is a true testimonial to the most outstanding decade of accomplishments in sports history that can be found anywhere. My sincere thanks and appreciation to Jim O'Brien for his dedication and determination in helping me—along with a championship staff—bring this prideful work to the people of Pittsburgh. My sincere thanks also goes to all who helped make this book a reality. Once again it is a one-of-a-kind in the nation, for Pittsburghers it was a decade unmatched in the annals of sports.

Marty Wolfson
Publisher